Crossing
the Border

Voices of refugee
and exiled women

Dedicated to my parents: Gerda and Hermann Striem

and in memory of members of my family who perished at Nazi hands: Wilhelm, Francisca and Hildegard Luster and Eugenie, Alfred and Frieda Striem and children Freddie, Giesela, Rita and Jonathan.

Crossing the Border

Voices of refugee and exiled women

Edited by Jennifer Langer

Five Leaves Publications
www.fiveleaves.co

Crossing the Border
edited by Jennifer Langer

Published in 2002 by Five Leaves,
PO Box 81, Nottingham NG5 4ER
www.fiveleaves.co.uk

ISBN 0 907 123635

Five Leaves acknowledges financial assistance
from East Midlands Arts

Typeset by 4 Sheets Design & Print Ltd.
Printed in Great Britain by Antony Rowe

Contents

Introduction

This is a pioneering collection of writing by women who are refugees or in exile, mainly in Britain. According to the United Nations High Commission on Refugees, women and children constitute more than 80% of the world's refugee population, having fled war and repression and frequently having become separated from male family members who may have been fighting, imprisoned, missing or killed. Women may have witnessed husbands and relatives being killed, and in flight they, themselves, may have been injured or maimed. In addition, they may have been imprisoned, tortured and raped. Women may have performed a number of roles of resistance such as actively fighting, as in Kurdistan and Kosova, being political activists, hiding people, passing messages or providing community services such as food, clothing and medical care.

The book covers some of the main countries from which refugees in the UK originate — Somalia, Democratic Republic of Congo, Afghanistan, Algeria, Iran, Iraq, Kurdistan, Northern Cyprus, Turkey, Bosnia and Kosova. The majority of the writers are in exile in London, their work reflecting the experiences of women in war and the after-effects of this. From the literature, an insight can be gained about how war and conflict affect women. Women are usually victims of war waged by men, although each political situation is different, ranging from genocide and ethnic cleansing in Kosova to the continued struggle for political rights in Kurdistan, factional warfare in Somalia, the complete suppression of the opposition in Iraq and ethnic war in Democratic Republic of Congo.

However, I was shocked and horrified to find that so many women were writing about being victims of a patri-

1

archal society where power structures and conflict connect with the oppression of women, in quite a frightening way. So much of the literature illustrates the depths of women's pain and despair.

The book is divided into themes rather than geographical areas, as it became clear that there was a commonality of experiences. These themes are women in conflict, women incarcerated, departures, exile, living memories and thoughts and cries of pain. Needless to say, there are, of course, differences, not only because each writer is an individual, but because of the differences in culture, languages, literary traditions, politics and sub-texts. The section entitled 'Departures' does not only refer to the physical sense of leaving, but also addresses the mental processes of departing from one culture to arrive in another. I felt it was important to provide background information to help the reader contextualise the work. These summaries consist not only of information about the conflict in the country of origin and how it affects women, but also information on women as victims in a patriarchal society, as politics and the role of women are frequently closely intertwined, often representing state policy. The background information also consists of a short summary about the voice of women and about women writers and literature inside the various countries and in exile. The reader ought to be aware that with fluid political situations, as in Afghanistan, the voice of women may reflect the changes.

My Motivation

Why did I undertake this work? There are many reasons. In my first book *The Bend in the Road: Refugees Writing* very few women writers were included and I became interested in this; were there in fact so few? I remember a woman colleague at the book launch gasping "where are the women?" when she saw the line-up was mainly men.

2

This was a challenge. I was not only interested in the literature but also in the insight it provided into how women writers perceived the terrible experience of war, oppression, displacement and loss and the subsequent alienation, exile and search for a valid identity. Through their stories, we can begin to understand what refugee and exiled women think and feel. They also challenge media stereotypes of women from many of these countries, who are portrayed as submissive rather than strong or assertive.

I had come across refugee writers in the course of my education work with refugees but at a deeper level perhaps I was also interested because of my own identity as the daughter of refugees who had fled Nazi Germany and started a new life in Britain.

As a child born in Britain, I felt a strange mixture of identities with perhaps the German one predominating at that time. This was well expressed by Karen Adler in *Second Generation Voices* — 'That marginality which I felt while growing up as a secular Jew, a not-quite foreigner who most certainly was not English, a child who understood the German her parents spoke but would never communicate in it herself.' At home we ate German food, I learned German nursery rhymes and songs, wore German clothes and shoes and vaguely understood my parents' secret conversations in German. At school open days when my parents communicated with my teachers in German accents, I became acutely aware of their origin and of the fact that they were different.

I was very aware of a kind of love-hate relationship with Germany and visited Germany with my parents on several occasions whilst a child. They were both quite assimilated, my mother's family having lived in an area of Zehlendorf, Berlin, with very few Jews. She had been the only Jewish pupil at her school. My father lived near Breslau (now Wroclaw, Poland) and was part of the motor-cycle racing fraternity. My mother extolled the wonderful youth she had spent in Berlin — balls, the tennis club, hockey team, a shared rowing boat on the Krumme Lanke, the expecta-

3

tion of study at university. All had come to an end with Jews being forbidden from attending normal schools, places or events and having to wear the yellow Star of David on their sleeves. Fellow pupils were members of the 'Hitler Youth' wearing a black uniform. In 1933, Jews were excluded from the civil service, the media and teaching. In 1935, the Nuremberg Laws forbade Jews to marry or have relations with non-Jews. Shops and even towns, displayed signs saying 'Jews not admitted'. By 1938, one third of the Jewish population had left Germany, many of them penniless after they had been forced to hand over everything to their Nazi persecutors. In November 1938, Hitler's supporters took to the streets and smashed or set on fire Jewish houses, shops and synagogues and killed Jews in the orgy of destruction that became known as Kristallnacht.

On one occasion in the early eighties, I accompanied my mother to Berlin, her first visit since she had been forced to leave in 1939. Although she showed me her school and area, she would not venture up to her former home as clearly this was too painful.

The sight of elderly men in the streets prompted me to question what their role had been in the Holocaust; most probably they would have denied all knowledge of what had happened at that time. When registering at our hotel, there were strange looks as my mother completed 'Place of Birth: Berlin'. Nothing needed to be explained.

In the living room at home, there were photographs of my parents' murdered relatives but I chose not to ask questions and shut off my mind about the way they had died. My father expressed anger about the fate of his family, frequently sending letters to newspapers about Nazis, while my mother preferred not to discuss it. Words like uncle, aunt, cousins and grandparents were alien concepts to me but occasionally someone with the same surname would telephone and there would be conversations about any tenuous links that could be established to ascertain if the caller was a relative or not. I delighted in the visits of an elderly, jolly, well-groomed lady who possessed the same surname, calling her 'aunt'. I was sad when she decided to return to Berlin. My parents could not understand her motivation given everything that had happened. Once a German, Christian, young woman who had found our name in the telephone directory, came to see us and surprisingly no inhibitions on either side seemed to exist, because of the possibility of her being related.

I realise my refugee roots permeate my being. The memory of loss is my history. Recently, I completed eleven forms to register the names and details of each member of my family killed. Tears dripped onto the forms. This is a family I never knew and each form represents a person killed by the Nazis: 'Place of death: Auschwitz or Monovitz or unknown'. They would have been my aunts, uncles, cousins and grandparents and unknown generations to come. I gaze at photos of happy children and family members leading normal lives, who never suspected the unbelievable events to come.

My parents were both the only survivors of their families. My mother was desperate to leave Germany and was intending to go to Uruguay and was, therefore, learning Spanish. Unfortunately, the consul was recalled, taking all my mother's vital documentation with him. She was finally sponsored by a friend in the UK but was unable to bring out her parents. Red Cross telegrams passed between them and then came to an abrupt halt. I still have the telegrams. My father was likewise desperate to leave Germany and was contacting all kinds of sponsors in the UK, even down to his contact at Triumph-Norton from whom he imported motor bikes for his racing. He knew the dark forces were closing in and that his days of freedom were numbered.

The following is a testimony he wrote for the Wiener Library, London, about events in November 1938 and his incarceration in Buchenwald concentration camp. It has been kindly translated from the German by Peter Prager.

The concierge of Koernerstr, 26 confirmed to the Gestapo that I was in my flat and she gave them the door key. Hence I was arrested on November 11 at 5am.

I was taken to the police station Victoriastr. In front of the station stood some people and some of the women said, "Throw them into the fire". They were referring to the burning synagogue. In the cellar of the police station, there were already ten to fifteen Jewish prisoners. After several hours, we were taken by lorry to a main police station. About 1,000 men and youths were already assembled there in the courtyard.

After several hours, top officials arrived and one of us dared to speak to them. He showed them his Iron Cross First Class from the War (First World War) and thought he deserved better treatment. The officer tore the medal from him, slapped his face twice and shouted that next time he would not get away so lightly. "How dare a Jew behave this way."

In the evening, several officers came again and said we were going on a mystery tour and we had to assemble in the open. Whoever tried to escape would be shot. Then we were marched under strict escort to Breslau station. Some of the older men had to be almost carried while the guards urged us on. We travelled all night and in Leipzig the train waited a long time in a siding. At Weimar station, the Breslau SS left and after a while, the concentration camp SS arrived. With much ado we had to leave the carriages in a hurry and had to run across the platform down the stairs which had been made slippery with soap and anybody who fell was whipped. When we arrived at the bottom, we had to line up, ten men at a time with our faces pressed against a wall. The SS pushed us further so that we could hardly breathe. We had to bow our heads and if we inad-

vertently raised them, they whipped our heads.
After this reception, we had to run to the lorries and
climb up into them without being given any steps
but they whipped us when we did not hurry. A tar-
paulin was thrown over us and off we went. The
journey took just under an hour. When we arrived,
we had to hurry down being whipped all the time.
Those who lost their hats had to leave them behind
or receive more beatings. We arrived between 9am
and 10am on Saturday and on the parade ground
already stood thousands who had arrived the previous day. They had shaven heads and soon it was our
turn to be shaved. That day, the next day and the
day after, transports continued to arrive. In contrast to those who already had prison uniform and
stayed in numbered barracks, we were called 'special section Jews' and through loudspeakers, we
were always addressed as Jewboys.

For us 12,000 new prisoners there were no barracks. They were being built by other prisoners.
Five barracks were built, each of which would house
2,500 men. At first we had to wait on the parade
ground in the glare of floodlights. The barracks had
been erected with rough boards about 100 metres
long and in the interior there were two or three
loose planks which were used as bunks. There was
so little space that we had to lie sideways. There was
no water, no washing facilities and for the first few
days no toilets. In the two weeks I was there, I could
not wash.

At Weimar Station, there had been some fatalities
of elderly men. For the next two weeks we had to
stand on the parade ground from 6am to 8pm. The
worst day was the third, when the commander said
that we could sit down. But our legs had to be
spread around the man in front and we were not
allowed to change position.

I had been arrested on Friday morning and received my first meal on Sunday afternoon consisting of strong fish soup. For days we had nothing to drink. On rainy days I collected water in my hat from a dripping roof. The ground around our barracks soon became a quagmire. Our shoes got stuck and soon disintegrated. In December, the elevation where our camp was situated became rough and cold; no heating, no blankets, no warm clothing and no regular food. Now and again food was brought to us, one day there was something, nothing the next day. The first nights the SS came into our barracks and anybody who was in their way was beaten to death. On the first evening we lost some comrades who had a heart attack. Some lost their nerves because of the hopelessness. The SS took these people, tied them to a tree and beat them. On some days we were compelled to sit; those who stood up to relieve themselves were given ten to twenty beatings. Anybody who started to cry out or pray was hung up along the barred windows of the administrative block in such a way that their toes just touched the ground. They were then put into a bunker and we never saw them again. Some were electrocuted when they touched the electric barbed wire in the dark. Others were driven towards the wire by guard dogs. The bodies were then brought to the gate. In the first fortnight about 1,500 died. Anybody who fell ill was lost. I was lucky because I wore a winter overcoat with which I covered myself when I lay on the loose plank and I used my jacket to lie on. Many inmates had frostbite on their toes because of the cold.

After two weeks we were forced to write cards saying we were well but required blankets, underwear, shoes, coats etc. Many of the parcels were stolen and of those which arrived we were obliged to hand some over to a winter charity. In this way I lost two parcels and only had rags on my feet. On one occasion we had to witness an execution.

Car owners were promised immediate release if they donated their cars. When they did this, nothing happened. On some occasions we had to stand the entire night on the parade ground because one person was missing out of 20,000. By the next morning nearly 100 had died. Then in the morning, we were immediately dispatched to the stone quarry.

In the two weeks I was in the camp, my weight went down from 142 pounds to 109 pounds.

My parents came to Britain as single people in 1939, before the age of the multi-cultural community. In total, about 70,000 Jewish refugees came to Britain in the thirties before the outbreak of the Second World War. Although the asylum laws are draconian now, they appear more liberal than in the thirties when very strict immigration controls were enforced and quotas operated and sponsors were required. The 1905 Aliens Restriction Act stipulated that all aliens needed means of support or a work permit and job, otherwise they would be refused entry. No refugee admitted was allowed to be a financial burden to the state. In Britain there was opposition to Jewish refugee immigration throughout the late 1930s. In 1938, the *Daily Express* demanded that restrictions be tightened not relaxed, and professional bodies such as the British Medical Association, opposed the entry of refugees with professional qualifications. My impression was that it was quite difficult for refugees to gain acceptance by the host community. There was the complexity of being both German and Jewish. Usually, however, the host community perceived my parents as German when they heard the German accent, which in itself posed problems during the Second World War. Generally I think that German Jewish refugees were too engrossed in the struggle for survival here, given that there was no benefit system in place, to be particularly concerned. In any case, they tended to move in their own circles and continue the cultural life they had had in Germany, setting up new organisations to meet their needs.

My father, like many others, was interned on the Isle of Man on suspicion of being a German spy. In the panic following the invasion of the Low Countries, Winston Churchill had ordered the mass internment of all refugees in case they harboured spies and fifth columnists. However, my father subsequently enlisted in the 'Pioneer Corps' of the British Army as did many of his compatriots, and contributed to the war effort. My mother initially worked as a domestic servant, as this was the only method by which she was allowed to gain entry to the UK, having been sponsored by a friend. In the last year before the War the British Government had made it easier for young Jewish women to come to Britain as domestic servants. During the War my mother carried out fire watching duties, but both my parents' over-riding concern was to extricate their families from the hell that was Nazi Germany.

Refugee and Exiled Women Writers and their Literature

I felt it was important to reflect exiled women writers 'voices' denied to many of them, in their countries of origin and in exile. However, the translated work may not truly represent the nuances and depth of the original work, and may therefore appear raw. For most, this is the first time their work has been translated and has appeared in English, making it accessible outside their communities. The work included is by experienced, and less experienced writers, some of the latter writing for the first time to express their feelings. Some writers have had their work published in community magazines or newsletters with a few having had their work published in books, mainly in their own language. There is a disparity between

10

the representation of different countries which reflects the history, culture and traditions of the female voice and its disempowerment in male dominated society. It also reflects my difficulty in accessing women writers as someone outside the communities and culture, and the enormous barriers to communication that language poses. Furthermore, in some cases, the main centres of exile may be in other countries such as Germany or Sweden. Moreover, I found that women's new burdens in exile, the heavy demands on their time and feelings of depression were also barriers. Women often feel frustrated, isolated and terrified in an alien culture and without comfort from their immediate family. For example, many Somali women in exile find themselves in the role of head of the family with sole responsibility for large numbers of children and with a succession of both practical and psychological problems to deal with. One Somali poet told me that she dreamed of returning one day to the fertile valley of the Juba River, her homeland in Somalia, and meanwhile found it hard to function in Britain. Similarly, a Bosnian poet cried out that she could no longer write, having lost her inspiration because of the pressures of life. However, upon arrival, her anguish had caused her to write prolifically to pour out her emotions "like a volcano erupting".

My original aim was to include literature by refugee writers; however, some of the writers preferred not to define themselves as refugees in the narrow sense of the Geneva Convention. In some cultures, the word 'refugee' has negative connotations and is considered pejorative. Some writers dislike being stereotyped as a refugee with its current unfortunate connotations of being a victim, a scrounger and a bogus refugee. In many cases, writers cannot now return because the political situation has changed, with freedom of speech abolished and censorship introduced. Some writers classify themselves as 'exiles' who chose to leave because of the change in the political situation which had reverberations on the cultural and social systems, as in the case of an Iranian writer who was

11

worried about her daughters and their education under the new regime. Another Iranian writer left because her son would have been forcibly conscripted into the army during the Iran-Iraq war and would, she feared, have become 'cannon fodder'. One Algerian writer told me that although she had been offered work as a television presenter, it would have been too difficult and dangerous to function in the current set-up in Algeria, where censorship was the norm and where the opposition would have endangered her life if she spoke out freely. Other writers may have left initially to study but were unable to return because of the new situation or war. Fear is an issue preventing many of the writers expressing themselves as freely as they would wish. The fear is caused by the repercussion their writing could have on their families still living in their native lands and by spies in the UK. This manifests itself in caution when writing about politics, the deployment of allegory or in the use of a pen-name. One writer told me that in order to retrieve her short stories from her country whilst a refugee in the UK, she had bribed her sister, who still lived in her country, with presents. Her sister had then embedded the writer's stories in letters. This process had taken three years.

The literature in the section on loss and memories is sad and moving. Women writers remember places, images, experiences, objects and people, with the sadness deriving from the knowledge that these are purely memories now that the writers are in exile. Darija Stojnic, from Bosnia, writes a humorous short story about the buses of Sarajevo which although inefficient, are much loved and missed. Fahrija Hodzic, also a Bosnian poet, describes the ear-rings she always wears that have been in her family for generations and symbolise the link with her lost family. Rouhi Shafii, from Iran, in *Scent of Saffron* describes childhood memories of her beautiful family house and sleeping on the roof in the hot south. Haifa Zangana, from Iraq, describes the interior life of the women's hammam.

One important theme is 'Exile'. This is not only a physical condition but also a mental one, the writer feeling alienated from the majority and unwelcome. Initially there is relief to have found sanctuary in the UK but the experience of displacement, with its associated socio-cultural and psychological trauma, is very hard and painful. The host society is often perceived as marginalising the refugee and expressing its resistance to new groups. The experiences of refugee women may often be marginalised because they are not articulate in the public domain. There is often the complete denial of the reality of refugee women's experiences of rape, with no-one here connecting with it or acknowledging it. The refugee feels in a kind of limbo, physically here but mentally there, unwilling to be in the host society but unable to return. According to Mahnaz Afkhami in *Women in Exile,* "Exile is a no-man's land, where one belongs fully nowhere," and "The pain of exile is palpable and long-lasting". Many writers remain rooted in a world that no longer exists, as their past has been destroyed and if they return, they often find that everything has changed and is not as they remembered. The angst of exile is expressed in Rouhi Shafii's evocation of leaving which is a mixture of joy and sadness. Her daughter is so relieved at no longer having to wear the hejab, that she leaves the mass of black material on her plane seat and when they arrive at Heathrow, they are amazed by all the bright colours and smiling faces. However, the settlement process is very difficult as she finds that Londoners are not genuinely interested in her life story or reasons for fleeing. Rouhi Sharifian in her story *The Traveller* expresses the pain of not belonging through the image of a homosexual who is shunned by the other passengers on a coach journey to Nottingham. The author, however, makes human contact with him as they are both outsiders and also she cares about their common humanity. Choman Hardi, a young Kurdish poet, expresses the pain of being stereotyped as a refugee rather than as an individual.

Afkhami also makes the point that "Along with the loss of their culture and home comes the loss of the traditional patriarchal structures that limited their lives in their own land. Exile in its disruptiveness resembles a rebirth for the women. The pain of breaking out of the cultural cocoon brings with it the possibility of an expanded universe and a freer, more independent self." One wonders how this can be reconciled with the feelings of isolation and rootlessness articulated by so many of the writers. In addition, almost all the writers are experiencing pain because of what is happening in their country. Many explain that even though they are living outside the country, they do not have peace of mind feeling "half there and half here". Although the women had suffered because of conflict in their own areas, many were concerned about all oppressed people, and common humanity.

The complex process of exile has been analysed in different ways, for example as consisting of three stages — uprooting, disjuncture and metamorphosis. Martin Tucker in *Literary Exile in the Twentieth Century* states that the exiled writer's pattern is that of flight from origins, then reconstruction of origins through revision of memory, followed by an artistic flowering. The length of time the contributors have been in exile varies and may change the writer's perspective. The writer may feel her identity is evolving and changing from feeling wholly alienated from the mainstream culture to absorbing mainstream influences and being involved in a process of dialogue. Some writers no longer classify themselves as refugees and a few such as Haifa Zangana, may start to write in English rather than in their mother tongue which reflects their perception of themselves as being partially integrated. In addition, they often wish to reach a wider audience to enable the reading public to understand their culture and experiences. Some writers have complex feelings about their interaction with the indigenous society. Fatma Durmush, whose parents were refugees and who came to Britain at a young age, has stated that she feels half British and half Turkish with much of her work reflecting her Turkish identity. Dr Miriam Hastings of Birkbeck College, has commented that second generation women often act as a voice for the first generation because the latter were not able to express themselves and felt alienated from society given that their priorities were their children and the desperate struggle for survival.

Some of the writers have found the angst of exile to be a powerful contributory factor which inspires them to write. Haifa Zangana says of her work, "Is it my charm for curing the leprosy that permeated my body on the day it was touched by whatever I hate; my charm for warding off forgiveness that comes with the passing of time, for repelling widespread failing memory, repelling the return to a country where they still practise insulting rituals, repelling the unconscious emptying of memory, of its rage, repelling oblivion, oblivion, oblivion?" The critic Andrew Gurr's thesis that exile is a constructive force for the writer may be compared to Edmund Wilson's earlier premise that the artist works from a wound that shoots its own arrows of artistic strength and stimulation while Ted Hughes, stated "Every work of art stems from a wound in the soul of the artist". He also felt that writing poetry had the power to comfort and heal.

Generally, I found it harder to locate women writers than male writers, although it transpired that there were significant numbers, many of whom wrote for themselves but wished their work to become accessible to a readership.

A fundamental issue concerns the hidden voice of women. Generally, there is a conflict between the traditional woman's role, focusing on the needs of others, and the role of the professional writer, which is self-centred because it puts one's own development and fulfilment first. Men have dominated and continue to dominate and control the world of literature and public space both inside most of the countries and in various diasporas. The work of women had not been published for a range of reasons.

Generally women's literature was traditionally an oral one with women playing an important part as storytellers within the private space. Also, even today, two-thirds of the world's illiterate are women and have less educational opportunities than men so that women are deprived of the power of the pen. In addition, because the women's role is circumscribed with taboos about entering the public domain, both in the home country and, to a lesser extent, in exile, it is harder for them to gain access to publishing and recognition as they are deprived of the same connections or networks as the male writers. According to Claire Buck in the *Bloomsbury Guide to Women's Literature*: "There has been a long history of the marginalisation of women's writing whereas male writers have access to the writing world and assert themselves in terms of their writing prowess." Many of the writers proclaimed with emotion "Our voice is not heard", "Our voice is silenced" and "We haven't got a voice". In many countries women are confined to the private space and are not expected to articulate thoughts or opinions in the public space. They are expected to be silent and submissive, often covered in a chador, veil or burqua.

At a School of Oriental and African Studies (SOAS) conference entitled 'Mapping Arab Womanhood', writers made the point that social taboos were very strong, leading to a process of self-censorship and censorship by the family. Furthermore, writers now were struggling with the same issues as those of a hundred years ago — love, marriage, divorce — and it was felt that presenting negative, pessimistic images of women was unhelpful. The opinion was expressed that all Arab women had a second layer of complexity and that in a non-democratic society, various devices such as deviousness, madness and exorcism ('zar') were deployed by women to gain their freedom. The conference participants argued for a common male-female discourse, rather than male-female polarity. What I found depressing was the discussion around 'Islam and Arab Women's Identity' where the focus was on interpretation of the Koran in terms of the woman's position, with the role of the state and religion seemingly inseparable.

The issue of feminism is a matter of life and death in many of the countries included, such as Algeria and Afghanistan. There is enormous pressure on women to conform to the norms of society and to deviate from these norms is dangerous. Women may be victims of gender-related persecution such as beatings, whippings or stoning. At the SOAS conference, referred to above, it was stated that if women behaved in a non-Islamic way, they were considered enemies of the state. Writers in many sections of the book are writing to expose the iniquities in their patriarchal societies and the connection with state policy. So much of this literature illustrates the depths of women's pain and despair. The similarity of experience is surprising and shocking and the anger expressed by the women writers is palpable. This is therefore literature with a strong message which tries to change the status quo and which would certainly be censored in many countries.

Is this western feminism transformed? The term 'plurality of feminisms' is now used with not only the western model being valid; scholars have begun to use the term 'feminisms' to acknowledge the diversity of cultures and situations. Interpretations of feminism are totally different in the societies included in the book. Some Arab women have claimed that Arab feminism is indigenous to the Arab world. New scholarship undermines the myth of a monolithic western feminism and refines understanding of feminisms as products of particular times, places, classes and races. One concern of feminist literary criticism was and continues to be the stereotyping of women in the work of male writers although some writers in exile, such as Nuruddin Farah and Mohamed Afraax from Somalia, have put themselves in the role of the oppressed woman. According to Margot Badran and Miriam Cooke in *Opening the Gates*, 'The feminist discourse of Arab women writers destroys patriarchially produced female arche-

17

types and replaces them with their own prototypes: women who have their own aspirations, desires, needs." According to Robin Morgan in *The Eye of the Storm*, "Women in the Muslim world have borne the brunt of especially invidious stereotyping but are courageously working for change." As stated earlier, I continually heard from the writers "We haven't got a voice. Our voice is silenced." In many societies, women's voices were not supposed to be heard and were even considered by some to be 'awra' — something shameful to be hidden.

Language is a key issue as language is very closely linked to identity, with a famous quote being "My language is my homeland". Clearly the majority of writers use their mother tongue to express complex feelings and ideas and are unable to write effectively in the language of the new country, feeling the loss of a language in which to communicate. They are, therefore, restricted to writing for their own community or attempting to publish work which could possibly be distributed in their own country, which is a complex, expensive process.

There is a general paucity of work in translation by women writers from the countries included. Most literature was written in mother tongue and it was therefore difficult to make a decision about the literature to be included without having all the pieces translated first. Most of the writers' work had never been translated into English. Translating was an area of great complexity with many of the writers talking about the difficulty of finding the precise equivalent to expressions or of trying to explain culturally embedded points. Salah Niazi, the eminent Iraqi Arab poet, has raised points about translation in his newly published book in Arabic *Alienation and the National Hero*. Cross-cultural issues are a real factor in that it is problematic to translate work which expresses another mentality and different social concepts, for example, communication in Arabic is direct, positive and certain, whereas in English it is more tentative and hesitant, expressing humility. Samia Dahnaan, for example, articulated the difficulty of transferring very different images from Arabic to English. I am very grateful to friends of the writers who worked collaboratively with the writers on translation; I usually did the final editing which often involved long discussions with the writer on interpretation.

Language was indeed a barrier, not only in terms of translations, but also in terms of being able to gain access to current information about women and women writers without being able to read reference books or journals in the original language, apart from French. I therefore needed to rely on material in English and on the writers and academics with whom I was in contact. In several cases, the background information was written by a person with the specific knowledge.

I hope that through this work being read and disseminated, many of the myths about refugee and exiled women will be deconstructed.

Jennifer Langer
October, 2001.

References
Mahnaz Afkhami, *Women in Exile*, University Press of Virginia, 1994
Margot Badran, and Miriam Cooke, *Opening the Gates: A Century of Arab Feminist Writing,* Virago, 1990
Claire Buck, *Bloomsbury Guide to Women's Literature*, Bloomsbury, 1992
Second Generation Voices, January 1998, no.7, Second Generation Network.
Martin Tucker, *Literary Exile in the Twentieth Century*, Greenwood Press, 1991
Refugee Council, Women Refugees, Fact File, April 1997

Acknowledgments

Niloufar Pourzand, UNICEF, Peshawar, Pakistan
Ahmed Yener, Turkish Community Library, Islington
Janette Griffiths and Jane Spender, International PEN
Moris Farhi
Iranian Community Library, Acton
Helena Scott, French Research Co-ordinator, Department of
    Francophone Studies, University of Westminster
Sami Aziz, Afghan Community Association, Harrow
Afghanaid, London
Estella Schmidt, Kurdistan Information Centre, London
Mohamed Afrax, Chair of Somali Section of International PEN
Fatima Giama, Organiser of West Hampstead Somali Women's
    Group
Jean-Marie Witele, Co-ordinator, Islington Zairean Refugee
    Group
Mai Ghossoub, Saqi Publishers, London
Quintin Hoare, Bosnian Institute, London
Predrag Finci, Editor of *SALON*, London
Milan Uzelac
Afsaneh Leissner, BBC Persian Service, World Service
Haifa Zangana
Hasan Sahan, Parental Outreach Worker, Haringey Council
Elia Lamani, BBC Albanian Service
Miriam Hastings, Birkbeck College, University of London
Xhevat Ademi, Co-ordinator 'The Unaccompanied Albanian-
    speaking Refugees Project', International Social Service of
    the UK
Farah Hiwad, Society of Afghan Residents in the UK
Sozan Mohamed
Valbona Ismaili Luta
Rouhi Shafii
Betulah Destani, Historian, Centre for Albanian Studies,
    London
Institute of War and Peace Reporting, London
St. Antony's Middle East Centre, Oxford
Camden Libraries and Librarians, West Hampstead and Swiss
    Cottage branches
Mildred Hillock, Refugee Council Information Centre and
    Library, London
Poetry Library, London
Aydin Mehmet Ali, For the Advancement of Turkish Speakers'
Art and Literature (FATAL)
Tom Cheeseman, University of Wales, Swansea
Suhaila Ismat

20

Women in
Conflict

A Drama

Valbona Ismaili Luta
(Kosova)
Translated from Albanian by Ragip Luta

NEVER fight against life
DO NOT let the horses get lost on the paths
REMEMBER the dogs barking like mad

and the sofra* laid without bread
DO NOT open the doors to the wounds
LISTEN!
THE BLOOD will flood
A WHOLE DRAMA on a small stage.

* *sofra — dinner table*

A Tale of Fear
Gjeraqina Tuhina
(Kosova)

The planes flew low last night and anti-aircraft fire responded from the ground, shooting into the sky. On the streets I could hear lots of Serbs shouting — cursing Albanians, NATO, America, Britain, Clinton, Blair, Muslims, Turks.

At about 10pm I heard sounds of boots running up the stairs of the building where I stayed last night. (I haven't slept at home for a week.) I heard the sound of someone knocking on a neighbouring door. "That's it," I thought, "they've arrived." Still, I was amazed how calm I felt.

I have always been scared whenever I see a policeman or anyone carrying a gun (though nowadays there's a difference: Serbs carry only big machine-guns). But this time I was cool. "The worst thing they can do is kill me, so nothing can surprise me." I thought. I made a decision: "I won't try to hide my identity or my mother tongue," — Albanian, of course.

Then I heard someone running again, but now the sound was heading downstairs. No-one knocked on my door but I just had to know what was going on, so I looked outside. It was a man I had spoken to before. I had met him on the street a week ago, and we exchanged a few words about the political situation (what else?). We were speaking in Serbian, and he seemed very open-minded and 'normal'. I was quite glad, as I didn't want to condemn a whole nation because of the government's politics. There are decent people among them, I thought. Until that night.

Now he was wearing a strange uniform, neither police nor military, carrying weapons and heading out into the

24

night. The knock came from his 'friend' who had come in a rush, and in the same clothes and gear to get him. Off they went, no doubt to try to kill an Albanian or to burn a house.

Next day I would have to find another place to sleep: I wouldn't want to run into him again now.

Until a few days ago, I felt sorry for the people suffering in the villages. But I don't any more. Now I too am fighting for survival. I try to stay alive but it's difficult. This morning I almost collapsed out of breath while running towards my parents' house to see if they are still OK. There's no phone, so every time I go to spend a night somewhere else, I kiss my father and my mother. I fear that I won't see them again. Yesterday I passed by my favourite café where I used to meet my friends every day. For years we met and chatted there. We were all so close that if you missed one afternoon, everyone noticed and wondered where you'd gone. Now it is destroyed, even the chairs were taken, and it doesn't look like my café at all. Inside five policemen were getting drunk on whisky in the middle of the mess they had made.

Maybe it seems ridiculous to think about this café now, but not for me.

God knows when we will gather again, and who will be absent at that time. How many of us are missing?

There is no way to find out. The telephone lines from Albanian houses have been cut, and the whole town is sliced into sections by police and armed Serb civilians.

No one can communicate, no one can move. For now, only names go through my mind. I try to remember faces but I can't.

Still, for the first time last night, I felt happy.

The MUP (police) building in the centre of town was completely destroyed by NATO jets. I watched it burning from the window. Now only ashes remain. At least something of 'theirs' has been destroyed. The big mushroom that lit the night sky looked so beautiful. At last there was something good in all this tragedy.

We just hope that it will go on, and that NATO planes will fly even lower tonight. But how quickly day goes now! My friends used to call me 'Nighthawk', because I adored the night, but now I hate it. I will have to leave my home soon, to hide in some other place. To avoid any more knocks.

I will take my blanket, stay awake the whole night, and listen to the sounds of planes, anti-aircraft guns, and shouting. It seems to me that every shot comes from the direction of my parents' house, and it fills me with fear.

The electricity shuts off about 6pm and it is not clever to light a candle, because that will just show that some one is inside. Everyone stays in the dark, waiting.

Trapped
Gjeraqina Tuhina
(Kosova)

The neighbourhoods of Dragodan and Taslixhe, entirely Albanian, were emptied yesterday. Now they have broken into almost every house in Dragodan and destroyed them. And they are doing the same thing in Taslixhe.

Vrenjvc, the last neighbourhood on the outskirts of the road to Belgrade, was emptied yesterday. I have no information about looting, it's simply destroying.

The streets are different. We used to have heavy firing at night but not so much in the day. Now there is shooting all of the time, day and night. It's not fighting, just firing in all directions. Everyone is hooting outside. It is going on now. I also saw a few jeeps on the streets taken from the UNHCR warehouse.

Only women dare go out; the men are too vulnerable. But there were no shops open and nothing to buy. Already we have started using the food we had set aside as reserves. Yesterday the people from Dragodan came and now we have four families living in a three-bedroom flat. So we have more mouths to feed.

No one else will write. No one else is around. Everyone is in hiding but I have no information about where they are. We have no leaders now; it is just us.

My friends from Belgrade and elsewhere are calling me, telling me to leave. God, I want to get out of here. I can't stand it. But I won't leave until I have rock-solid guarantees, a document that I am allowed to pass, or something so that we can get through. There was a big convoy that left yesterday from the city for the Macedonian border. But we hear that they haven't been allowed through yet.

27

I check the Internet to find out what is happening in my own town. Kosova press, the KLA agency, reports shootings in Pristina and shelling in Taslixhe. I can hear the shooting but not the shelling. And then I understand. I see why those people came last night into my parents' house. Both of these neighbourhoods, Dragodan and Taslixhe, are up on the hills. Now that they are 'clean', it is very easy to set up artillery there and target anything in the town.

> *At noon, the family is told to leave. The dispatch cannot be finished. there is only time to write one more e-mail.*

NO STORY — sorry. We have been ordered to leave the apartment. We're going NOW. I don't know where...

Pray for me, and I'll call you when or as soon as I can, but as for now, it seems that I will have the status of the people that came some days ago to my house. Goodbye.

Shortly after the family departs, the Institute in London calls: "Is X there?"

"He had to go."

"When do you expect him to come back?"

"I don't think he's ever coming back."

Calvary

Aida Derguti
(Kosova)
Translated by Lindita Derguti-Pajaziti

Each passing day
resembles the one today
I'm one of those
narrators of the
modern age
in the Golgota* of the Balkans,
monotonously observing
the usual empty corners
noting persecutions sowing fear
and Calvary stands dignified
outside the ancient walls of the fortress
the ancient altar of savages
gorging on the blood of askets*

* *Golgota — place of destruction, pillage and slaughter inflicted by evil,
mythological army*
* *askets — a religion; the followers believe people should enjoy pain and
sacrifice in order to ensure a better life in the other world.*

Searching for Saleem
Farooka Gauhari
(Afghanistan)

The author's husband has disappeared; he may be in prison or dead. So begins a long search for Saleem.

Saturday April 29, 1978

I was not myself at all. I was aware that what was happening was real, but real only in the way one reads a novel. I was stopped many times by soldiers who inspected the inside and the trunk of my car. Somehow, through some small streets that I had never seen before, I came to the Bibi Mahro Road, which ran past the American embassy and the Kabul Radio-Television station. The road led to my destination, the Khoja Rawash Air Force Base, as well as to the Kabul airport. It was heavily guarded with tanks. All army personnel were armed and ready for action, and among the tanks were a few civilians armed with machine guns. No matter how many roads I tried that day, I always encountered soldiers who blocked the main road leading to the base. I was not concerned with my own safety; my only goal was to reach Saleem's office.

After three hours of driving in circles, it seemed hopeless. I was getting nowhere, so I headed back home before curfew. Home at last, Rahim ran and opened the garage door. Oh God, mentally and physically prostrate. Rahim said that we had many guests and he had served them tea. I nodded and asked if he could make some fresh tea for me as well.

I stood silently by the garage door a few minutes to catch my breath and calm down before facing my relatives. I wasn't expecting them or ready to meet with them. Nor did I know how they had been informed — perhaps Yonus and Mariam had told them. When I stepped inside, practically everybody was there waiting for me. My sisters, brothers, in-laws and their families entirely filled the two large rooms. My daughter, Sahar, was playing outside happily, unaware of what was going on. Omar and Ali were among the guests, knowing that something was very wrong. I watched all three of them quietly for a few moments. I prayed to God to grant me the strength I needed so desperately at that very moment.

As soon as I entered the room all conversation stopped. Everyone's eyes were fixed on me. I almost broke into tears, but I pulled myself together and told them with a sad smile that it was too early to come to any conclusions. I added that I simply didn't know much at the moment. I went around the room and greeted each one of them individually. I knew that if I showed the slightest trace of the turmoil inside me, everybody would break out crying, especially my mother and my mother-in-law, whose wailing would be audible miles away. What the outcome would be and how it would affect my children, I didn't know, but certainly it would hurt them very badly. So, for their sake, I attempted to be strong as a rock. My actions calmed everyone. I was scared to death, though, wondering how much longer my contrived confidence could possibly last.

Rahim brought my tea. After a short while most of the guests left except for my closest relatives. They thought I should not be left alone. Night came and the curfew began. We all sat quietly. There seemed to be nothing to talk about. Everybody gazed at the TV or listened to the radio. I didn't know what was going on in the kitchen, but Rahim was there doing his best. I did not feel hungry, even though I had not eaten since breakfast. At dinner I reluctantly joined the guests. I couldn't swallow a single morsel of food; my throat felt swollen shut. I couldn't stop thinking about Saleem. It seemed that the parts of my body were separate — my hands, my lips, my ears, my legs, my eyes simply would not function together. I felt myself drowning deeper and deeper in a vast ocean of hopeless-ness.

An hour after dinner I excused myself and went to bed. Before I left the room, I was careful not to spoil the evening by any foolish actions. I forced myself to act nor-mal. I kissed the children good night as usual and told Rahim to arrange for everybody's bed. The guests slept all over the house, on the floor, on benches, or any other place they found to be comfortable.

As I lay down, I felt that there were thousands of miles between my husband and me. What a drastic change! Just three short nights ago he was right beside me; now I could not reach him. It made me even more angry and depressed. I wanted to sleep but couldn't. I lay staring at the ceiling for hour after hour. It was one of the longest and most difficult nights of my life.

Hours passed in the darkness. Whenever I heard the roar of a jeep, I would sit up, hoping it was Saleem's car returning home. As soon as the car passed, my hopes died. More than a hundred cars passed and I lost count. Every time my reactions were the same: hope, prayers, and hap-piness mounted at the rumble of the approaching car, then misery returned as the noise faded away, I don't know how long I lay there languishing in this condition. I don't know whether I slept or not. Around four in the morning I jumped out of my bed as if it were on fire. In this cool spring morning I was hot and perspiring; my clothes were soaked. I needed some fresh air, so I carefully tiptoed through the two long hallways and out onto the front ter-race. I begged God to help Saleem wherever he might be. I prayed, "O God! I can't lose him. Please, God, give me a chance to tell him how much I love him."

Somehow the cool, fresh air made me feel better. I returned to my room and slept the rest of the night.

Saturday December 8, 1979
On this morning I got up a little late and missed the uni-versity van, so I walked to school. On my way I met Sultan,

the school storeroom keeper. He stopped his bicycle and asked me about the type of ditto paper that I had ordered months ago for our department. As I was giving him instructions about the quality required for our use and where to purchase it, I noticed that a black Benz taxi had stopped at the west end of the street, about a hundred yards away. The driver's big, reflecting eyeglasses attracted my attention. A few moments later the cab left while I continued talking to Sultan. Soon another black Benz taxi drove up and parked about fifty yards from us, this time to the east side. Nothing seemed unusual. When Sultan went on his way, I continued walking toward the university. As I passed the parked taxi I looked at the driver and my whole world began to spin. He wore reflecting sunglasses and had a ferocious face. He was watching me carefully through the side mirror! The idea that he was following me scared me to death even though I didn't have the slightest idea why I was his target. I had heard from colleagues that most of the cab drivers were secret police.

I passed him without losing control, but I did not want him, whoever he was, to follow me. Something — probably all the detective books I'd read — gave me the idea that he should not know my place of work or my home address, so at the first intersection I did not take the road leading to the university but instead turned toward the bus stop and boarded the first bus that arrived. I didn't even check its route.

From inside the bus, I saw the cab driver still watching me. After riding half an hour or so, I got off at Puli-Baghi Umomi, a very crowded area of town, and ran. I ran into the mall. I turned around and saw the cab driver with his mirror-like sunglasses. My God, he was following me! I turned back toward the door I had entered and, ducking behind a tall man, left the shopping centre. I looked back; the cab driver was still milling with the rest of the crowd and looking for me. I jumped into the nearest bus. Its destination was a village outside Kabul called Waisal Abad, but I didn't care. I wanted to get out of there, and fast!

After an hour's ride, I reached Waisal Abad and from there I took a cab, finally arriving at work about noon. For at least a month afterwards I took the faculty bus to school and avoided crossing the street again.

Sunday December 16, 1979

People say, "Take one day at a time." For me, a day at a time became too long. To survive, I had to hang onto minutes, rather than days. In fact, I took one minute at a time. To keep my mind off the problems and to do my regular daily work, I lived only from minute to minute.

For example, on my way to the university I always counted the chimneys of the Darul-Malamine and Ibnesena schools, which flanked the road. One, two, three, four... no, I counted wrong and I would start all over again; one, two, three, four, five... fifteen, sixteen... thirty... I had counted them a thousand times during the previous twenty months. If there was nothing else to count, I counted the cement blocks of sidewalks — one, two, three... five hundred sixty, five hundred sixty-one and so on — till I reached my office building. The next day I counted the tall shrubs, then the houses on the mountainside. In fact, I was counting like a robot, almost anything and everything that came in sight. The only satisfaction I derived from counting was that it passed the time and kept my mind off my troubles. No doubt I was getting very close to insanity.

September 1980

At nine in the morning the small window of the police office facing the hall, opened. When my turn arrived I explained to the plainclothes officer my name and the nature of my application. He went to the end of the room, pulled out a large, heavy blue binder, and found my application. He looked at the secret police report, closed the binder, and said, "Yes, of course... of course... You can go. I don't see any reason not to."

Then he signed a special form, handed it to me, and told me to complete the rest of the steps. I took the papers but did not move away from the window. I asked him politely, "Sir, what about my husband? What did the report say about Saleem?"

He looked at me with surprise for a moment and opened the big binder again. He read the information silently and answered in a hurry, "Well, he is fine and will come home. And... now... you can go."

I still didn't move away from my place, but insisted that he let me read it for myself. He refused and closed the binder. He took the binder back to its original place while I stood still in front of the window and gazed at him. How dearly I wanted to know what information those pages held about Saleem. After all, those were the police reports and must be correct.

The policeman came back, sat down again at the window, and shouted, "Next!"

I reluctantly walked away from the window and stood in a corner as the well-dressed gentleman behind me approached the window. He asked for his papers, which were supposed to have been signed weeks before but were not completed yet. The man insisted, "My application has been here for months and I don't know what the reason for the delay is. How long must I wait?"

His words hit the officer like a bullet. He began shouting, loudly enough that everyone in the hall could easily hear him: "Brother, all you can think about is yourself. We all work hard day and night to rebuild our country and you apply for a West German vacation?"

The man said, "Sorry, sir; I didn't mean to upset you. I apologise. The goods I'm exporting are waiting for shipment and the delay is costing me a fortune."

The policeman didn't hear. Still shouting, his face red and with puffy droplets of spit flying out of his mouth, saturating the air around the window, he cried, "Dishonest agents of the CIA — people like you want to leave the country when you're needed here the most!" There was no

35

end to his insulting speech even though the gentleman kept apologising.

The situation was getting worse and was attracting everybody's attention. All the policemen in the office gathered around the window. I took advantage of the moment. With a great courage very unfamiliar to me, I went from the far door at the right end of the hall and crossed two large rooms until I was inside the office right behind the policemen where no one was permitted to enter. I ignored all the signs on the doors that said 'Authorised Personnel Only Beyond This Point.'

I approached the rows of shelves filled with the big blue binders and pulled out the one that had the secret police report on us. I took the binder into the far corner of the room, I even stupidly sat on one of the police desks and opened it. I found the right page and read it. The report was very brief: "Saleem was an anti-revolutionary element and was eliminated the first day. We do not have any information on his wife in our records." I crossed the room again and put the binder back in its place. Then I quickly stepped out of the office, recrossing the restricted areas once more. Nobody had even noticed my presence there.

Now whenever I think about that day, I wonder why I didn't leave the binder on the desk after reading the report rather than crossing the entire room again to take it back to its original place. Probably all of those secret police, so well trained in East Germany, would never dream that a person like me would ever do such a crazy thing in their presence.

After I left the police office I went to a corner of the hall and stood near a window, my face bathed in a cold sweat. My hands shook and I could not speak. All the world in front of me became blurred and dark. Everything hid behind the shadowy curtains of my vibrating teardrops. I heard someone say, "You need to sign the forms in this office before you leave." I didn't care anymore. Whoever he was didn't matter. My body felt numb all over and the whole world turned around me in circles. My insides heaved and I began to throw up. The pain in my stomach was excruciating. A couple of men and a woman passed by and noticed my condition. They came forward to help, and I told them I would be all right.

I leaned on a windowsill. I don't know how long I was there, but long enough to feel a little better. I looked at my watch. I had got there before nine in the morning; it was now two-thirty in the afternoon. I went to the nearest bus stop and got on a bus. I felt so miserable that I didn't want my children to see me in my present condition, so I got off at Dehmazang and went into the Kabul Zoo. All the guys at the office knew me, but I wasn't ready or willing to talk to them. Reluctantly I put my hand in my pocket, pulled the money out, and bought a ticket. I didn't wait for the change. My world was dead. I was breathing like a dying person who still hangs on to this world, trying hard to breathe all the last breaths of air that are possible.

I wasn't there to see the animals. I was there to overcome my shock and needed some time and space. I needed a quiet place to think and to be left alone. I'd lost track of time. I needed to pull myself together. I selected a table in a far corner, facing the Chamchamast River and the mountain that the Noon Cannon stood on. The air was fresh; the earth was covered with a green carpet of low plants. The trees had just begun to change colour and the rows of poplars already displayed their bright fall colours. Once in a while a cool breeze swept gently across my face from green fields. Nature had always fascinated me. It gave me peace and comfort. I loved the soothing quietness of its fresh, slow breezes. There I always found the beauty and greatness of God. In fact, I saw the presence of God right next to me.

After some time, the busboy brought me a pot of hot tea with a small plate that held a few sugar-coated almonds. He said something, but I didn't answer, nor did I move. He stood there for a few moments and then left without a word from me. I heard his low murmurs as he walked away. He must have thought I was totally deaf or insane.

(from *Searching for Saleem* by Farooka Gauhari, University of Nebraska Press, 1996. Reprinted by permission of the University of Nebraska Press)

The Glass Marbles
Pari Mansouri
(Iran)
Translated from Farsi by Katy Wallace-Kianush

The man hurriedly opened his black briefcase, taking out the papers inside. He looked at them carefully, one by one, and quietly put them back.

The woman, who had followed him into the hallway, asked anxiously, "Were you looking for something?"

"No" he said, "I just wanted to make sure I had the files of the two critically ill patients with me. I brought them home to study last night."

He then put on his black coat and, with a worried look in his dark eyes, said "So much snow! I have to leave earlier this morning and it's so cold! I tried to start the car first thing, but the engine's frozen. It is really falling apart. I called for a cab while you were in the kitchen. Hassan Agha, as usual, was flattery itself, but he said, 'You know that we are devoted to you, doctor, but this damn snow makes it impossible for the cab to get into your road.' He is right too. Anyway, I have to walk to the top of the road now, and wait for the cab."

"But it's too early now. I have made breakfast. Come and eat something before you go," the woman said with sympathy and kindness. "When is Hassan Agha sending the cab?"
"Simeen, I haven't got the time to eat anything," he said.
"Don't worry, I'll eat something as soon as I get to the hospital. The cab is coming at 6.30. It is such a cold day and the snow is badly frozen over. I hope you won't have any excuse for leaving the house today."

She noticed that, as usual, he was in a world filled with his own problems, and did not realise that to ensure there was food on their table, she had to spend hours in different queues everyday. She was silent but indignant.

The man who sensed something was wrong, said in a self-righteous tone, "I don't want to have to worry about you too. Just look after yourself and Taraneh."

Then as he was about to leave, a little girl of about four or five came out of one of the rooms. In her woolly nightdress, she was like a playful, white rabbit as she hopped towards him and said, "Daddy, Daddy, wait a minute! Don't go now! I want to ask you something."

He picked her up, embraced her, kissed her rosy cheeks, and stroked her shiny brown hair, saying "Why are you up so early? Now ask your question, my dear, because I have very little time. I have to leave earlier this morning."

The little girl bent down her head and said sulkily "I don't want you to leave earlier; you're always leaving earlier!"

The man lifted her chin with his hand and with kindness looked into her bright brown eyes and said, "Taraneh, look at me, my pretty little girl. I must leave early. There are many sick and injured people waiting for me at the hospital. Please ask your question dear."

"When will those sick people get better, Daddy? They are always sick!" she said sadly.

"No, Taraneh, they are not always sick, my dear. Some of them get better and leave; but there is war; so, every day many injured people arrive at the hospital from the South."

"I know," she said. "I have seen them on television. They are always dropping bombs there, Daddy. Will the bombs come here too?"

He held his breath in horror at the thought and hugged her more tightly saying, "No! No! They will not come here. They wouldn't dare! But what did you really want to ask me? Have you forgotten it?"

"I wanted to know if you had ever seen a rainbow?" she asked hesitantly.

The question confused him. He had not expected it at

such a time. He was not even sure if he had heard her properly. "Yes dear, of course I have seen one; but why do you want to know now?"

Her eyes lit up as she said, "Banafsheh was here yesterday. She had a really pretty book with her, full of nice pictures. It had a rainbow too Daddy. Banafsheh told me no one has seen a rainbow."

There was a brief silence, as he slowly put the little girl down and kissed her again. "Banafsheh is wrong, my dear. Everyone has seen a rainbow. I'm sure you and Banafsheh will see one too some day. But now, I really must go. I'm sure your mother can answer any other questions you might have."

* * *

The man was walking carefully across the frozen ice and snow trying to keep his balance; but his daughter's question seemed to linger in his mind, haunting him. How could she know a rainbow, if not through pictures in a book! In this polluted city of concrete, with its sky of smoke, his own memory of a rainbow had become like a distant mirage. His heart was heavy with a sad longing, as he finally reached the top of the road.

Akbar Agha, the cab driver, knew him. Once they were seated, and he was behind the wheel, he said with humility, "Good morning to you Doctor. I hope you are feeling fine today. Please have the heart to forgive me for not picking you up at your door. It's this wretched ice and snow."

"Don't worry, Akbar Agha, a little walk is good for me. Tell me, how is your stomach? Did the last tablet I prescribed help you at all?"

"Oh yes," said Akbar Agha, "I'm much better. I pray that God will always keep you for us! God knows these are troubled times, Doctor. Everyone's suffering; it's stomach complaints and stress. I put it all down to all the worry. You have to work like a dog, just to feed your wife and kids. Last

41

month, my eldest son volunteered and was sent to the front. He is only 15. His mother has been crying and worrying the whole month. She's restless, can't sleep. I come home every night, dog-tired but I have to forget how I feel, to give her some comfort. These last few days, she has had a fever and the shivers. Her face is as yellow as turmeric. I really want to try and take a day off, Doctor, and bring her to your hospital. I don't know what it could be. Is it malaria? Maybe it's TB? What kind of fever could it be?"

"Please don't worry," the man said, "Make sure you bring your wife to the hospital tomorrow morning. I will examine her carefully. If necessary, we will run some tests and prescribe something for her. I'm sure she'll recover very soon."

* * *

The cab moved slowly along the road. There were chains on its tyres to stop it from slipping, but it was still very hard to control. Akbar Agha was managing to drive the car very well, talking constantly of the cruel times and singing the doctor's praises. Yet the doctor did not hear every word. He was deep in his own thoughts. His daughter's question and the image of the rainbow kept creeping back into his mind.

He realised that everything had changed; he had changed so much himself. He remembered, years ago, he knew what Nature was. He rarely stayed in the city during the weekends and spent many happy hours in the mountains with his friends. They used to set out at dawn and when the sun's first rays had spread gloriously through the sky, they would be at the peak of Tochal[1]. How sweet was the mountain air that filled his youthful lungs, while the music of the water and light, the birds and life itself, embraced his whole being.

Those were the days when he had time at least to remember that he liked music, specially classical music. He would often go to concerts. It was ten years ago when he had first met Simeen. He had been working as an intern in the hospital and Simeen was finishing her last year at the college of music. He could clearly recollect the night the students of the college of music were performing Beethoven's Sixth Symphony and Simeen was playing the clarinet. He fell in love with her instantly and a year later they were married. He then recalled the day all those years ago, when together they had gone to the village of Demavend,[2] but before they could start climbing the mountain thunder and lightning shook the sky and it started to rain heavily. Yet it stopped as soon as it had started and the triumphant rays of the sun pierced the clouds and painted the most beautiful rainbow on the turquoise sky. They stood in awe at the wonder of it all.

That was the last time he had seen a rainbow.

* * *

His mind wandered to the time when he was four years old. He was with his brother who was a year older than him. They were in the garden which was filled with the scent of summer roses. They both had some colourful glass marbles and they were swapping them, one by one. Then, closing one eye, they held them up against each other in the bright sunshine and in those crystals of light they saw thousands of merging rainbows.

* * *

He was swapping the last glass marble with his brother in his mind, when a terrifying explosion tore the cab from its place, embedding it in a gaping hole in the ground. He could hear Akbar Agha crying out twice "Oh, Ghamareh Bani Hashem![3] Oh, Ghamareh Bani Hashem!"

Then there was silence. He tried to get up and help him. He mustered all his strength; it was no use. A metal rod had pierced his side, from where he could feel the gushing of a warm liquid. His eyes were closed. He felt extremely

43

weak. He opened his eyes with great difficulty. Blood trick-led down slowly from his forehead and covered his eyes and face. He struggled to think what had happened but he had no control over his mind. There was a horrific storm and his body was thrown into a vast field. Through his dying eyes, as though in a dream, he saw a crystal and bright sunshine spread over this field. Simeen and Taraneh were by his side and together they could see boys with large glass marbles strapped to their waists. They were happy and content and started to jump and skip through the field; but with every jump, a rainbow emerged. The whole field was adorned with thousands of rainbows and the boys disappeared.

Light and dust mingled and rose up high; so very high, becoming one with the clouds, the sun, the moon and the stars. Now everything started to fade, dim and dimmer. The black void was engulfing him. It was as if from a dis-tant land, on the other side of the world, at the beginning of time, or perhaps at the very start of creation, he could hear the sound of the sirens; and all was fading still... and then, the whole universe stood still.

[1] Tochal — one of the peaks of the Elburz Mountains
[2] Village of Demavend — the village situated at the base of Demavend, the highest peak of the Elburz Mountains
[3] Ghamareh Bani Hashem — The moon of the Bani Hashem family, the nickname of "Abbas", Imam Hussain's brother, one of the martyrs of Karbala

The Dedication
Aydin Mehmet Ali
(Northern Cyprus)

"I want to welcome you to this special evening..." she begins. Her deep, resonant voice is distilled of any emotion.

"It is an evening we can't organise in our own country. We are no longer together, we are forced apart... divided, we live apart. It is a... a historical moment for us to be together." The silence seeps through the cracks, her voice controls the emotions. He stands next to her dressed in grey, his white head and beard propped up by the gray body. He holds onto his beard, caresses it gently. He will read the Turkish poems in Greek. About Cyprus.

"We want to project onto this screen the unity of our separate images. Even when we are physically apart, we search for that unity... that moment of togetherness. The images of Cyprus... the images can only come together on a screen. Only our images can unite. Thousands of miles away. In the cold distances of another world... here in London."

Her voice slowly cracks. The lights hide the moment and provoke dust particles into a frenzied dance. Shifting feet. Low murmurs. A slight controlled cough. The perpetrators safe in their invisibility. The only signs of an unseen audience. She catches sight of the slim body of the poet walking on stage. His glasses create a flash of light. He stands in the spotlight wearing a white shirt and black waistcoat, his curly head slightly bowed, a book in his left hand.

* * *

I sit at a table in a pub. Lewes, a comfortable British town. Miles from where I was thought of, given birth to, where I grew up, was moulded. The sons and daughters of generals, officers, soldiers, unaware of the history they have created for me, sit around tables, sipping their drinks, enjoying each other, their identities, their smugness, on a lazy Sunday evening.

Cypriot... Cypriot... Turkish... Turkish... Turkish-Cypriot... Cypriot-Turkish... Cyprioturkish...

Which one? Which ones? My brain processes the words at speed, my soul lingers on meanings, Turkish-Cypriot-Woman. Is the relationship as simple as the dash-in-between? The divided person of a divided land, continues her division even further in another land. Searching for the pieces to put together, to claim, searching for "wholeness".

Words on the cover of a book symbolise and eternalise my permanent split state. CYPRUS. I am reading about identity. My eyes are captured by the words... "by July 1958 TMT were able to force Greek Cypriots out of a Nicosia suburb."

I feel the pain of a loss. My loss is mentioned in a book I read thirty years later. What I had suffered becomes history. History on pages. I, as a woman, using my intellect, have to abstract, remove my feelings, remove my childhood pain from it and present it as a piece of polemic for winning arguments and maybe struggles.

Maro! How I had loved you! How I had missed you! One day you were my friend. You were there. Then you were not. The rules had changed. You disappeared one night. I woke up and the night had taken you away. Not even a good-bye! Not a hug! No tears! The unshed tears of losing you. The unshed pain of 30 years overwhelms me.

The morning came without you. As though you had never existed. But you are there. In my photographs. On my eleventh birthday. May 29. By July you had gone, you had become part of history.

Where did the night take you? Where? Did you live through the wars? Did you survive? Are you 40 today just like me? Where are you Maro? My other self. The child inside me escapes from the mask of the grown up and howls.

* * *

"Today has a special meaning for me. I would like to dedicate this evening of poetry, in our three languages, Turkish, Greek and English, to my childhood friend, Maro. I don't know where she is. I don't know what happened to her... She disappeared one night with her family. Her house was left empty. It stood opposite ours as it had always done. Its shutters shut, doors closed. The jasmine wrapped around the balcony. I expected it to wait for them just like me. To sulk, to refuse to blossom. But each day white blossoms opened into the night and offered themselves to the long-tongued moths. And they were shed by the following evening, making a lace carpet on the brown earth. One day the windows opened, a ginger-haired man looked out. Turkish voices seemed so strange coming from Maro's house."

* * *

That day I walked across and dug out the tin of marbles I had buried for safekeeping under the orange tree in her garden. I took it home. Somehow I knew she was not coming back.

How I resented them for taking Maro away from me. At a stroke, part of my existence was wiped out. They came in the night... lined up petrol bombs against the wall next to the door of our balcony. Why? To throw at the Greeks? Who were they, these night visitors? My protectors from the Greeks? Maro is Greek. From Maro? But she is my friend! Why doesn't anybody believe that we are friends? Why? How an eleven-year-old child resented your unseen faces, hands. I can hear the child's voice inside me, resisting. The unshed tears of 30 years of pain, fall. What my 'identity' did not allow me, what I did not allow myself to do, as a young Turkish-Cypriot girl of eleven.

* * *

"I would like to dedicate this evening of poetry about peace, love and optimism, the poetry of my friend who has gone through another war 15 years after the one I lived through, to my childhood friend, Maro. With the same conviction and stubbornness of the poet who believes in the power of love and poetry, I want to believe that she has survived the wars and is alive!"

Baghdad Diaries
Nuha al-Radi
(Iraq)

Day 1

I woke up at 3am to the barrage of exploding bombs. I let
out a huge groan that I can still hear. I couldn't believe
that war had started. I went out on the balcony, the sky
was lit up with the most extraordinary firework display —
the noise was beyond description. My dog, Salvador Dali,
was chasing frantically round the two houses looking up at
the sky and barking furiously. I couldn't get an answer
from Ma and Needles' phone so tried Suha who answered
in a hushed voice from her shelter under the stairs, and
told me to put out my lights. "What for?" I asked. "All the
street lights are still on." Suha, being a fastidious and effi-
cient person, had taped all her windows and doors against
nuclear fallout, and organised the windowless room under
the stairs as her shelter and stashed it with provisions. I
refused to take any such precautions, but Ma insisted on it
and made a variety of designs on my windows, scrimping
on the last ones as she ran out of tape.

Later on I ventured outside to put out the garage light.
Salvador was very nervous. Shortly after that we lost all
electricity, I needn't have bothered with putting the lights
out. The phones followed suit and went dead. I think we
are done for, a modern nation cannot fight without electricity and communications. Thank heavens for our ration
of Pakistani matches. Thinking of you Handy, glued to the
television in Karachi — are you with us? Why are we being
punished in this way?

With the first bomb, Ma and Needles' windows shattered, the ones facing the river. It's a good thing their

49

shutters were down otherwise they could both have been badly hurt. One of poor Bingo's pups was killed in the garden by flying glass — our first war casualty. Bingo is the mother of Salvador Dali. Myra, Ilham and the boys came in the morning, went and then returned to stay the night.

Day 2
Myra, Ilham and the boys went off to Khanaqin, they think they will be safer there. Amal and Munir, whose house is also on the river, lost all their windows the first night they moved in. Ma and Suha come and stay the nights, during the day they all go off to check on their own houses. Needles prefers to stay with Menth. My closest neighbour M.A.W. joins us for dinner, his wife is away in London.

Said came by and picked up Suha and me to have lunch with Taha. Said has a good supply of petrol but is not ready to give us any of it. We had kebab and beer; delicious. They were both quite unfazed by the situation and think that we are doing quite well. I can't think what they mean. No air raids en route. Salvador still barks wildly when the sirens go.

Today, all over Baghdad, government trucks threw bread to the thronging crowds.

Day 3
Suha and I spent the day merrily painting in my studio while the war was going on full blast outside. I wonder where the detachment comes from, whilst others are gnashing their teeth with fear. This afternoon we saw a SAM missile explode in the sky. I also caught Mundher Baig riding around on his grandson's tricycle, scrunched up with his legs under his chin, pedalling round and round in his driveway. He said he was enjoying himself. He misses his grandchildren and is convinced that he will not see them again.

At night we had a fire in the orchard. At first we thought it was war damage but in fact it was Fulayih's fault. He had been burning some dry wood near the dead fuel of a palm tree, trying to turn it into coal. We used up all our water, Dood's house and mine combined, plus the fire extinguisher from the car to put out this fire. Now we have no water, and Fulayih has no fuel.

Day 4

Woke up to an air raid at 5am. Went to Zaid's house to leave a message and saw his two old aunts, each probably 110 years old; one was bent double over the stove while the other never stopped chattering beside her. Because of the constant air raids they are afraid to go upstairs to their bedrooms so they sleep in their clothes on couches in the sitting room, missing their familiar mattresses and pillows. They seem oblivious to the enormity of what's happening around them, concentrating only on the immediate things, so old and frail yet so alive and entertaining. Their phone still works so I tried to call Assia and Suha whose house is right across the river from the Dora refinery. A huge black sky covers that part of Baghdad. It must be horrific living there. No one answered the telephone.

Mundher Baig started a generator for their house on precious and scarce petrol. Ten of us just stood around gaping in wonder at this machine and the noise it made. Only four days have passed since the start of the war and already any machinery and mod cons seem to be totally alien, like something from Mars.

Suhas is experimenting with making *basturma* (cured sausages) from meat in her freezer. Our freezers are beginning to defrost, so it's a good thing that it's so cold.

Salvador continues to attack M.A.W. who aggravates him by brandishing his walking stick at him, we now have to escort him in and out of the orchard. At dinner M.A.W's stomach growled and Ma thought it was an air raid. Cooked potatoes in the fireplace, trying to save on gas. M.A.W. said one could taste the potato in the smoke, admittedly they were charred. The sky is a wondrous sight at night, every star clearly shining amidst the fireworks and the continuous noise of explosions. I hope Sol [the author's sister] and Dood are not too worried about us. They should know that we are survivors.

Made a dynamic punch tonight with Aquavit, vodka and fresh orange juice. We ate fish and rice.

Day 5

Munir gave me a calendar today. It's 21 January. My painting of Mundher Baig and family is nearly finished. Got my bicycle fixed. It's a brand new one, never been used, and we had been trying for days to inflate the tyres. They both turned out to have punctures. I told the guy who was mending it that it was new. "They always come like this," he said. Does someone actually puncture them before they leave the factory? It's an Iraqi bike, imaginatively called Baghdad. It's a good thing they didn't call it Ishtar; her name already dignifies fridges, freezers, soap, matches, heaters and hotels. You name it, it's called Ishtar. That proud goddess of war would not have liked her name being associated with such lowly things. Imagination is not our strongest point when it comes to naming things.

We are now all going to the loo in the orchard, fertilising it and saving ourselves some water which no longer flows out of the taps. Janette comes by every day. She says everyone has gone off to the countryside because it's the best place to be during a war. Then she said "But your house is like being in the country anyway, and that's the best place to be in. Lucky you." She's so right. None of us is budging from this orchard paradise, which it truly is. She is looking around for a bedfellow today, quite crazed. I said it wasn't uppermost in my mind right now.

Basil came by and I told him to put his mind to work on basic agriculture. Now that we are back in the Dark Ages, we have to figure out a way to haul up water from the river. He is cooking up all the foodstuff he had in his freezer and feeding it to his cats. His wife and daughters can't be bothered.

Apparently people have taken off for the countryside with their freezers loaded on their pick-up trucks. They eat their way through the food as it defrosts — barbecues in the country. Quite mad. Only we would escape from a war carrying freezers full of goodies. Iraqis have been hoarders for centuries. It's a national habit. Since one never knows when anything will be available on the market, one buys when one sees, and in great quantities. Most people automatically queue up when they see a line forming, not caring what's at the other end; boot polish, soap, tomatoes or a useless gadget. Needles says she is running out of chickens when she has twenty left in the freezer.

Day 6

Got up for the regular 8am air raid. It finished an hour later. We go and queue for petrol — our ration: 20 litres. Amal, who never remembers to wear her glasses, backed into a wall.

The entire country has collapsed and disintegrated in a few days. They say that outside Baghdad everything appears to be normal. I wonder how long we can survive this kind of bombardment. This afternoon Muwafaq and Ala brought a hysterical, crying Hind. They wanted to come and stay here. Hind screamed and cried all the time. She insists on dragging everyone down to their cellar every air raid, now she wants to drag the entire household (grandmother, mother, brother, fiancé and herself) to Khanaqin. No one wanted to go there; the alternative was to come here. Poor Maarib, who is not well and had trouble with her eyes, does not want to be parted from her own bathroom. In normal times she takes about five baths a day and puts cream all over her body after each one. I go to their car. Hind is still crying. I am very stern with her — rules of the house are no crying, no guns, no smoking. She continues to howl, saying "I'm scared, I don't want to die." No stopping her waterworks, they leave undecided.

Today is the sixth day. I hope we get water tomorrow.

Day 7

The worst has happened — beer without ice. Cleaned out the freezer and removed a ton of different kinds of bread. All I ever had in my freezer was bread, ice and bones for Salvador. Asma has so much chicken in hers that she gave some away and grilled the rest. Now Nufa goes around chewing on chicken rather than her usual chocolate bars. She is keeping those for harder times, she says.

Following Suha's recipe for *basturma*, Ma began making her own. None of us has ever made *basturma* before and we thought that it would be a good way to preserve our meat. We minced raw meat and mixed it with a lot of different spices and salt, and then stuffed the mixture into nylon stockings, in lieu of animal intestines, which were not available. Suha's hand mincer was resurrected and put to use. We are using Dood's house as our fridge — all that marble, what a come-down. My bread covers all the tables and the *basturmas* hang above.

We have to eat an enormous amount of food so as not to throw it away. This means we shit so much more — all is done in the garden. If we use the bathroom, we fear that the sewage will back up on us — I have only now discovered that electricity moves it. One takes so much for granted. Wonder whether the Allies thought of such things when they were planning the bombing. I don't think we will be seeing electricity for a long time to come.

Started burning the rubbish today and clearing the orchard of dead matter. Amal was helping, wearing her usual high heels even for collecting brambles.

Rumour has it that we are going to have a difficult night ahead. This is the seventh night, maybe Bush thinks he is God too. But it clouded over, so maybe God was on our side tonight. Now there are three gods. Who will win?

We got some water today but the pressure was too weak to get it up to the tank on the roof. Never mind. I'm not complaining. At least we got to fill up all the buckets. All our drinking water must be boiled now.

I finished Mundher's painting so we had a little party to celebrate its unveiling. Everyone was impressed and thought I deserved a prize. We opened a bottle of champagne and ate *meloukhia* (a type of vegetable stew) and a million other things. I wish that our stock of food would finish so that we could eat a little less. M.A.W.'s sister and brother-in-law fled their house in Fahama and came to live with him. Now there are two more for dinner. She left dressed in a green suit, which is all she possesses now. They huddle together for security. She is sweet but hardly says a word. He never stops talking and is as deaf as a post. He is probably the last surviving communist in this country. In his youth he was well-known for singing old Iraqi songs, so he entertained us and lulled us all to sleep with his nice voice — sleeping heads lolling in different directions.

Day 8
Silence reigns. It's six in the morning, and no air raid. I ate so much last night that I couldn't go to sleep. Depression has hit me with the realisation that the whole world hates us and is really glad to ruin us. It's not a comforting thought. It's an unfair world. Other countries do wrong. Look at what Russia did in Afghanistan, or Turkey's invasion of Cyprus, or Israel taking over Palestine and Lebanon. Nobody bombed them senseless the way we are being bombarded now. They were not even punished. Iraq has had many high and low peaks in its long history, we have certainly become notorious. This will be neither the first nor the last time. "Too much history," as Sol always says. At least Baghdad is now on the map. I will no longer have to explain where I come from.

I had these two dreams before the start of the war: the Americans in battle fatigues jogging down Haifa Street and lining up in the alleyways, kissing each other. They were led by a girl dressed in red who was running very fast. Then suddenly the scene switched and I was coming out of the house and everything was dry as dust, just earth, and I was all alone. I said to myself, "I will build and plant it so that it will be the most beautiful garden." Later, what bothered me about this dream was the loneliness of it. Am I going to be the only survivor?

(From *Baghdad Diaries* by Nuha al-Radi, London, Saqi Books, 1998. Reprinted by permission of Saqi Books.)

The Raid
Shehrazad
(Iraq)

It was one of those very hot summer days in Baghdad when the search took place in a hall of residence for female university students.

Shireen and Samar, both twenty-two years of age, had been friends for three years. They were studying in the School of Engineering and lived together in Room 22 alongside 1,500 other female Medical and Science students from different parts of Iraq.

The students used to call it the Gulbenkian Building, a prestigious affair, even after the oil nationalisation. The building had been established by Mrs. Gulbenkian through her donations to charities, since Mr. Gulbenkian held a big slice of the shares in Iraqi oil.

Shireen was short with a round face, blonde hair and dark brown eyes. Her family lived in the ancient region of Kirkuk. The city had recently been renamed Al-Ta'ameem. This made her very angry so she was constantly making comments about the whole situation. "What kind of a world are we living in? It's Kurdish and they want to call it Ta'ameem! If they called it Ta'ameem in Kurdish, okay — maybe that would be possible... what a Shiite world."

Samar was from the South. She was very tall with blonde hair and green eyes. She had a southern accent but she considered the Baghdad accent to be much higher class. Unfortunately, however much she tried, her southern accent could still be heard in her speech.

It was the middle of May. The academic year was nearly finished. Most of the students had taken their exams.

Some had already left to join their families for the summer holiday.

The whole atmosphere was soaked in lethargy. Files were everywhere: in the rooms, passages, showers, toilets and kitchen. The building had not been cleaned, nor the rubbish collected during the exam period. Shireen and Samar's room was very hot because the fan was broken. Shireen wore a black bra and waist slip. She held a large towel in her hands to drive the flies out of the door. "Samar, what about seeing the French Alain Delon film? They say it's very good. Every five minutes, Alain wears a different outfit." Shireen continued to drive out the flies as she talked. "No... What about the new Egyptian film, *Mahmoud Yassina and Nilli*. It's got love and romance, lots of kissing and beach scenes where they're half naked."

In the end they decided to have something to eat before going to the four o'clock show. Shireen volunteered to go and prepare some tea. Using the kitchen and especially the cooker was a major headache because there was only one that was shared between 200 girls and the kitchen was just four by four metres. The floor was layered with dirt: crumbs, grease, egg shells, potato skins and burnt paper that was discarded after being used to light the only two gas rings that were working.

Shireen entered the kitchen and started talking and joking with the girls waiting their turn. In this way she charmed herself to the head of the queue. Shireen served the tea, while Samar carried on her war against the invading flies. "Samar should I put on my blue jeans and red shirt?" Shireen inquired. "No, please, my dear, for God's sake, I'm not in the mood for trouble. Anything but trousers or a short skirt." Samar replied quietly. "But I want to wear them. When am I going to wear them?" Shireen answered. "Why are you wasting my breath? You know what men are like? God bless them! Bum pinchers will be two a penny after dark down there and the film ends after seven. Al-Sadon Street will be packed with men. Just wear a long skirt, so we can be a bit safer."

As Samar said this, four men and the matron invaded room 22. The girls were shocked and became very nervous in the presence of the strangers. Shireen was still in her bra and waist slip. She fumbled quickly to put on her blue dressing gown but in her panic got it on inside out. The four men and the woman smiled coolly. "We're checking the inventory. It's the end of the year," said one of the men by way of an excuse for their abrupt visit. Shireen and Samar looked at him in amazement. The speaker was fat with a thin black moustache. He wore a bright blue summer suit, a short sleeved light jacket and wide trouser legs typical of the Party style. His shoes were the standard red patent leather with high in-step and heel.

Room 22 was a square shape, with four single beds and four wooden fitted cupboards. The short fat man went towards the two posters fixed on the wall. "Who are the people in these posters?" he said angrily. "Franco Kaspari and Alain Delon," Shireen answered. "Don't you know it's against the rules to put up posters in these halls of residence?" The fat man's tone was hostile. He put a matchstick between his teeth and began sucking. Then he went to the other wall and glanced at the posters. "Who do these belong to? You don't have to tell me who they are. This is Mahmoud Yassin and the other one is Hussien Fihmi." Samar looked frightened and was becoming more nervous. Shireen remained angry. Shireen came from a poor family and had a lot of brothers. The two eldest had finished their studies and had completed two years' military service. Now they worked as agricultural engineers. As a result, the financial situation for her family had improved and she was over the moon about their change in circumstances. She'd always dreamed of wearing foreign clothes. "I want to wear brand names with 'made in...' on the label." And she would say "made in" in English.

Nowadays, Shireen went every week to Al-Nahire Street, which was the biggest shopping centre in Baghdad, to buy imported clothes. The political situation did not interest Shireen but being Kurdish and harassed every day for it, she knew how to avoid even very short conversations with Arab nationalist students or government party students. She believed that Arabs were responsible for the misery suffered by the Kurds, although Shireen's friends and boyfriend were Arab.

The second man was tall, pale-skinned and balding. He had two gold teeth which stuck out prominently from his mouth. He wore a very dirty, bright purple, light nylon shirt with tight, white trousers. He had sat on one of the beds as soon as they had burst into the room. After systematically searching the bed and pillows, he had found some photographs. While staring at them carefully, he asked casually "Who sleeps in this bed?" "Me," Shireen answered but this time with more fear in her voice. "Your fiancé's or...?" he gestured with his hand and a fake smile and moved his eyebrows up and down waiting for her answer. "No, he's not my fiancé, but God willing, he shall be soon — very soon." Her round white face was turning very red and she had begun to sweat. They were photos of Shireen's boyfriend taken last year when he had gone to Paris for the summer holidays. Most of the photos were of the boyfriend standing in front of the Eiffel Tower and in cafés along the Saint Michel.

The third man was tall, olive-skinned and very handsome. He was wearing a foreign suit and had a Rothman's cigarette in his mouth. While the search progressed, he and the matron talked and flirted together. They all addressed him as 'Sir' — a term reserved exclusively for military and secret police officers.

The 'Sir' walked towards the wooden cupboard and looked at the pictures which were tacked on the inside door of the cupboard. "Which one of you likes ballet?" the 'Sir' asked in a friendly tone. "None of us really... We just cut out the pictures from magazines to cheer up the room," Shireen answered. "This one's okay, a ballerina dancing, but..." he indicated the picture next to it... "Male and female together?" In a sudden movement he tore all the pictures off the inside door. Everyone stood in shocked

60

silence. All they could hear were the flies. Everybody in the room was waiting for some disaster except the matron who continued to flirt with the 'Sir'. "You know posters aren't allowed," she said as if to justify the 'Sir's' behaviour towards the girls.

The 'Sir' took some of the books and magazines out of the cupboard and put them on one of the beds. He sat next to them, opened his legs comfortably and started reading the titles imitating a police officer or detective voice in American movies. *"The Political Report — The Students' Voice — Arab Revolutions — Montalakat — Nationalisation — Michael Aflak — Alyass Faraht — Saddam Hussain.* Who do these political books belong to?" he asked politely. "They're mine," Samar answered. "Are you a member of the Ba'athist party?" he asked. "Yes," she answered more quietly. "The comrade seems very intellectual but I think you have too many political books," he said. "My eldest brother teaches at the Nationalist and Socialist college," she replied, smiling. This was a newly established training centre for élite secret police.

Every two or three minutes the golden mouth would stop searching and walk to the mirror to check his appearance and cover his balding head with the few strands of hair which still grew at the back. He then began to take the foodstuff and tins out of the cupboard. "Beef, Cream, Cheese, Toothpaste, Tea." He rummaged with his right hand in the teabag container as he spoke. The short man in the purple shirt was busy searching through the pots of food on the table with a spoon. "Mash Allah! You are very good cooks! Our girls are real housewives! Your cooking is delicious! As you know Iraqi men are very fond of their stomachs." While he was commenting, he tested and then ate from each pot he opened.

Shireen and Samar were very bad cooks, so they never bothered. Shireen's father travelled to Baghdad every week, from Kirkuk to buy produce for his fruit and vegetable shop. He visited his daughter with food cooked by Shireen's mother. Shireen loved to see her father but she always made sure that none of the girls from the halls ever saw him. Shireen's father used to dress in traditional Kurdish clothing. When the Kurdish political movement failed in the mid-seventies, and after the oil nationalisation, there were thousands of jokes about the Kurds, how stupid and foolish they were.

In Shireen's first year, some of the girls had spotted her father and had made fun of his outfit, particularly the long, wide belt which was worn around the waist. Shireen learned her lesson early. Since then, she had always managed to find a reason why her father should not meet her at the halls of residence.

The fat man was busy searching the other beds. On Samar's bed under her pillow, he found many photographs. He stared at each photo. She became nervous again, watching the fat man holding her photos and walked towards him quickly. "Are these girl friends from your university?" the fat man asked. "No," she answered. Samar had been looking for a wife for her eldest brother. She always managed to persuade other girls to let her take their photograph at students' parties and trips. Then she chose the most beautiful one and found out as soon as she could whether she was available. Often her brother ended up meeting these girls thanks to Samar's hard work. But so far none of her hunting had worked out. She used to visit her brother's hall of residence once a week and usually really enjoyed herself. Each time she would talk for days afterwards about the building. "Dear, the minute you enter my brother's halls... you forget that God created poverty when you see the flooring, the garden, the furniture, the walls..."

The 'Sir' opened Shireen's cupboard again and started taking out items of her clothing one by one and commenting on them. "Skirt, bra, knickers, trousers, bra..." He spoke with palpable relish. Shireen looked very red and angry and moved quickly towards the 'Sir' until she was as close to him as she could get. The 'Sir' was still taking out her clothes and commenting happily. He got hold of a big, fat, closed paper bag. Shireen grabbed his hand. "No! Please don't open it! This is private stuff. Please." The 'Sir' held onto the paper bag tightly and said "Let go! I want to see what's in it." "Please! It's private. It doesn't concern you at all." Shireen pleaded. The 'Sir' pushed her onto the bed. "Leave me alone bitch, let me see what you are hiding." The other two men restrained her violently. By this time Shireen was sobbing uncontrollably.

He put his hand in the bag and felt something wet. He pulled out a bloodied sanitary towel. Everybody stared at the disgust on the 'Sir's' face as he held the soaking fresh pad in his hand.

Women
Incarcerated

The Executions

Shahrnush Parsipur

(Iran)

Translated from Farsi by Abbas Milani

Bored as I was, I began, along with a few other inmates, to make worry beads. The dough of the bread was the material we used to form the beads and we used powder paint to colour them.

At this time, prisoners were being regularly taken for interrogation. They usually wore oversized slippers to these ordeals. The reason for this was that they were regularly whipped on their feet, and in consequence, the feet would swell. Had they not taken their oversized slippers, they would have had to walk back to the cell on bruised feet.

The daily departure of these prisoners to the prosecutor's office created an incredible atmosphere of terror in the cell. I continued to make worry beads and observe my cellmates. The number of prisoners had drastically increased.

The number of prisoners beaten was also on the rise. I remember well Shahin, a dark-faced girl. She belonged to one of the leftist groups. I asked her to show me her bruises. She laughed and said that because of her dark skin, the bruises could not be seen. I followed each case with avid curiosity. It seemed in some cases that the whole body was one big bruise.

The next night I saw Shahin in the bathroom again. She seemed happy as she chatted to her friend — apparently she had gone to another interrogation, and now felt that the danger had passed. A couple of days later, she seemed rather nervous again, and that night she was summoned once more to the prosecutor's office. The next day her name appeared on the list of those who had been executed. I had by then become a friend of her friend and I asked her about Shahin. Apparently, Shahin's crime was to have been the driver of a car in the trunk of which a small printing press had been hidden. On the last day of her life, Shahin had told her friend that she thought she was going to be executed. She knew this because the interrogator had fondled her breasts and that was a sure sign of doom.

The truth is I have never seen a political prisoner who had been sexually abused or molested. There was a rumour that virgins condemned to die were married to the Revolutionary Guards before their execution. According to tradition, if a virgin girl is buried, she will take a man with her. Since no one who was ever executed ever came back to speak of their experience, I was never able to verify this rumour. Shahin's words are my only proof. I also knew of a couple of prisoners who came very close to having sexual relations with their interrogators. In one case the cause was the girl's clever attempt to avoid torture. The second case was a heated love affair between a prisoner and her interrogator.

Toward the end of September, the number of prisoners who could not walk was on the increase. They had been badly whipped on the soles of their feet. After a while, a swollen lump, the size of an orange, would appear on the bottom of their feet. One of the biggest problems for these prisoners was walking to the bathroom. Some found a clever solution: they turned a big metal cheese container into a chamber pot. They installed a thin layer of foam around the rim of the pot; three people would embrace the wounded prisoner and gingerly lower her onto it.

One night, as we all lay in the dark, I decided to go to the bathroom, hoping to avoid the long line in the morning. It was one o'clock in the morning. Prisoners were lined up next to each other on the floor. They were all awake. There was absolute silence in the cell. Something ominous was in the atmosphere. There was no line for the toilet.

Instead, a few prisoners stood around and took turns to climb up on the water-heater and look out. When I approached, I saw one of the girls trembling. Although we were not friends, she held my arm and quietly said that the bodies of prisoners were being lined up in the yard. From about eleven o'clock that night, a piercing sound had been heard at more or less regular intervals. One of the prisoners suggested that the authorities were constructing a new visiting centre and what we heard was the sound of steel being unloaded. The girl I was with became visibly more shaken when the sound was heard again. I asked her about the sound. She said it was machine-gun fire.

By the time that long and bitter night finally passed, we had counted more than 250 *coups de grace*. In the newspapers the next day, I found the names of more than 300 people who had been executed.

The following day was even more awful for everyone in the block. They took a few prisoners from each block to the office of the prosecutor. There, after summary trials lasting between two and five minutes, the prisoners were divided into two lines. One line was taken to be executed; the other was returned to the cells. The intent was probably to bring terror to everyone. Many of the prisoners who were called to trial that night behaved abnormally for many months afterwards. I saw one of them occasionally fall as she walked, and then get up and continue as though nothing had happened. Another sat the whole night gazing at the toothbrushes, the towels and the jackets of the executed prisoners...

That same day they brought Holou to our block. She was a shy girl and stood in a corner, motionless. I asked her her name. "Houlou," she replied. It was a habit of the Mujahadin to give a false name at the time of arrest. In prison, they would call one another by names of flowers, fruits and animals. The leftists also had the same habit. Houlou, Persian for peach, truly suited her.

I told Houlou that I would like to know her real name. With tears in her eyes, she said she had already died four times. She explained how from the moment of her arrest, up until our conversation, the guards had simulated her execution four times. Twice the Revolutionary Guards had stormed a bus ferrying prisoners, pretending to go on a rampage. On another occasion, they had stood her against a wall, told her she was going to be shot, and then fired blanks at her. I forget the details of her fourth experience. As we talked, it was clear that something had truly died in her; she was only 15 years old and I was filled with silent rage about her torments.

Another of the prisoners, named Golshan, seemed deeply melancholic. I was told that only last week her father, along with other monarchists, had been executed. I tried to help this young girl and soon became friends with her. Before her incarceration, she had performed her prayers religiously, but had quit them upon her arrest. She had been at an engineering college somewhere in England; around Easter time she had returned to Iran to marry her fiancé. Her father was a member of a monarchist group and as bad luck would have it, when Revolutionary Guards raided her father's office to arrest him and other members of the group, she was in the office. As she claimed, and I have no reason to doubt it, her only participation in the group was typing one of their letters. She was arrested along with everybody else. During interrogations she had behaved badly, being utterly intransigent on matters of rather dubious significance. For instance, she had refused to wear a veil or to remove her nail varnish from her fingers. The sight of her father's execution had changed her radically. I think she tried to compensate for her father's timorous behaviour during his trial by her own valour.

While in Evin prison, she had a dream that she related to me. She dreamt that she was engulfed inside an octopus. A big tendril forcefully entered the entrails and plucked someone from inside each organ, placing them in another tendril, Golshan began to scream, 'Take me too! Take me too!" and she ran after the big tendril. The tendril deposited the abducted people on top of a hill and Golshan heard the voice of the Octopus saying "I just had this hankering to bring them out here."

The dream was important. In prison, the killing grounds were called 'hills'. In hindsight, I regret I did not try at the time to analyse her dream for her. I only told her, "Golshan, be careful." As was her habit, she took some pills and hid under a blanket. Under the blanket was her only place of solace.

Towards the end of November, overcrowding in the prison reached an explosive point. There were more than 350 people crammed in our few cells. Every night, a group of prisoners was forced to stand in a corner, because there was not enough room for everyone to sit down. Summary trials and mass executions had become routine... I was tired and disheartened. I felt the weight of all the corpses on my shoulders. In one way, though, I felt happy to be in prison in these treacherous times; I knew that if I had been free, and had not taken any steps to protest against the executions, I would have forever hated myself. But the unfolding catastrophe was much bigger than anything I could do, bigger even than anything a political group could do. In captivity, one is not tormented with these problems, for there is definitely nothing one can do. I knew that when the sad history of these days came to be written down, then at least my role would be clear.

Albert Camus, in his interpretation of the Sisyphus myth — the man who had killed his son and was commanded by the gods to spend eternity pushing a rock up a steep hill so that it can roll down again — claims that the man is happy because he need make no choices. Now, in prison, in times of bloody and banal brutality, I too was happy because I need not make any choices. I had not asked to be in this position, but I made no efforts to escape from it, leaving my fate in the hands of the Hezbollah.

71

A Woman in Exile

Amba Bongo
(Democratic Republic of Congo)
From Une Femme en Exil *(A Woman in Exile)*
Translated by Jennifer Langer

That Saturday was a special day for the whole family. On the first Saturday in May, grandmother Anna, whose name the young woman proudly bore, assembled all her nine children, 41 grandchildren and 16 great grandchildren. Grandfather, from whom she was separated, had remarried a young nurse by whom he had had five other children. Grandmother Anna had practically brought them up single-handed and considered them as her own children.

Everybody had been invited to the celebration which started at the beginning of the afternoon. There was a big barbecue in the garden behind the house and everyone brought a dish and cooked it on the embers. There were so many things to prepare: well-seasoned grilled chicken, tilapia and cat-fish marinated in a mixture of peppers and onion, salted, smoked fish, ginger fritters, ripe plantains, red sweet potatoes, potatoes, huge yams... The kitchen was clearly too small... The male members of the family dealt with the drinks which they had already stacked in a corner, packs of Primus, Skol and other sweet drinks. The brothers-in-law worked hard to please their mother-in-law. Chairs had been borrowed from neighbours who had also been invited. The celebration was in full swing under the African sky and the light conversation punctuated by bursts of laughter. Disagreements were put aside, if only for this one day, and the whole family was happy. It was a really vibrant festival of colour, music, dance and joy.

Young Anna felt happy as well. She had invited Christopher who all the family knew and with whom she was very much in love. He embodied her ideal man — tender, intellectual and virile. Christopher was a domineering partner when he wished, a friend who knew how to take care of her, at the same time respecting her independence and her accumulated experience. He had taught her so much and had opened her eyes to the world; Christopher had known how to awaken in her a languid sensuality and dormant feelings which had surprised and amazed them.

In addition, he had taken her to the 'Must', the nightclub which was the talk of the town. They had left the family celebration at about midnight and had gone for a lovers' stroll along the Boulevard of Trente Juin in the centre of town. Then they had danced to the rhythm of Koffi Olomide. Anna was a fervent fan of this singer with his raucous and sensual voice. All Africa was dancing to him. Anna had never been able to resist *'Rue l'Amour,'* *'L'homme de la rue,'* *'Ngobila'* or *'Diva'*. The young woman stood up abruptly and threw herself on to the dance floor already packed with dancers, arms up, eyes closed, mouthing the song, rocking sensually to the gentle rhythm of the music. However, sitting on a recliner at the bottom of the garden savouring this smooth voice with eyes half-closed and face turned towards the burning sun, was from afar a more vivid sensation, with the melody reaching every inch of her soul. So then the young woman gave thanks for having created a being as much endowed with love as with pleasure.

The young couple had met up with friends and acted the fool together. The evening was merry and romantic. Christopher could not take his eyes off her. Anna loved his looks of desire, which made her feel like a real woman...

However, Anna did not want to abuse all of this, because she needed to be fresh for the following day. She had to pack her parents' suitcases as they were catching the plane to Inongo. Anna took great pleasure in packing her parents' clothes, deciding what each parent would wear during their stay in the village of Inongo. Occasionally, feeling mischevious, she buried at the bottom of the suitcase an object, a photo or a picture which would surprise one of them and make them aware that she was always with them, whether near or faraway. She imagined their astonishment, which made her smile and filled her heart with joy. That would chase away that feeling of heaviness and emptiness which she always experienced when they went away. Anna buried this little melancholy secret in her heart until her parents' return a month or two later.

Although her brother Melongo was seeing to everything, her parents always took a real pleasure in helping with the harvest. It was a ritual that Loseno and Sisika would not miss for anything. Each year, around June, while the men kept an eye on the picking, drying, crushing and the packing of the coffee and other products from the plantation, Sisika saw to the buying of the fish and game. She preferred to buy them in the village rather than in the capital because they were fresher. The Manga women were used to keeping the best products for him and they in turn were well-rewarded with large tips.

Loseno, as deputy of the sub region of Mai-Ndombe, had political responsibilities for conscription. He always managed to reconcile his two important areas and had no difficulty in working for his people as well as for his family.

On her return from the airport, the young woman had helped Temiko — her little soulmate as she liked to call her — find some missing jigsaw puzzle pieces, but she had ended up falling sound asleep under the pergola, rocking peacefully on the swing. It was early evening and there was a slight breeze. A gentle wind caressed her face and a bird on one of the young fruit trees added a melody to the young woman's dreams.

She was jolted awake by the abrupt screeching of brakes. Had she had a nightmare? No, her dream still seemed delightful.

* * *

74

Four large men dressed in uniform got out of a black car which had stopped in front of the gate. Soldiers! The young woman's heart skipped a beat. As she stood up from the garden swing, Moseka emerged from the living room. They were both standing on the verandah as if hypnotised by the appearance of these soldiers. The soldiers walked up the few steps which separated them from the two sisters and one of them asked:

"Miss Anna Elykia?"

"That's me. What do you want?"

"We have been ordered to take you with us."

"Have you got an arrest warrant?" asked Moseka. She was frightened for her little sister. She had never seen this kind of uniform before.

"We don't need one. We take whoever we want, where we want and when we want. We use any means to achieve our ends. It is not in your interest to resist."

Anna shook with fear, all of a sudden feeling goose pimples covering her forearms.

"Let me change," said the young woman.

She needed time to reflect. She thought of Kola and of his warning three weeks ago when he had threatened her and told her that she would not survive because of her behaviour and that there would be trouble in store for her. Anna had not really paid any attention but she had been distracted from her work. She had not spoken about it to anyone, not even to her father because she had not wanted to worry him pointlessly but now she regretted it.

"There is no need to change. That's quite good enough."

The young woman wore a flimsy, cotton, ankle-length nightdress which she liked wearing in very hot weather because it made her feel cool. On her feet she wore wooden clogs.

One of the soldiers gripped her firmly by the arm and Anna felt his fingers sinking deep into her flesh. She shivered with fear. They went down the steps, taking her with them.

"Let me come with her," begged Moseka.

"Stay where you are!" replied the fourth man. He softened a little, turning towards her to say:

"Get her a loincloth, otherwise she might catch cold."

Moseka ran into the bedroom and grabbed a loincloth and a blanket, and... She wanted to take more things but her head was buzzing. She could not think clearly. Her sister was being kidnapped in front of her very eyes and she was powerless to prevent it.

A long honking sound from the car horn brought her back to reality and she hurried out of the house. As she held out the loincloth and the blanket to her sister, one of the soldiers snatched the blanket and threw it through the car window. He walked away laughing and started the engine.

All this had happened so quickly that Anna had not even had time to speak to her sister. Her parents had flown off that morning. She had taken them to N'djili airport. If only they had been there, they could maybe have prevented the soldiers from taking her away but maybe not... These men seemed so determined. Anna thought of her sister who looked frightened and powerless.

Anna had heard so much about kidnappings in the last few years. People talked about organisations that killed people and then sold their organs to distant Western research centres. Would she suffer the same fate? Perhaps they would simply torture her, tearing out her nails or one or two teeth. Anna shivered. She would die for sure, she who almost passed out just thinking about an injection. "Good Lord, help me, don't abandon me. I still want to do so much... so much."

Anna was terrified. She found herself wedged between two soldiers; one drove and one was sitting in the front seat. They were deathly quiet. She felt so afraid. Her heart was beating so fast that she felt ill. She groped for her watch on her left wrist. Although it was there, Anna did not dare look at the time. The man beside her moved slightly, took a scarf out of his pocket and leaned over the

76

young woman. "Don't move," he said. He tied the scarf over her eyes and knotted it at the back of her head so that she was in utter darkness. Anna told herself that she must find a way of calming herself. The whole car seemed to resonate with her heartbeat. Breathe in, breathe out, again and again. She repeated this several times until her breathing returned to normal. One thing brought under control.

Feeling a bit calmer, Anna tried to work out where she was, but it was difficult to do this blindfolded. She was sure they were still in the centre of the capital because the traffic was still heavy and she could hear the hooting and braking of cars as well as passers-by shouting. As they drove along, the traffic became lighter and the young woman sensed they had left the town behind and were penetrating the adjoining bush with the noise of cars and people replaced by bird song, toads and other insects. Anna was so tired, but she could not manage to close her eyes. She was so frightened. What were they going to do to her?

The car turned right abruptly, reducing speed, and they drove slowly for a few more minutes. Then as the driver hooted twice, the young woman heard the grating noise of a gate and the car slowed down again. They had definitely entered a military compound because she could hear the sound of soldiers' feet coming and going. The blindfold was removed and she was pushed out of the car. Although she could not see very well, she could see she was in a large villa which must have had two or three floors. One of the soldiers took her by her left arm and pushed her towards the house, in front of which was a guard. The soldier led her down a corridor and then pushed her into a small yard which they crossed in a few paces. Then they entered a red brick building and descended to the basement where they headed along other narrow corridors. Everything was so gloomy and cramped! The badly lit corridor gave off an unbearable smell of urine and dampness. The soldier holding her walked briskly, propelling her in front of him.

There were several iron doors with little rectangular openings. He stopped in front of one. One of the guards quickly came up, saluted, opened a door and the officer pushed her into a minuscule cell full of a greasy, sour smell which made the poor woman's stomach heave. The officer slammed the door shut and Anna heard him lock it. She was alone.

Because she had been forthright in denouncing the injustice in her work situation and above all, because she believed in democracy in her country, Anna was imprisoned for five months in a detention centre. She spent the most terrible months of her life in this prison where she existed in unbelievably inhumane conditions, incarcerated in a wretched underground cell with only a tiny ventilation hole. The furnishings consisted of a thin mattress; no chairs or toilet. On the beaten red earth floor enormous cockroaches ran around. And always, night and day, that greasy, stomach turning, indefinable smell lingered in the air. A naked light bulb, which hung from a four metre high ceiling, gave a yellowish glow, showing up the dark red stains all over the cell walls. A guard took her to the toilets when necessary. She was entitled to two quick showers a week and these became a real luxury for her.

In the depths of this cell, Anna lived as if on another planet. It was impossible to make contact with the outside world, Anna's only human contact was with the silent guard who escorted her to the toilets and whose icy demeanour stopped any attempt at conversation. She had one meal a day, which generally consisted of a bowl of suspect, poor quality rice. She spent at least twenty minutes removing the filth mixed in with the rice and after this, nothing much remained. Sometimes, when the rice was accompanied by some unidentifiable cooked vegetable or a bit of meat, so tough that it was impossible to chew, she stopped eating altogether. Some days, she received a bit of bread from a kindly guard and for her, this constituted a little feast.

Anna had never really been a practising Christian. Sunday morning Mass bored her and Sunday morning used to mean a charmed morning with breakfast taken in the sun at the bottom of the garden or on the verandah whenever the rain put in an appearance. Rain had never bothered Anna; on the contrary, at those times, she felt a deep peace whilst watching the huge raindrops washing down the leaves and the entire garden. Anna liked the burning sun as much as the torrential rain. Rainy or sunny Sundays were for loafing around and for admiring nature which life had made so perfect. Sunday Mass had not truly inspired Anna; she lacked concentration and spent three-quarters of her time observing the serious and devout manner of the parishioners. Prayer was, for Anna, an intimate dialogue between an individual and God. To be in ecstasies over a child's smile, a good deed or the beauty of a plant, was for Anna the simplest form of prayer, a way of thanking life for the most extraordinary and sublime things that busy humans had decided to treat as normal. Here in prison, the relationship between Anna and her God had intensified profoundly, she had become accustomed to asking Him for so many things, the courage to remain optimistic... She asked Him to give her sufficient strength to resist hunger, to be indifferent to food. Anna drew sustenance from her prayers, a strength which allowed her to continue to live in this hell, everyday, day after day.

The cell was cramped and very grubby. Hygiene was never respected in prisons, but Anna, somewhat naively, had never imagined a place like this in her worst nightmares, let alone that she would undergo this. The walls were soaked, and when it rained, huge water drops fell from the leaking ceiling. Every evening, before bedtime, Anna hunted insects, spending hours killing mosquitoes, spiders and centipedes which came out of cracks in the walls and ground. She slept very little, partly because of the nerve-wracking noise of the mosquitoes who victimised her as soon as she tried to get some sleep, partly because of the uncertainty she felt about her future but mainly because of the screams and cries, which came from prisoners being tortured every night. The wailing pierced the brick walls, like a dreadful nightmare. It was frightful, inhumane, unbearable. She blocked her ears in an attempt to stop thinking about the other prisoners' ordeal. It would soon be her turn.

What was most humiliating, was when the prison governor, remembering her existence, ordered the guards to confiscate her few remaining clothes. The guards had very quickly taken her watch, which had been a twentieth birthday present from her parents. Anna loved it and had never taken it off. They had also taken her clogs and since then she had been barefoot. The soldiers forced her to remain naked for several days with the guards frequently making foul remarks about her body. She had not suffered any physical torture during her imprisonment but the periods of enforced nakedness were for her, the worst of all tortures. It was prolonged violation, the deepest violation of her person. Over a long period she felt stripped down to the depths of her soul. Also, from the first night she had spent frightened and alone in the pitch black, the heat and lack of air had provoked asthma attacks which had returned in full force to weaken her.

The Silence of the Living
Nafissa Boudalia
(Algeria)

The silence of the living
Is deafening
The dead are there
They question me again
The assassins are there
Now, howl louder
They shout again
You are a spy… you are a spy

Bring hither
The pincers
Bring here
The syringe
It's easy to confess
You are a spy… you are a spy

We found this feather
It's all so clear now
The nib in the end
The spacing of the ink
The shapes of the faces
And the expression of the eyelids
You are a spy… you are a spy

We found this frame
It's all in the canvas
You believe in the spirit
Where you dip your brushes
Ethereal in different sizes
Your blues are threatening
Your reds are too deep
You are a spy... you are a spy

Departures

Scent of Saffron (extract)
Rouhi Shafii
(Iran)

Spring of freedom turns into a chilly winter

By summer 1983 hundred of thousands had left the country. There came a time when we were all frightened for our lives and our families' lives. Although we had not done anything wrong, it did not matter. Possessing a wrong book could send you to the gallows. I had thousands of books in my library. In those days of horror, every morning piles of books were often dumped at the rubbish collection centres. In the shadow of the night people put their precious books in sacks and threw them into the rubbish. Out of fear I did it several times but still I had many more books at home.

One night, while Iraj was out, I began to burn my books in the basement. It took me until four in the morning to burn all those I thought might jeopardise our lives. By the time he arrived here, at five in the morning, I had already cleaned the house of the traces of knowledge we were forbidden to acquire. I pretended that I had been asleep throughout the night, having sweet dreams. In our unusual circumstances we learnt quickly to deceive, even our closest ones.

Now it seemed that all signs of pleasure or happiness had gone out of our system. Now I felt that I had become like those people who walked with heads down, fearful, and frowning most of the time. I did not see a path to happiness anymore. To me, all hope was gone, withered away with the cyclone that swept us around and crushed us under its dreadful power. In the early winter of 1983 Iraj planned to go to the US and stay there a while. Over the years I had constantly refused suggestions to leave Iran. Although I loved travelling abroad my roots were here, in the rivers, mountains and deserts and the orange gardens of my home town. How could I leave my mother and Manuchehr behind? I visited their graves regularly and talked to them. I still loved the people, the majority of whom had turned their backs on us. I still hoped I would be useful some day, some time. I thought it was a good idea for Iraj to go. At least one of us might find happiness on some other soil. Finally, he left for the US and I busied myself with the centre. The first week he arrived in Dallas he called me and cried for a while. I asked him the reason. He said he could not stand the colours, the plentiful goods in the supermarkets and the happy-go-lucky people. He had almost forgotten that people had normal lives in some parts of the globe.

The war with Iraq was in its fourth year now. All the country's resources were diverted to the war. We had driven Iraq from most parts of Iran. It was the expansionist ideas that took the war onto Iraqi soil. Hundreds of thousands of youths were being killed in the battlefields, by mines or under heavy Iraqi artillery. Boys as young as twelve and thirteen. Most streets and alleys in Tehran were renamed after a martyr. Every week hundreds of corpses were carried into Tehran and other cities, buried in lengthy processions.

I sell the childcare centre

In December 1983 suspicion was building up about our centre. We felt we were being watched. Although most of those who had originally helped to establish the centre had already left the country and many politically minded parents had taken their children away, we did not even trust our workers. Could anyone accuse us of something? Did we have to apply for a licence? Fear invaded our minds. Every knock at the door or unexpected phone call made us jump to our feet.

Finally, we decided it was time we closed the centre, like many other establishments which bloomed and died in the coldness of fear. As the last resort, someone suggested that we find a buyer for it. Businesswise, it was prospering and whoever bought it would gain from the business. At the time we had about 65 children. At the end of the second year we had paid all our debts, the workers were paid good salaries and we had some savings as well. At last a buyer was found and we sold the goodwill, cheaper than the market price, and left the centre we had built with so much effort.

Iraj returned from his trip to the US after only four months as he could not settle down there. He missed us and saw no life in America without us. In February 1983 Aunt Iran, who had been ill with cancer for years, passed away. Her death reminded me of the young brother I had lost and although I loved Aunt Iran very much, at the cemetery I cried for Manuchehr and his wasted life.

In the winter of 1984 the war stretched to Tehran and the major cities. Saddam Hussein, angry at the occupation of some territories by the Iranian army, began bombing the big cities indiscriminately. His air force was much stronger than ours, which gave him the upper hand. Tehran was constantly being bombed, creating fear and chaos. We often had to rush to school to take our children home in fear of bombardments. In the early evening, cars raced to get home for fear of being caught in the open. Although our house was a mile away from Ayatollah Khomeini's residence in Niavaran and we were well protected by an anti-aircraft missile system, we were still frightened all the time.

At night we were not allowed to turn the light on when the siren sounded. Silence, darkness and the sound of explosions created a fear inside each of us which frequently led to nervous disorders. The general use by the population of anti-depressant drugs had increased dramatically. The elderly and the children suffered most. Once a bomb hit an apartment block where a family was having a birthday party. Twenty-five children and some adults were killed. My children were frightened to sleep in their own rooms. Parham started sleepwalking and perspired heavily at night. I moved them to our room. The four of us now shared one bed and hugged when the sirens began. Many families did the same. The worst experience was the time you knew another area had been hit and sighed with relief, which showed the depth of human selfishness.

Apart from the bombing of the cities, oil tankers, ships and remote ports were also being destroyed by bombs. It seemed that the world had left us alone to destroy ourselves. By March 1985 most of our neighbours had emigrated. They were forced to leave because of their male children. Boys were forbidden to travel abroad from the age of fourteen. The war machine needed fuel. Hundreds of thousands had been sent to the front just to walk on mines. Among the shanty towns and lower classes children became a human resource for the war machine and material resource for their parents. Once they were martyred, parents received money and became part of an umbrella foundation (The Martyred Foundation) which provided them with privileges and services. Widows were in constant battles with their in-laws over the remaining children and the fringe benefits. After long legal disputes a decree was eventually issued to give widows the right to keep their children and the benefits of their husbands' martyrdom.

Now I had a deep anxiety. Parham would be fourteen next year and banned from leaving Iran. Could I let my child go to the front to fight in a futile war — the child I had never let out of my sight. What would happen to Parastou in a country which was so hostile to women? In March 1985 Alex came to visit us, despite our warnings of the bombings and the dangers. It seemed that she was more adventurous than us. When she experienced the first night under the sirens, she knew what we meant. While she was in Tehran she insisted that I obtain a visa from the British Embassy in Tehran, although the embassy seemed reluctant to grant visas to Iranians. I didn't want to go to America and we were no longer welcome in Britain. However, I managed to obtain a visa which was to expire in three months' time.

Since we had closed the childcare centre, I had done nothing except read and garden. With publishing houses closed and censorship firmly in place we could not publish anything. I had no job, no future and it seemed the doors were closing in on me, one by one. Everyday I lived in fear, uncertainty and despair. What would the future be in a country with a never-ending war? What future would my children have in years to come? Time seemed to have lapsed now. In March our next-door neighbour, Mr Moradi's family, emigrated to Britain. Parham lost his best friends. So far about 40 families from three nearby streets were gone. Every day somebody came round to say goodbye; kisses, hugs and promises to let us know where they were. I began to think seriously about our life in Iran. In April, I told Iraj that we would leave.

Packing my life in cardboard boxes, 1985
It took me two months to prepare ourselves for the final journey. Apart from the big pieces of furniture which I sold, the rest of our belongings were packed in boxes and left in the basement, hoping we would return soon. Although I had disposed of many of my books, I still had many left. I shipped some to London and I was careful in my selection. At the post office all the books were examined before I was permitted to pack them. I still had a certain number of books which I wanted to leave with a friend. The last act of terror happened when one morning I put the books in the car to deliver them to the friend. I was stopped on the way by a police motorcyclist who asked me to accompany him to the station. Giving me no explanation, I panicked to the point of collapse. If I went to the station and they inspected the car, which was the first thing they would do, I would be detained immediately.

89

Carrying books in those days meant asking for trouble. I wished I had hugged and kissed Parastou when I dropped her at school. I wished I had said goodbye, left a note. Did I water the flowers this morning? So many untold words, so much unfinished business. I might be gone so easily. We reached the station after a few minutes. I parked the car further down the road to avoid inspection. I went to the station to find only that my rear number plate was lost. I left my licence with them with a written promise that I would get the plate immediately. For three days my mind would not function properly. Was this the land of Hafis and Sa'adi and all those great poets who preached eternal love for human beings and happiness ever after?

A week before we left my father came from Jiroft to say goodbye. The day before we were due to leave we went to Iraj's parents. His mother cried for the grandchildren she might never see again. She said she had always been sure I would not leave Iran and that she would be near her son and grandchildren. Tears were welling in Iraj's father's eyes but he did not let them flow. When we left the house he stood at the door, his eyes following our car until we disappeared round the bend of the street.

In July 1985 the heat was intense even in the early morning. We said goodbye to my sister and her children whom I loved very much. None of us cried at that point. The door closed behind us when the taxi moved away. Crowded streets, noisy cars, the early morning bakeries and the dusty trees of Pahlavi Avenue were lost in my tears.

At the airport the woman custom inspector in her black chador went through our belongings for two hours. At last, tired and disappointed at not finding any valuables, she asked why I was taking so many unimportant things with me, for example my son's teddy bear. I looked at her for a moment and asked her if she knew what *kooch* (migration) meant. She went silent. Later, there was a misunderstanding about our reservations and we almost missed our plane. Parastou insisted that we leave our hejab on board the plane when we landed at Heathrow. Here, we joined the three million Iranians who had already left the country.

Escape
Ayesha Tarzi
(Afghanistan)

"And those who became fighters for the cause
of Allah after they had been oppressed, we
verily shall give them goodly lodging in the
world, and surely the reward of the Hereafter
is greater if they but knew."
Surah An-Nahl
XVI,41

A warm misty midsummer morning. We were leaving
Kabul, leaving Afghanistan. A week before, my husband
and I had reached this decision. Our daughters had been
expelled from school for taking part in an anti-Soviet
demonstration...

It was dawn when we drove out of Kabul, and there were
not many people about. Some were wrapped in light *keshes*
(shawls), were going to the mosque for morning prayer.
Thin spirals of bluish smoke rose from the bakeries; early
donkey trains passed, their bells tinkling in the quiet
morning air. How peaceful it all seemed and yet here we
were, fleeing because our very existence was threatened,
fugitives from an ancient city now at the mercy of the
Russian army. Although the veil obscured my view, I
craned my neck for a last glimpse of this city which held so
many memories. I tried to swallow the lump in my throat
as the Maranjan Hill loomed in the morning mist. No one
was allowed now to visit the cemetery on the hill and it
was over two years since I had seen my parents' graves. I
had tried to go once, but my way had been barred by soldiers, their bayonets gleaming in the morning sun. On

Wednesdays I used to take flowers, but now, no doubt, dust and weeds choked the gravestones. My throat ached. The bus moved steadily onwards.

A charred building came into view, while nearby a crooked sign, hanging from a small roadside post, pronounced the village school. Obviously it had served as a meeting place for party members, so it had been burnt down. We had encountered so many of these gutted ruins on the way, I wondered whether I would live to put it all down on paper.

The thoughts in my head became more frantic when the familiar sound of firing shattered the silence. I peered through my veil and saw two of the dreaded Russian helicopter gunships circling the nearby mountains on the right, swooping down over the peaks. The gunships were strafing the mountain tops. I could see bursts of dust, like puffs of smoke, when they scored a hit, and the fragments of rock spurted into the air. I could hear the staccato rifle fire of the *Mujahideen* as they replied. A number of trucks and buses were standing in the road, the drivers and passengers huddled together, undecided and scared. One of our guides got down and joined the group. I could see him waving his hands and speaking to other drivers. There was some sort of altercation as to whether the vehicles should proceed or not. Meanwhile the firing continued and the helicopters circled the mountain tops like birds of prey. I hated them. For two years now we had endured the sight and sound of these death machines hovering over the capital. They lunged again and again; a new model, khaki coloured for camouflage.

I looked at my husband who was watching. His lips were set firmly, their whitish line a sign of his fear for our safety. The head of the guide appeared through the window of the bus.

"No one wants to go first," he muttered; then turning back, he shouted, "You cowards! If I didn't have women with me, I'd have gone first."

93

His words were drowned by the noise of a military tank, which came rolling along in our direction. Four Afghan soldiers were perched around the gun turret. "Don't turn back," they shouted, "it's nothing much. We'll go ahead and clear the way. Then you can continue your journey." They rumbled off in a cloud of dust.

One of the guides accompanying us muttered, "Give me the bottles." In accordance with the head guide's instruction, I had brought along two boiled chickens in a paper bag, a quantity of lemons and two bottles filled with drinking water. The lemons were to quench our thirst so that we would need to drink only very little water, as the bus could not stop for us to relieve ourselves.

"You mean these?" I asked, pulling the bottles from beneath the seat where I had hidden them.

"Yes, yes," he replied impatiently. "If we meet the *Mujahideen* they might think it's alcohol, and if the soldiers find it, they will suspect any 'nomads' travelling with a supply of bottled water."

Silently I handed him the bottles. He jumped down and then, standing in the shadow of the bus, emptied them out and kicked them into the ditch. I could see them lying there, the glass reflecting the sun like a brilliant unblinking eye.

One of the helicopters flew over us, very low, skimming the air above our heads. The men in the middle of the road scattered; some threw themselves into the ditches at the side of the road, others ran for cover under the trees.

Our guide's patience snapped. "Are you women, that you hide from planes? We are going first; you cowards can follow us if you wish." The men looked at him sheepishly as they emerged from cover. One of the truck drivers spat into the dust and scratched his head. He said he would follow us. I shifted my aching back slowly so as not to dislodge the heavy veil that covered my face. My second daughter pressed my hand gently; her fingers were cold. I responded with what I hoped was a reassuring grip, but in reality I felt far from confident. Had we made a terrible

94

mistake, my husband and I, and in attempting to save our children from danger in the capital, only brought them into yet greater danger? I felt a core of nervous tension at the base of my skull, and began to pray feverishly. Hugging the little cloth bundle which was all we had been allowed to bring, my fingers felt the familiar shape of the Koran, and I became calmer. "Allah protect us, thou who are Merciful and Compassionate." I felt stronger and ashamed of having panicked a few moments before. My husband, looking over, saw the bundle and smiled reassuringly. My eldest daughter murmured softly. "Don't worry, mother, we're not alone; Allah will protect us." We would be on our way any moment now, and soon would reach the narrow part of the road, bordered by mountains on one side and hemmed in by thickets on the other. The helicopters had flown off towards Kabul, no doubt to refuel or collect more ammunition. Sporadic bursts of gunfire continued.

The road was getting narrower. As we turned a corner and saw grey smoke billowing to our left, I realised why the tank had not returned; it was lying on its side, half in the ditch, licked by tongues of fire, its shell belching forth great clouds of smoke. The four soldiers were there also; I glimpsed one of them briefly, sprawled on the tank, charred beyond recognition. Two more lay on their faces, dark stains spreading across their backs. The fourth, spread-eagled on the roadside, stared sightlessly at the sky, a scarlet bloom on his forehead. I felt nauseated; they were 24 years at the most, and as a mother, I felt like weeping. I wished the bus could move faster, but the road was narrow and the driver could do nothing. Further up, another tank half-blocked the road; ten or twelve soldiers were trying unsuccessfully to move it out of the way. With great difficulty our driver managed to pass, wrenching the bus to the side of the road. It took time, but at last we were clear, and the bus increased speed until we were careering down the hill at breakneck speed. I heard shots overhead and realised that the driver was trying to avoid the crossfire. Twenty minutes later the bus slowed down and we resumed our journey at a normal speed.

I felt drained of feeling, empty and cheerless. Though I tried to forget everything, those dead men, grotesquely sprawled like broken dolls, were before me. Each detail stood out with frightening clarity: the thin rivulet of blood running from the mouth of the young man, the scarlet seal on his forehead. My mouth was filled with a sour, metallic taste. And yet perhaps death came as a release to them. At least now they were free.

The hours dragged by. We passed one checkpoint uneventfully, and I was relieved. "That's one gone," I said. The guide looked at me, then pronounced, "That checkpoint is not dangerous, it's the next one that we've to worry about. You see, the three hour delay because of the fighting in Logar was unfortunate, and now we will arrive in Gardez at the worst possible time." He looked out of the window and stroked his beard. He said: "That's my home over there," and he indicated a mountain range that loomed bluish-grey in the distance. He went on to describe the village. I caught certain words but was not paying attention, being too concerned over the next checkpoint. I wondered what it was they did to fugitives. The bus ground to a halt. One of the guides explained. "Your husband will have to walk and bypass the town of Gardez, because of the checkpoint. One of us will accompany him through the fields. You see, if he were recognised there, you might all be suspected. You will go by bus to the checkpoint. Whatever happens," he said with urgency, "don't speak, don't utter a single sound. You are supposed to be nomads and you know well enough that nomad women never speak to strange men." I nodded assent.

My husband and one of the guides got off the bus and walked together to the side of the road, then descended into the fields. I felt a near unbearable sense of loss.

"What happens if we are apprehended?" I said shivering inwardly. "My husband will wait, he'll return eventually and they will arrest him also."

"Pray," said the guide. "Pray as you've never prayed before, pray that we won't arouse suspicion." I couldn't see my daughters' faces but I could see their fists clenching and unclenching, twisting the corners of their veils.

"It will be all right," I said. "Just pray to God for our father's safety and for ours."

The bus entered Gardez, and my fears were realised. A large group of men stood around the checkpoint, some of them soldiers, some party members, dressed in tight-fitting dark suits and loud shirts, sporting huge moustaches. I looked at them in horror — so many people, surely it meant that someone had informed on us? The bus drew to a halt. "Don't utter a word," the guide hissed. "I'll do the talking." The door opened, a head appeared. "Yours is the first vehicle to come this way today," said the officer. "We've received reports of fighting in Logar. Did you see anything?" "Yes sir," replied our driver. "We were in the midst of it, but it's all right now. The army is in full control of the situation." "That's good news," cried one of the party members, evidently a senior official. "On your way now, you've been delayed too long already." He grinned and slammed the door, waving us on. I unclenched my hands, and my palms were glistening with sweat in the noonday sun.

A few moments after leaving Gardez, the bus slowed down. "Look! There's father," shouted one of our daughters, pointing towards the fields. I made out two small figures approaching, growing more and more distinct, and then I was gazing into my husband's face, my heart light with relief. We resumed our journey. As we progressed the land became greener. The bus climbed narrow passes and slithered over dry river beds and rumbled through gushing streams and we saw women working in the fields, carrying water jugs gracefully poised on their heads, their colourful skirts swinging in the dust as they made their way through the trees.

We reached a quiet place, a narrow stretch of road that sloped towards the river, bordered by mulberry trees, and there the driver parked the bus. "You can get out and stretch your legs," said the guide. "We will wait here until it gets darker." And then he explained that because of the delay in Logar, our timing had been disrupted, and it would be dangerous for us to reach the area near the frontier, which we would have to traverse on foot. He went on to say that as provincial staff and patrols would be around in the late afternoon, it would be safer to set off at dusk. I got up and stretched my weary muscles. My legs were stiff and numb.

The children climbed down, clutching their veils, and walked on to the river-bank. As I descended, the cloying scent of mulberries reached me. The mulberries were ripe and many had fallen from the trees, crushed to a pulpish-white underfoot. A thousand white butterflies, attracted by the scent of the ripe fruit, circled the trees, fluttering in and out of the branches. It was like watching snowflakes, and from a distance, it seemed as if the trees were in blossom. Slowly, I followed my daughters. My husband sat on a boulder talking with the guides. I slithered down the grassy bank, clutching my veil to prevent it from falling. When I reached the water's edge, my daughters, their veils thrown back, were washing their hands and faces. I followed their example and perched on a small flattish boulder, trailing my fingers in the water. I heard one of the guides ask my husband if he liked mulberries. He must have replied yes, for two of the men them ambled towards the trees, one of them taking a large cloth from the bus as the other climbed a tree. After enlisting the driver's help, the second man began to shake the branches, and ripe mulberries came pelting down. A cloud of white butterflies rose upwards and fluttered in agitation. It was peaceful by the river. No tanks, no helicopters: a sanctuary.

Another sanctuary came to mind: the Shahi-do-Shamshera shrine in the capital, the mausoleum of the King of Two Swords, which I had visited on the evening before we left Kabul. It was nearing six o'clock when I entered that holy place. I had greeted the old *mullah*, who sat near the arched gateway selling millet. I remember the calm that descended on me as I stood in the dying rays of the evening sun and prayed for a safe journey. The pigeons circled around, their feathers reddish-gold in the setting sun, the soft swishing sound of their wings filling the twilit air.

"Mother, which one shall I take with me?" My youngest daughter's voice broke in on my thoughts. "What do you mean?" I said. "Which stone shall I take as a souvenir?" I withdrew my hand, which had grown cold from trailing in the water, and rubbed it to restore circulation. I looked at the pebbles: they shimmered in the water, a muted kaleidoscope of colours. A bluish stone, not unlike a pale turquoise with brown veining, caught my eye. I dipped in and withdrew it, my movements disturbing the sand and clouding the water.

My daughter chose another pebble. I dropped mine back and heard its forlorn plop as it settled back on the river-bed. I looked at the large smooth pebble resting in my daughter's palm: it was black and white, stark and uncompromising as truth.

One of the guides brought over some mulberries. I asked him when we would move on. "In half an hour, we'll be on our way," he replied. I returned to the bus. The silence was broken by the sound of an approaching vehicle. I drew my veil over my face and huddled into a corner of the seat, my husband and daughters still sitting by the river, their backs towards the road. At a distance they looked like nomads, and, unless the vehicle stopped, there was no danger. A few minutes later a lorry rumbled up the road. It didn't stop; I breathed a huge sigh of relief. The shadows were lengthening on the grassy bank and the ripe smell of mulberries became more pungent.

Everyone returned to the bus and once more we were on our way.

The sun had set when we reached a small cluster of mud houses. The senior guide leapt out of the bus. "I'll be back in a minute," he said, and ran towards two men who were rolling a tyre towards us. They stopped and began talking to him. One of them ran off towards the houses; the other leant against the tyre and watched his friend disappear into a dark doorway. "What is the guide doing?" I asked the driver. "He is waiting for a gun." The nonchalant reply shocked me. "Why does he need a gun?" I asked my husband. "We've come so far, why does he need a gun now?" My husband looked at me and answered, choosing his words carefully: "The gun is for protection, you understand."

I did not understand, or perhaps, chose not to. Who, after all, would attack a group of ragged nomads? But there was no point in asking question that nobody wanted to answer, and I lapsed into silence. The guide reappeared, carrying a gun and its glossy stock gleamed in the dusk. It was familiar: a Kalashnikov. I had seen such guns carried by Russian soldiers, and I shuddered.

On we drove. After half an hour the bus stopped and we climbed down. Night had fallen and the stars were winking in the velvety sky.

"The bus will meet us on the other side of the border town of Tsamkanai," explained the guide. "The driver will signal us. There is a full moon tonight. It will help us find our way but..." here he paused, as if searching for the right words "...the moonlight could also prove dangerous, so take care."

My husband, our daughters and I, accompanied by three guides, set out on foot. I asked the chief guide how long it would take us to reach the bus, and he replied that while the men could cover the distance in an hour, for us it would mean nearly a two-hour walk. I did not realise that he was not telling the truth. He was not a liar: he simply did not want to alarm us. It took over six hours to reach the bus, a gruelling trek that left us all exhausted, and our feet blistered and bleeding.

We started off, led on by the chief guide, his gun set at a jaunty angle. He moved swiftly. The first 20 or so minutes were not bad: indeed, after having sat for the entire day in a bus it was a relief to be walking. The landscape grew more and more rugged; we scrambled up rocky slopes strewn with boulders that gleamed white in the moonlight. It reminded me of a landscape by Doré: beautiful, awesome, terrifying. The moonlight traced silvery fingers on rocks and bushes, leaving the rest in darkness. I began to have difficulty breathing, no doubt a consequence of having smoked too much. From time to time I turned back to look at my husband and daughters behind me. I found comfort in the sight of my husband's broad shoulders outlined against the light. My daughters walked gracefully, their veils thrown back, their faces pale in the night. The guide looked over his shoulder at them. "They walk like gazelles, don't they?" he grinned, his teeth gleaming. "But then they are young. Are you all right?" I detected a note of concern. "Oh yes, yes I'm fine," I said, my chest constricted, my lungs feeling as if they would burst. "Might I remove my veil? I'm very hot." "Yes, of course, but cover your face if anyone approaches." I threw back my veil. The cool air came as a pleasant relief, and I forgot the difficulties I had in breathing. Pushing the sticky strands of hair away from my face, I made a renewed effort to walk faster. "It seems as if we've been walking for more than two hours," I told the guide. "Just another twenty minutes and we'll be there," he answered. It sounded too glib and realised that we had a long way yet to go. We trudged along, my chest rasping each time I drew breath. I tried to forget it; the going was downhill now, and this made it easier. In a burst of confidence, I walked too fast and stumbled over. I had twisted my ankle, the ankle with the torn ligament, and all through sheer carelessness. The pain shot up my leg. "You shouldn't have gone so fast," my husband said, taking the cloth with which he had been mopping his face. He soaked it in a trickle of water running between the rocks and tied it around my ankle. We had now reached ground level. "Be careful now, don't talk any more," whispered the guide. "We are now approaching some *qualas**, and we don't want to wake anyone"

We walked on slowly, the scent of *Senjed* ** trees heavy in the air. We were walking through a dark leafy tunnel of trees, their upper branches thickly intertwined, shutting out the stars. The earth was soft and moist, and our feet made no sound as we moved forward. Then a dog barked, shattering the silence. I stiffened, then relaxed when the noise was not repeated. The narrow path led past a *quala*. We tiptoed onwards. A lantern hanging in one of the windows glowed feebly in the brilliant moonlight, illuminating that impregnable and forbidden structure. Then the silence shattered about us, and I gazed in horror as a huge dog bounded forwards. It checked and growled, a deep-throated, menacing rumble, its fur bristling, its eyes slitted like silver crescents against the moonlight: a watchdog. I held my breath, sure that we would be discovered.

Apparently the men of the household were sleeping on the rooftop because of the heat; someone shouted and the dog turned back reluctantly. We waited with bated breath for a few seconds and then sped on swiftly. The *qualas* left behind, we breathed more freely. The sound of rushing water reached us. We had come to a small river in full spate, and the water foamed along, looking quite deep. The guide indicated a narrow plank the width of a man's foot. "We cross here," he said. "You join hands and move sideways along the plank." He smiled. "Try not to look down." First the children passed, holding hands, flanked by the guides. Then my turn came. I held onto the guide and gripped my husband's right hand, while in the other he held that precious bundle containing the Koran. Halfway across, the plank felt as if it must give way. I tried not to look down and, failing, shut my eyes tightly. I could not tell whether it was the plank that quivered or myself. At

102

last I was once again on terra firma. "One more river and then we reach the bus," said the chief guide. One more river; I wondered if we would ever reach it.

Tilled fields stretched ahead of us and beyond them the river gleamed like molten silver. Our progress was slow, for the fields were muddy, and to avoid sinking ankle-deep into the mud, we had to walk on the narrow ridges that divided the fields, where the soil was firmer. Several times I slipped. I took off the cloth bandage. The pain persisted. I wrapped my ankle again. Then, at last, when it seemed that I could go no further, we were walking on the pebbly sand and drawing close to the turbulent river. I could not see any kind of crossing, but I decided to keep silent.

The guide peered into the darkness beyond the river. "I can't see the signal. The bus should have arrived an hour ago." He strained his eyes. "Can you see any lights?" he asked. My hopes sank. Had we come come all this way for nothing? We drew close to the water's edge and then we saw them, two beacons that flickered once, then once again, then were enveloped in the darkness of the opposite bank. The guide was jubilant. "It's them, it's the bus," he cried. "We'll carry you over." The tallest of the guides waded into the river with my youngest daughter on his back, his turban wrapped firmly around both their waists. "Hold on tight, don't be scared," I called, as breathless, we watched their progress. They reached the other bank safely. The guide returned after having let my daughter down on the far side. She stood, a solitary little figure, watching us. Her sisters crossed the river in a like manner, but I refused to be carried over. I made the crossing clinging to my husband's arm and gripping the guide's hand with all my remaining strength. The initial impact of the cold water took my breath away. At a certain point, beyond the halfway mark, the water was deeper and the current stronger, and I felt it pulling me, dragging at my clothes. "Don't panic, go slowly," cautioned my husband. "You can make it." I did make it. I staggered out, my wet skirts dragging at me. It was only then that thousands of red-hot needles pierced my flesh, stabbing at the soles of my feet. I stumbled once or twice and then collapsed on a grassy ledge. "I'm sorry," I mumbled. "I can't walk. I just can't go any further. Go on, don't wait. I'll try to follow as soon as the pain lessens." "Look, the bus is waiting; just another ten minutes and you can rest." The guide indicated the bus, a dark silent shape not far away. "I know, but I can't walk. My feet are burning." My husband removed my shoes. The gritty river sand had found its way inside as I crossed, and the razor-sharp particles had cut through the blistered soles: they resembled slabs of raw meat. Blood oozed from countless cuts onto the grass. I felt deathly tired and only wished to curl up on the damp soil and sleep. My husband, seeing my blood-stained feet, pulled up a clump of soft ferny leaves and gently rubbed my feet. Meanwhile, one of the guides cleaned out my shoes and lined them with more leaves. After a few minutes' rest, I put them on and hobbled up the slope, leaning on my husband's arm. My feet were still burning, but at least the pain was bearable. We reached the bus and climbed aboard. The driver was relieved to see us; we had taken a long time, much longer than he had expected, and he feared that we had been arrested. I shivered in my wet clothing.

The guide said that we must spend what remained of the night in a *quala* belonging to an acquaintance of his, a teacher. We reached this *quala* after a 15-minute drive. One of the guides banged on the massive wooden door, and a few moments later it swung open and the teacher was ushering us inside. We walked up a steep and narrow flight of stairs, our host lighting the way with a lantern. The grotesque shapes of our shadows moved with us. We were led into a small room furnished with goat-hair rugs and large cushions covered in gaily-patterned floral cotton. A prayer rug was hanging on the wall. The only other objects in the room were a row of painted wooden pegs near the door and a pot of green plants hanging in one of the small arched windows. The *quala* owner placed his lantern on one of the windowsills while the guides settled themselves on the cushions near the doorway and we sat down opposite them under the windows.

"I'll bring you some hot tea," said our host. A few moments later he returned bearing a tray and followed by a woman — probably his wife — her face partly obscured, who carried another tray of sweet cakes. The tea was delicious: sweet and milky. An hour later, everyone settled to rest the best way they could. My daughters curled up, their veils pulled over them, and were soon asleep. I huddled up against the wall feeling damp and dejected. My feet felt as if they were resting on hot coals. I closed my eyes. Once or twice I woke from disturbed dreams to find my husband still awake; he kept watch all night, and only later did I discover that he was worried lest the *quala* owner betray us for the sake of the reward.

Early the next morning my husband woke me with a touch on my shoulder. I opened my eyes; everyone was awake. I was stiff and aching, and my clothes were still damp. I forced my sore feet into soggy shoes. Outside the *quala* we washed our faces in a little stream.

After a short drive, the bus came to a halt and we disembarked; we had reached a small village. The guide led the way into a courtyard where a cow, some goats and two donkeys were tethered. Chickens fled cackling at our approach. We entered an arched doorway and stepped into a room furnished with cushions. After we sat down, I looked around me. A string of prayer beads hung on a nail and a transistor radio in a sequinned velvet cover stood on the windowsill. After a breakfast of tea and bread we were on our way.

It was only then that I noticed that my younger daughter was limping badly. The rough leather sandals had chafed her feet leaving raw and bloody patches of flesh where they had blistered. The others had also had the skin rubbed off their heels. I looked at them with love, while my husband tore his handkerchief into strips, wrapping the raw places as best as he could.

105

We walked through the muddy fields. The sun was shining overhead and the morning mist had lifted. Coming out of the fields, we continued on a narrow meandering path, bordered by trees on one side and by fields on the other. An hour had now passed since we set out. We crossed a small stream and the guide stopped. "This is the end of your journey," he said. "You have just crossed the frontier. You are safe." I was overwhelmed with a sense of relief but did not experience the heady joy that I had anticipated. "That is a frontier stone," said the guard, indicating a small white rock not unlike a milestone standing by the stream. "You are now safe. I bid you farewell. God be with you."

We bade him farewell. My husband and daughters were already walking on as I turned back and looked at the mountains rearing their majestic heads against the brilliant blue sky. I felt my tears falling, blinding and hot.

I turned around and walked forward to where my husband and daughters were waiting for me.

(Reprinted from *Red Death*, by permission of Islamic Texts Society, 1995)

*A quala is a mud structure resembling a small fort, with watch towers at all four corners.
**senjed — Russian olive.

Voices in a
Strange Land

Another Day – Another Life
Amna Dumpor
(Bosnia)
Translated by Gianna Salkovic

This road that everybody follows
for me is just a path.
And this light, which is for me
only a shadow,
for them is a precious life.

There are no words spoken
while travelling,
as you grow like a special tree.

There is no way
which is their own way.
You will always reach the end.

Only the death at the end
Will remain in each case the same.

Then you see the clock,
it's midnight just for those
who write and yet it's another day.

Pristina in Exile
Gjeraqina Tuhina
(Kosova)

Kosova Albanians in Skopje feel strangely at home: on the streets and in the cafés, everyone is there. But something is wrong, and many are still missing.

When I arrived from Kosova, I expected to find the Macedonia I have always known, the Macedonia I saw on my last visit a few weeks ago. But instead I saw Pristina.

Throughout Macedonia, in Tetovo, in Gostivar, in Kicevo and especially in Skopje, the capital of Kosova is in Macedonia. Everywhere I went I saw a friend from home, some I hadn't seen in a week, some I hadn't seen in a long time. The streets belong to another town, but the feeling was that you were walking in the middle of Pristina.

At first, it looked wonderful, and it seemed like people were even having fun. The cafés were full, with everyone you knew. I saw all of my friends. We went to the big open market in Skopje to buy personal items we hadn't brought with us. And the people in Macedonia — that is, the Albanians in Macedonia — are so welcoming. The Macedonians themselves talk about "changing the demographics" of the country, and are in a bad mood; you can feel the tension. But the Albanians — they offer the Kosovars so much hospitality it hurts.

Most of all it is a time when we can be sure who is alive. We don't speak about the dead yet, because nothing can be confirmed. But at least we know who is alive, because we have seen each other.

For me, the best was seeing many of my journalist colleagues, whom I hadn't seen for at least a week. And of these, the most important was Baton Haxhiu, the *Koha*

Ditore editor everyone thought was dead.

I first saw him in the huge queue at the border. I recognised his car and his registration plate, seven kilometres back within Yugoslav territory, but I never thought it would be him.

He was wearing a hat, and had shaved his beard. Of course, he was still officially dead, so obviously he was terrified and wanted to hide. There were a lot of rumours about Serbian agents and no-one felt safe until they got through the border.

When I finally recognised him I went crazy. I wanted to jump and kiss him. But the look from his eyes was clear. You didn't see me.

Many other Albanians, people smarter than me, saw him too. But they didn't acknowledge him at all. They just only needed to see him, to know: "Baton is alive."

I felt as if I were dreaming. As if I wouldn't believe it until I could touch him. The next day, when we finally met again, we just cried and cried. I screamed at him that he had cost five years of my life. He just smiled.

And just below this sense of carnival, people really do cry in Pristina. I was amazed, especially with the men. Crying and crying, over everything they have been through.

For we are still in shock. We are too proud to admit that we are refugees. People are using new expressions, like 'deportees'. Anything to avoid admitting what has really happened.

In many of the cafés, people are talking seriously about how they will be back in their homes within two weeks. They believe that NATO will continue and win the war, and they will then be able to go back. They are even impatient.

But really all they have is this hope — for me, I'm afraid, it is a dream. They want these two weeks to be something temporary, itself a dream. They want to pretend that it didn't happen and that it can all be reversed. Even though we have no organisation anymore. Even though many are dead. Even though we are, in fact, here in Macedonia.

To remember, it's enough just to spend half an hour back at the border. To see the huge numbers of refugees trapped there and waiting in the cold, you feel sick. And when you sit with people at the cafés and talk to them, the stories are all the same: the policemen, the expulsions, the trains.

Others have even tried to call home. I spoke to seven or eight friends who rang up their houses. Again, always the same. Someone answers in Serbian. They ask, "Is this the house of family so-and-so." The reply is clear: "I don't know whose it was before, but it's mine now."

So despite the atmosphere in the streets, something is wrong. Something doesn't fit. We know what it is. But we don't want to think about it.

There Me Here

Nazand Begikhani
(Kurdistan, Iraq)

I am a white shadow
Between HERE and THERE

My past
Was a Goddess in the East
At dawn
My mother would cover her with a veil of light
Mystics would meditate her
Mullahs feared her
At night majestically
Malak Tawus would hold her hand to the dome of
  self-knowledge
In the mornings
The young would kneel to her chestnut plaits
And she
Like Inanna[1]
Inside her temple of beauty
Would wait for Dumuzy[2]

My present
In the pale evenings of Paris
Is lost in search of the diamond of logic
In the darkness of loneliness
Threatens death
And promises marriage to eternity

My future
Is sleeping between Here and There
Dreaming of both of them

[1] Innana became Ishtar. She was the Goddess of Love during the Sumerian epoch. She is considered the most important Goddess in Mesopotamia, with many temples built in her honour, including one in Erbail (Erbil of today).

[2] Dumuzy became Tumuz. He was the lover of Innana and was responsible for promoting fertility.

Scent of Saffron (extract)
Rouhi Shafii
(Iran)

Exile

"I am a breed of trees
Breathing stale air
Brings me to my knees
A dead sparrow told me
Just remember the flight
Otherwise, the birds will always cease."

Farough Farokhzad, *Rebirth*

From above, London seemed green and peaceful. Clouds
were scattered in the sky and I could see the Thames and
the rush of traffic on the motorways. Approaching the
runway I could even see flowers blossoming in the small
gardens. When our plane landed I looked at Heathrow
differently. A group of young girls in fancy dress
attracted my attention. Tears filled my eyes. On the
same planet, six thousand miles away, people had forgotten about colours. Broad smiles on some faces drew
my attention. The scarf and the long sack which distinguished us Iranian women as forbidden, untouchable
creatures, were no longer there. My daughter was right.
It was good to leave the symbols of our enforced womanhood behind us on the aeroplane seats. Parastou's face
was shining, her long brown hair dancing in the breeze.

It was nice to see Mehdi and his family among the
crowds; hugs, kisses and countless words poured out. They
had recently moved to a two-bedroom maisonette in

115

Hayes, Middlesex. We were given one of the bedrooms for the time being. The first thing I did was plant some vegetable seeds in the rear garden. I had brought these with me. We did not know what to do next. For the first two weeks friends and relatives came to visit. We bought a small car to become mobile. We listed our priorities.

Just a month before our departure from Iran, Iraj had been offered a job taking over a company whose owners had moved to Germany. While in Tehran he had not been sure if he would accept the offer. Now after a month in London, he decided that it would be best if he returned and took up the job. The salary was being paid in sterling, which would help us in London until I got a job. Deep in his mind he preferred to be with his parents, rather than us. By August we were left on our own to make something of our lives.

The first thing I had to do was to find a place of our own. Living with my brother's family was becoming harder by the day. I began to look at the properties and before long I secured a mortgage and bought a flat in the street nearby. To move to the new flat, however, took us to the end of October. It was difficult at first to register the children at school. When school started they were still at home. Finally I managed to register them at Barnhill in Hayes which was a few minutes from where we lived. I bought them uniforms and accompanied them on the first day. I could see anxiety in their eyes. Back home they were familiar with everything. Now the environment seemed alien. Although their knowledge of English was fairly good, for the first two weeks they could not understand what the teachers or the children said. Colloquial language was different from the English they had learnt. Parham often came back soaked in perspiration and filled with anxiety. Parastou was by nature a more relaxed and sociable person so it was easier for her to adjust. New concepts entered their vocabulary: whites, blacks and Asians. The children did not know where to place themselves. I did not know either.

I was beginning to learn a new identity. I discovered that we were no longer part of 'a big nation'. The status that had been accorded Iran in the early 1970s, exhibited by the London cabby, no longer existed. We were categorised as an Ethnic Minority. I also found out that I was in the category of single mother; having two teenage children and being by myself. Now Britain began to open its true self to me. I began to learn that I had some rights as a single mother but I was constricted by the unwritten rules as I belonged to the minority and not the majority. Fear began to swell inside me. I realised that I was not even respected as the big sister by my brother any more. Rather, I was the woman who was confused and sad most of the time. "Why don't you take it easy? You are in Britain, safe and sound," my sister-in-law wondered. I was worried about the country and the loved ones I had left behind and the unknown path I had taken. Despite all the familiarity of London, smells, people's gestures, the way they looked at us seemed unfamiliar. How long would it take us to make London home?

Living in London was very different from visiting it on short trips. It was like rewriting a story to make it ready for a film. Gradually, I noticed that my living standards had dropped. Although after the revolution I was living on a limited income, still we had a big house, two cars and enough money to live on. Now the three of us had to shrink into the tiny bedroom of my brother's house and later into one tiny apartment. Apart from my student years, I had never had to worry about bills, taxes and expenses. Now I had to live on a tight budget, with few friends and, above all, had to stand on the sidelines, marginalised from society.

No one in Hayes, Middlesex was interested in knowing my story, although I had some lovely neighbours; an old woman painter who gave advice to Parastou on her drawing and a young man who had just got married. Nevertheless, they were more interested in our kitten and her welfare than us. I could not blame them. These were people with few complications in their lives. Well-protected by the security of their peaceful country and content with their TV, electricity and gas stamps and the pennies they could save on their daily shopping. At the beginning I used to explain myself to people I met. Soon I found out that I bored them. These people could not understand the complexities of my life. Even the few intellectuals whom I happened to know soon had their interest diverted. Nevertheless, I liked these people. I could learn a lot living among them. I could learn to make peace with myself, to experience normality, to walk a different path, away from dust and noise.

We moved to our flat on a cold early evening in November. It was on the first floor with two bedrooms; in total, the size of two rooms in our house in Tehran. Immediately, after we had put things in order, I began looking for a job. Having much pride in my diverse experience, I was certain that I would find a good job. After a few months of filling in applications and waiting, I understood that life was not going to be as easy as I had first thought.

In 1988 my son Parham was about to finish his O-Levels. My daughter Parastou was starting her GCSEs. By then she had firmly established her reputation as the best student in her class and the envy of others. Bullying at her school, Barnhill, was rife. Children, especially the Asians, often kept quiet about being bullied and harassed. Parham talked about children being beaten in the corners of toilets. Parastou was not the type to keep quiet if she was being harassed and this created hostility with her peers. On a winter night in 1988 she attended a school party at Barnhill. Parastou argued with a group of girls from her class at the party and on their way back from the party they began beating her, "to teach her a lesson." When I arrived at her friend's house, where she was taken after the incident, I saw Parastou covered in blood, her face swollen and full of bruises. The ambulance was about to take her to hospital. Her best friend Alison and her mother stayed with me until two in the morning, disgusted with what had happened. This was the ugliest face of London I had seen so far.

I did not know what to do or how to help Parastou to cope with her mental suffering. I did not want a permanent scar in her mind. She was not to be frightened of the environment she now lived in, I had to convince her that this was an isolated case. The police took action. The children involved were suspended for a few days and cautioned by the police and the schools gave reassurance this would not happen again. But these were not good enough to heal the mental wounds. Did she have to put up with the abuse and harassment which was inflicted out of jealousy or racism? I had brought her out of my country so that she would not have to put up with harassment and abuse. I did not believe she should put up with it at all. I decided to change her school but the principal convinced me that it was best if she stayed until the end of year. It took Parastou a long time to forget the incident. She was frightened of being attacked again and had to be accompanied to and from school for the rest of the year. Nevertheless, at the end of the year, she got the best grades in her GCSE exams and proved that she had the courage I had expected of her.

A Tale

Dieudonnee-Marcelle Makenga
(Democratic Republic of Congo)
Translated by Jennifer Langer

At last I am going there
to the country of liberty

I have read the guidebooks
on the country of liberty
the pictures, the dreams
will become reality
at last liberty
no more nightmares
I will be able to breathe freely

I am here, my Lord, I am here
everything is delightful, everything is beautiful
better than in my wildest dreams
Never have I seen anything like it
everything is novel
the land of wonders
like no other
definitely unlike the one I left behind
nothing here is the same
I just have to settle in

It won't take long
I just need to wait a little
I am a foreigner so must be patient
I will end up being happy
they are not all nasty
as my people here say
despite the sniggering and jeering
they will eventually give me

my papers
It should not be long
in the meantime I can't do anything
there is nothing to be done
other than go round in circles
and watch the others
feigning contentment
when I arrive here

"papers"
That's all I hear
throughout the day
It's unending
when I reach here
So I remain isolated
and in my head the insults
the abuse resound
I am

a foreigner
They insult me, are aggressive
in my head despair
point the finger of scorn at me
I am trapped like a deer
my dreams disintegrate
I never imagined it
I believed I would lead a good life

121

I believed those guidebooks
I had read about it in books
glossy magazines
they had deceived me

Now my eyes are opened
it was nothing but a nightmare
the land of wonders
was only a nasty story

papers

Close to the Truth
Choman Hardi
(Kurdistan, Iraq)

I'm me today
  and life is curling around me
    I can spin
      spin
      spin
  I can jump and reach to the sky

I'm full of beauty today
  I love the glasses
    the windows
      the mirrors

    I sit among the flowers
    and add one
      to the number of flowers
        on earth

   I feel the soul of a tree
    and notice the presence of a stone
I whisper to the wind
    and whistle at the dancing leaves

    I am full of songs
   and life is accepting the darkness
    and yet still searching for the light

I'm full of freedom today
   robbed of
     illusions of love
      and needing
    and this face
     once reminded me of my mother
      it is not her
      it is all me today

I smell like a newborn tree
  I smell wet
   like earth after the rain
 and my little hands
   can achieve the unthinkable

Oh Lord!
  I am full of happiness.

High Heeled Shoes
Choman Hardi
(Kurdistan, Iraq)

High heeled shoes
little black dress
glinting earrings
    under dark curly hair

a mysterious smile
a secret in the eyes
smelling of spring
    in a dark miserable winter
   surrounded by soft light
   with two unseen wings
   headings towards somewhere
    that no-one ever knows of
   even she doesn't know
   "but who cares" she says:

it is good to be on the way
it is good to try to get somewhere
it is good to be a woman.

A Kind of Dance

Samira Al-Mana

(Iraq)

*Translated by the author
and edited by Charles N. Lewis
from the novel* Look at Me! Look at Me*!*

The song was going round and round, droning on and on inside her head like a fly trapped in a jar, buzzing from one side to the other; it felt like a silky, black *abaya*[1] bearing down on her pate.

*O la la la la,
He is the knight of knights...*

Fatima reached the bus stop and the drone eased off. A few seconds of peace. She mopped her brow in relief. Blissful silence, like healing balm.

Suddenly another song started up just like the first one, strident and persistent, as broadcast on official Iraqi radio and heard by listeners in London during the war with Iran:

*Well done, you soldiers of the Arab world,
You did a wonderful job.
Clap, clap, clap, clap...*

Rhythm-like slaps, one after another. Songs like this had become the norm after Iraq's invasion of neighbouring Iran. A succession of calamities. Clap, clap, clap. Slap after slap. The tune was an old one which used to be played in Basra city by a band called The Drummers, which included boy dancers. That was before the war with Iran,

when they had changed the words from sex to politics.
Such things are possible.

She fidgeted as she waited for the bus, praying that no
more songs would assail her — so-called 'patriotic' songs
with rhythms like the well-known Iraqi ditty which mocks
slaves:

Go on, farty-pants, get up and
Dance for your master,
Go on, make him laugh!

With the aid of modern technology, these songs bridged
thousands of miles, crossing mountains, seas and countries in the twinkling of an eye to reach her in London. For
years, the radio had been her only means of knowing what
was going on in her own country. All letters and telephone
calls had ceased when the war had been declared out of the
blue, killing thousands and petrifying millions of hearts in
both nations. But the dancing lips of the official radio station still insisted:

We love you, O President, yes, we love you,
You love everybody
And everybody's in love with you.

OK, OK, take it easy. You're free to love whoever you
want. But what have *I* done? Why should *I* have to listen
to this? Some people in her land struggled desperately to
become enslaved.

She wandered a little way down the street and lifted her
head to the sky. If only she could repel the song, shake it
off. She walked towards two old ladies who were standing
nearby, chatting serenely. They made liberal use of words
like 'theoretically' or 'logically', and although there was no
real certainty in the way they talked, they exuded quiet
confidence and contentment.

I wish I had someone like you to walk with in the
street and chat to like my mother, my sister, my friend.

127

Fatima felt a horrible loneliness. Her fears seemed to increase tenfold. She propelled herself towards the two women as if they were her last refuge. They were deep in conversation:

"That antique shop looks interesting, my dear."

"There's another one just as good at the end of the street." "You're obviously an expert on antiques, dear." "No, dear, I'm still learning."

Both about eighty. For Fatima they represented harmony, homeliness, innocence.

* * *

The radio and TV news bulletins were endless: Sri Lanka: There has been a wave of communal violence among ethnic and sectarian groups," the BBC reports.

Meanwhile Baghdad is still thundering and foaming at the mouth: *Oh how we relish the slaughter of the villains. We slaughter them like sheep. Yes, a thousand times, yes, pounce on the filthy Iranian dogs and jerboas.*

The dial moves and then returns to where it was before: *The decision is irrevocable...* Baghdad again, of course, 1985, the Iran-Iraq war.

Beirut Radio kept appealing for blood donors all day yesterday: "Give more blood, all you who have so far escaped the bloodshed. Reuter reports that both sides, Christian and Muslim, sustained losses of thirty people in two hours. The newspapers claim that the violence erupted without warning and shattered the peace for no reason." The strong versus the strong, it seems. Splendid environment for both to grow up in. Arms sales in the area in dollars: 1982-1985: US, 26 billion; France, 15 billion; and last but not least, Britain, a paltry 6 billion. That's only the capitalist West; for the socialist countries the figures remain secret, though their exports are confined to arms as providers of hard currency.

* * *

Fatima jumped as the sound of her husband's voice interrupted her thoughts. He sounded as excited as when he had received a letter from Iraq during the war. "Fatima, Fatima, come and hear the news!" She laughed when the news was over. "Nothing in the world will change as long as greed and arms factories exist." She returned to the newspaper she had been reading before the interruption. "Listen," she said. "A journalist flew to Washington to investigate whether the restrictions on arms sales to the Middle East were being observed. He found that munitions factories were itching to get back to supplying arms to the region, given that some Middle Eastern countries, even before the Gulf War, were spending around 20 billion dollars a year for the rat-a-tat-tat and the bang bang bang... From now on, I don't want to hear the news any more. I've had a bellyful. I wish we could live in a place where there were no people and no radios."

"Fatima, do you really want to shut yourself off from what's happening in the world?"

"I don't know."

She does want news. She craves it. But where is the bearer of good tidings? Where is the radio that will bring her news of decent countries with rulers who do not abuse their power, and news of peace and quiet in her native land? There she is now. She emerges from the plane, steps down onto the tarmac, no need to kiss the ground, and waves to her loved ones far away in the airport building, behind the passport desk. They are longing for her to arrive, and wave back, their faces wreathed in smiles. Here she comes. The passport officer hands back her passport without showing the slightest interest. Proceed. She picks up her luggage and walks on. Her mouth can barely contain her huge smile.

The reality is too frightening to think about. A petty official, frustrated and angry, with a thick black moustache hiding half his face, sits there scrutinising her passport with hatred and loathing. He interrogates her testily: "You've been away twelve years? Where've you been all this time? Well, you didn't take part in Saddam's *Qadisya*[2] nor in the "Mother of all Battles." He takes her passport inside to check it. He looks at the list of persons forbidden to travel, the list of the expelled, the outlawed, the bereaved, the hated, the trouble-makers. Success at last. He glances at the passport for the last time, flipping it over as her walks towards her. He points a stern finger at her, signalling for her to stand aside.

"I came across two old ladies yesterday. I wished I had a friend like that. They were talking about completely different things from what we hear on the radio. You know, old women in the streets of London are assured of esteem. Poor Fadela, our neighbour in Baghdad! She was mortified at the way people treated her. A bus conductor shouted at her when she was a bit slow getting off the bus. "Get a move on, you old hag!"

Men considered her finished because she was no use to them any more," her husband said. "We used to call another of our neighbours 'Mother', you remember? She never had a child, but we always called her 'Mother' just the same, as a mark of respect."

"Because she was known to us personally. I'm not talking about that, I'm talking about women we don't know."

"We always used to say 'Do you think so, Mother?' Or we liked to please her by asking 'Is that so, Mother?' although she looked down on us and was never friendly towards us. She seemed grumpy all the time for one reason or another."

"She saw through your hypocrisy. She was a spinster, never had a son, what's the big deal? Never had relations with a man. But she defended masculine honour, of course, just the way you men want it." Her husband started to sing:

If he betrays his love, don't tell anyone,
If he breaks his promise, don't tell anyone,
Don't tell anyone, don't tell anyone.

"Please, I beg you, stop it. Don't ever sing that song again, it gets stuck in my head. I'm plagued by the songs I hear nowadays. Two of them latched onto me so firmly yesterday that I thought I'd never shake them off."

"Where did you hear them?"

"Baghdad Radio. They call them 'patriotic' songs. Remember the lovely old patriotic songs when we were children in Iraq, the ones we learned by heart? Yet they fade away the instant we choose to forget them."

Long live the Flag! High above us.
Our devotion to you is second only
To our adherence to God.

"The Flag is an imaginative and beautiful symbol. It's not a deeply flawed individual made of flesh and blood, a brutal despot who robs us of our possessions and orders us about."

"You're right. I wonder if, when radio first started, the inventor realised just how much dreadful hypocrisy, egotism and delusion it would spread over the world."

"Radio waves are capable of penetrating every part of the globe now, forcing their way into people's sitting rooms. People had better watch out." He launched into the song again to tease her:

If he betrays his love, don't tell any one,
If he breaks his promise, don't tell anyone,
Don't tell anyone.
Don't tell, don't tell, don't tell...

She put her hands over her ears and screamed at him in fury "Please stop it! Please, please stop it!"

* * *

131

She was taking a fortnight's holiday and no one would be able to locate her. An escape from the worldwide web of communications: a remote village deep in the British countryside. She had seen landscapes like this many times from the air. The countryside looked embroidered like children's clothes, or combed in parallel plaits, Afro-style. Fatima was taking refuge with an indifferent British landlord who had nothing to do with the conflict, didn't even know where Iraq was, let alone why she had left her country. And there'd be no politics. All that concerned him was the weekly rent for the room. He'd usually fall asleep at nine in the evening before the main BBC TV news.

She recalled:

Jan 16 1991: CNN Television announces that war has been declared on Iraq after the latter's refusal to withdraw from Kuwait by the deadline. The so-called 'Desert Storm' operation unleashes the biggest aerial bombing in history.

Feb 13 1991: The US attacks a shelter in Baghdad, killing 200, including women and children. The White House quotes reports indicating that it was being used for military purposes and is therefore a legitimate target.

Feb 25 1991: Iraqi forces set fire to nearly 800 Kuwaiti oil wells. The oil slick which Iraq has allowed to develop in the Gulf, is still spreading, threatening birds and wildlife in the whole area. Iraq finally orders the withdrawal of its armed forces.

She was perpetually gazing at the TV screen in horror. At times, she was all eyes, at others, she was all ears by the radio. The military planes, the rocket launchers, the satellites, the computers, all deployed for the modern art-cum-dance form of war. Oh, people, what happened to you over there? She turns to this or that wavelength for help. Here is the news. Here is a commentary. Here is a programme all about the Gulf war, dubbed the 'Mother of All Battles' by Iraq. Destruction par excellence. Saddam Hussein issues threats from his shelter. The power stations are demolished. The water tanks. The streets are full of sewage in Baghdad and other Iraqi towns, leading to outbreaks of cholera and typhoid. If the innocent are not killed by megaton bombs and explosions, they will die of hunger, thirst, disease. Shiites, Sunnis, Christians, Kurds are all mentioned and she follows everything as if her own children were being discussed.

What more do you want? Chanting? Here's plenty of it. Applause? *Clap, clap, clap*. Loyalist demonstrations? Easy. Also we have the islands of Tum el-Kubra, Tum el-Sughra, and Abu-Musa, all of them deserted but originally Arab. We must wrest them back from Iran, even if millions die in the process. And now we want to annex Kuwait. The Iraqis love wars and are always looking for a fight. Well, we found the 'Mother of All Battles'. The birds and fish of the Gulf have not been spared, nor the camels. Not even the camels. They gaze in bewilderment at the oil wells burning in the desert. *Ayee, ayee, ayee*, they bray as if crying for help.

* * *

The landlord opened the door for her and she walked into the room. A bed, a small table and a wardrobe. He showed her the kettle for making tea if she wanted. That was the only cooking allowed. He smiled and opened the window to show her the view of the countryside. He left it fully open and turned to fiddle with the old radio dial behind the bed. *Cha cha cha*. Dance music. "You like it?" he inquired, mimicking an exotic dancer's movements as he left the room. *Cha cha cha*.

Hesitantly she went over to the radio and placed a tense hand on the dial. The room was very still, as if all eyes were on her. *Cha cha cha*. What's happened to Kuwait and Iraq now? *Cha cha cha*. What's become of the camels, birds and fish? *Cha cha cha*. Are there any other stations on this decrepit old radio? *Cha cha cha*.

[1] *abaya* — black cloak
[2] *Qadisya* — battle of Arab Islamic forces against Persian forces in the 6th century. The Islamic forces were victorious.

133

Futile

Shadab Vajdi

(Iran)

Translated by Lotfali Khonji

Ignorant graveyard priests
have uttered their final, mortal pronouncement
on life
and sent all our dear ones
to the slaughterhouse of war,

.......and
comrade Morteza
in a Paris street-corner café
breathing Parisian air
blended with smoke from 'Winston' cigarettes
ruminates worthless philosophy
in his latest ideological analysis
and philosophises
on the confrontation of the bourgeoisie
with the proletariat.

Alas......

Daughter-in-Law
Aydin Mehmet-Ali
(Northern Cyprus)

She sat in the narrow little entrance waiting room of the hospital. She was frightened. She had retracted her arms, legs and neck, just like a turtle. Her eyes looked around with suspicion, watching anything moving. Anything that cast a shadow. She held a newborn baby, wrapped in a soft, white blanket, close to her breast. And a white, plastic carrier bag dangled from her wrist.

It was early afternoon. A light day... traces of sun were left behind. Short-lived sun rays poured through the window behind her. There was no-one else in the waiting area, only her. Nearer the door, the porters minded their business, occasionally looking at her from under their eyebrows. Not knowing what to do with her, hoping that they would not have to deal with her.

She was Turkish — they knew or rather they had guessed. She wore a *yemeni* on her head hiding everything but the central part of her face. A white *yemeni*, embroidered with love. Little black eyes darted quick glances like a trapped animal. A young mouth with lines of pain and a body under a heavy coat, ready to spring into action, just like an arrow in a bow.

They had tried to understand her. She wouldn't look at them. She looked down to the floor and mumbled something in her language. They had worked out from the name she wanted that it must be Turkish.

"What do you want dear?"

"Fatma'yi istiyorum!"

"What dear?"

"Fatma, Fatma... Fatma burda calisiyor!"

135

"What did she say?" He turns to his friend for help. Did he understand? No. Back to her again, "What did you say?"

"Who? Name? Name?" the other one chips in.

"Fatma... Fatma... Turk... Turk abla."

She was getting agitated, her face twisting up, her eyes watering. She was swaying from side to side, beating her breast lightly. She was so small. She was so desperate.

"Oh, you want the Turkish lady, the translator. She is not here dear! Not here!" He tried to make definite hand and face movements to indicate to her what he was saying. She didn't move. She didn't hear him.

"Not here dear! Not... h-e-r-e!" Speaking louder and spelling the words as though she had difficulties with her hearing. As though she could decipher lip reading any better. She stood her ground. He looked at his watch. Nearly two o'clock. The worker should be arriving soon. But how to get it across to her? He pointed at the chairs in the corner and indicated for her to sit down. And she understood and moved. Walked backwards to the chairs. The baby was asleep across her arm and the plastic bag dangled.

* * *

"Hello! I want to speak to Fatma Beyaz."

"Yes, Fatma Beyaz speaking. How can I help you?"

It was hectic again. She was trying to complete a form while squeezing the phone between her shoulder and ear. The paper slipped under her fingers. She pulled it back, her green eyes a little agitated, her face flushed. One of the other workers touched her on the shoulder and signalled that she had to go to the ward to deal with an emergency. Fatma signalled that she had understood. She still had a queue of women to see. Women from all walks of life. Some born in villages in Turkey, some from Cyprus, some Kurdish women who went to Cyprus, then came to London and asked for political asylum.

136

She didn't want to answer the phone but she was caught. She had a woman on Turner Ward who hadn't been near a doctor until she was six months' pregnant. She was in her mid-thirties. Fatma didn't know what difficulties she might face. She still had to get through all the tests including Thalassimia. The woman hadn't even heard of it.

Another one was having her second baby and Fatma was anxious for her. Her first child had been born blind. The woman was terrified. She was terrified that she might give birth to another blind baby. After the birth of her first baby she had cried for days, heart-rendering uncontrollable sobs talking to Fatma through her strangled voice; indecipherable sounds. Fatma was so shocked and felt so sad for the woman that she had spent hours listening to the strange sounds of this deaf and mute woman.

"How are we going to communicate?" she had asked through her tear-stained face, her mouth making awkward noises, her hands wringing and beating her chest, blaming her God for such punishment. Demanding answers from Fatma. "How are we going to communicate, he blind, and I deaf and mute? He won't even be able to see my lips so I can't teach him to lip-read. I can't hear his voice, so I can't respond to teach him anything." Fatma had felt so helpless, she had cried with the woman and yet she knew the woman expected her to hold herself together and help her. Somehow against all the odds, she wanted Fatma to help her.

Fatma was now praying, the unbeliever was praying, that the woman's second child would be a seeing child so that she could stop blaming herself for giving birth to deformed children. A punishment from God for her sins. That was what people around her had said. Every time Fatma thought of the deaf and mute woman she felt a kick in her belly.

And now the never-ending phone...she had made the mistake of picking it up... but it could be an emergency...

"Yes, Fatma Beyaz speaking..."

"Listen you whore! You better watch out! If you don't stop taking our women away and putting them in houses you will be sorry! We will make you sorry you were ever born! Who do you think you are... you whore!"

"Who is this?" She was taken aback. She stopped writing.

"None of your fucking business who it is! You know what I am talking about! You better send our women back to their homes, back to their husbands or else... I don't have to tell you again! You know what's coming! You will pay for this!"

"Who do you think you are? Do you think this is Turkey? Do you think this is a remote mountain top in Turkey? Do you think you can threaten me... cave man!" She had pulled herself together almost instinctively and was moving into the attack. Sheer survival instinct!

"We can get you any time we want, you whore! We are watching you! We know you are on your own! We know you don't have a husband. You better watch it, you feminist whore! We'll beat the shit out of you! You better tell that other feminist whore to stop giving speeches to our women or we will shut her up for good!"

"Go to Hell! Fuck off! You can't threaten me!" She was screaming into the phone. She had forgotten where she was. Her whole body was shaking, her free hand made into a fist with a pointing finger thrust at the invisible man on the phone. He had obviously hung up. She was shaking with anger, her green eyes scattering furious glances everywhere, her flushed face slightly perspiring.

She took a deep breath and wiped her forehead. She squeezed her eyes with her fingers. She hit the table with her fists and stood with her head hanging low. She thought for a moment. She needed to act quickly. She stood up, holding onto a table... she was shaking. She needed to deal with the threats. This was not the first one this week. She thought of her daughter, if anything should happen to her. She needed her friend. She needed to talk to her, to warn her of the seriousness of the situation, to agree some action with her. She would be in danger too. They were expecting the threats, but every time it happened it still shook them.

* * *

"God please help me! Please have mercy on your servant... I am so much in pain! I am trying to cook. I am in agony. I am trying not to cry. The lower part of my belly is on fire. Full of pain. Knives are cutting me up... I am so scared. Any moment, the bottom half of my body will open up and I will look down and there... on the floor... a pool of blood with all my innards... on the kitchen floor. I can't sit down properly. I sit as though on a sharp piece of glass. I have a daughter now. I've called her Umut. Hope. I gave birth to her ten days ago. My nipples are so sore from her suckling... I want to scream. And my breasts are so full, hard as stones. She is so strong. She is my little pink rose.

Oh mother! Mother... mother... oh my beautiful mother! My selfless mother... Where are you? Where are you, oh mother of mine? Why did you send me to these strange lands to these strange people? Oh my beautiful mother... Didn't you feel pity for me... pity for what was going to happen to this poor daughter of yours... so many thousands of miles away?"

She wipes her tears as they fall with the corner of her embroidered *yemeni*. She continues to stir the pot with one hand as she holds her daughter across her other arm. Her breast is bare, full, gently moving in rhythm to the baby's lips buried into it, sucking.

"I miss you so much my beautiful mother. So much... where are you? There is no one here. I can't talk to anyone. I see no one. No one comes to see me. And my mother-in-law... forgive me, I can't call her mother as I should, as you taught me to. She is not a mother to me. She is not. She is cruel, oh so cruel to me. She doesn't care. Look at me... ten days *loghusa*[1] and I am up cooking for the family. I don't even need to cook. They have the restaurant,

139

they can bring home all the food in the world. But they just do it to torture me. I've worked my guts out for them. You know I am not lazy. You know your daughter. You know how hard I work. And I worked even harder, worked my fingers to the bone. Just so they wouldn't say I am lazy. That I don't pull my weight, that I am a burden. You know how proud I am. I would never allow anyone to say I was lazy or... oh I worked so hard, so hard... in the house, in the restaurant. Day and night seven days, seven nights a week... non-stop. Non-stop, my beautiful mother. You would have been proud of me. I did everything you told me and even more...

And I don't know what to do beautiful mother of mine... I don't know how to feed a baby. My nipples hurt and I don't know what to do. They bleed. And there is no one I can ask. When I ask my mother-in-law she gets angry and shouts. You are not the first person to have a child... why do you make such a fuss... look at me... I've had five! God bless them and they are all like lions! And all sons! You had a miserably skinny girl and you act as though you've achieved some great feat! Just a girl, that's all you have produced! A daughter! More trouble... girls are trouble! You couldn't even produce a son for your first born.

Oh mother... beautiful mother of mine... and they beat me for nothing. I don't know what to do. I can't do anything right. He tells my husband to beat me for nothing and my husband obeys and beats me and my father-in-law stands there and watches and tells him to hit me harder like a man. Sometimes he doesn't and my father-in-law gets angry and threatens to beat him and hits him in front of me... oh mother, mother what should I do? What can I do? I wish you never sent me to these strange lands... to this London. I don't know it. I don't know its people. I don't know its language. I can't go anywhere, not like our village where I went everywhere... anywhere I wanted... into the hills, down to the fields, to my friends, to the weddings, to fetch water, even to the nearest town to buy material and sweets... oh mother I miss you all so much!

140

No one teaches me what to do with my child, how to look after myself. I am trying to remember the customs of the village. The 40-day custom after the birth of the child. I remember all the village women bringing food to the new mother, washing her clothes, massaging, oiling the baby, wrapping it up tight to make sure its bones grew strong and straight. And what do I do with these stone-hard breasts full of milk, dripping... and I am so sore under there. Good job there is this *abla* at the hospital who helps me when I need to ask her something. But she is so busy, she looks after so many women. And I can't go when I need her. They even complain when I ring her sometimes...

He is at home today. I don't know why he is here... he should be at the restaurant. He is angry again. I haven't done anything wrong. I am even scared to breathe. He shouted at me when my little Umut cried. I've picked her up and I'm trying to keep her quiet. Hush... hush my little one... hush... come, have some milk. Here... there is so much of it... here my rose. Open your mouth... come."

"Yes father... I'm trying to shut her up. I am trying to feed her. Don't worry she will be quiet now... any minute now!"

"Come my rose... don't make me cry. Don't... look your mummy is crying... don't cry my rose... take this nipple... come, open your mouth. Yes father, don't worry, I'll make her quiet... don't be angry father... I am really trying..."

* * *

"You good for nothing bitch! You can't even shut up your bastard. You useless shit! Shut that bastard up! You went and got yourself another bitch, one wasn't enough! Weren't you enough? Didn't you bring enough misery to this house! You had to go and get pregnant... not one year in this country and you go and get pregnant! You couldn't wait, could you? You bitch on heat! You had to have it, you had to fuck and get pregnant! You couldn't keep away from it, could you? Now another mouth to feed. Another one to clothe. You, then another one... another bastard to look after! Tomorrow or the day after you'll shit another one into the middle and who is going to look after it? Who? Who? That husband of yours? That good for nothing, that weakling? He can't even wipe his own nose! And then he wants a wife... he wants a wife to fuck, to fuck all night, get her pregnant, and there... there it is, another bastard for me to feed. Do you think this is a bottomless pit? You think you can do anything you want, anything you feel like? Do you? I'll show you what you will get in this house... I told you to get my dinner, where is it?"

"I'm coming father. I'm trying to get the child to be quiet father. It's cooking. Just another five minutes and it will be ready."

He walks into the small kitchen on the landing in his trousers, bare feet and white vest. His short hair is greying slightly at the temples, wild in contrast with his dark moustache. His slim, muscular body is tight and tense. He is ready to spring into action; to explode. Very little holds him back. She sees his arm muscles flexing, his neck going red in patches as she turns in fear to look at him. He is holding a belt as he comes towards her.

* * *

"He beat her mercilessly. I couldn't bear to look at her. A mother of ten days and he beat the shit out of her. And she is only eighteen... so young!" Fatma's voice becomes gentle. "So young... alone in this country. No one but no-one she can turn to... not one friend!" Fatma sips her drink, her eyes full of tears. "What about her husband?" asks Alev. They are in a coffee bar in Hackney drinking red wine aware of all the rules they are consciously breaking. "What did he do while his father was beating up his wife? Watch? Applaud?"

142

"Nothing!" says Fatma. "He is scared of him too. Do you call him a man? He is only a kid himself. Even worse... he is shit scared of his father. The father beats him too. If he tells him to beat up his wife and he doesn't, the father beats the son for disobedience. Would you believe it. But you know the power of patriarchy in some of these feudal families. The man is the ruler... next to God! He can even kill you... he has every right."

"And religion is on their side too," adds Alev, getting angrier, moving her body relentlessly, squeezing the stem of the glass in quick movements. "And I suppose the husband is 19, dependent on the father for a roof over his head, for his food and for his pocket money. Working for it but in the restaurant owned by the father and the promise that one day this will all be his... if he doesn't go bankrupt in the meantime! Even if he wanted to, at the age of nineteen with a wife and child, what the Hell...? Shit! The fucker! Where were his brains when he went to marry this poor village girl? Between his legs I suppose... the bastard!

Marry her in some village in Turkey, bring her here, make her pregnant immediately, have a child, make her work like a slave and have no responsibility for her... none... and when your father tells you to beat the shit out of her, do it! AND if she dares, if she dares to complain, she becomes the ungrateful, lazy slut, good for nothing; if she says let's go and make our own home she is Satan herself, she is trying to destroy the family and lead him astray; and if she dares to run away to escape the beatings and possible death, she is a whore! Straight and simple!"

Alev is squeezing the stem of her wine glass, pushing it backwards and forwards so unconsciously that Fatma gently puts her fingers at the base and stops her. She lifts the glass to her lips and looks at Fatma with her black eyes on fire. "You've got it in one Alev," Fatma says and looks at her friend, admiring her fearlessness, quick thinking and the eloquence with which she seems to move people into action. Sometimes she looks at this five foot nothing slim body and wonders where she gets such power. On a platform arguing her case she is unstoppable, she mows down any opposition in sight. She has such power with words, it's inspiring to be around her. She remembers a Rastaman calling her a lioness, "Man, you are powerful! Nothing can stand up to you! Respect, sister!" He had saluted her with a clenched fist.

"But we have a bigger problem..." says Fatma. "I received another phone call today. A man, of course... threatening me. And I need to take the threats seriously. And you too. You are vulnerable. People know who you are and what you do, despite the fact that you don't move around in the normal Turkish community circles. They know you. And they know where I am, where I work... they could hurt us if they wanted to."

"Yes, I suppose we have known it for a long time." She is more thoughtful and watching Fatma's face to gauge the seriousness of the threats. She knows Fatma will not panic and she will tell her the bare minimum, not wanting her to worry about Fatma's safety, unnecessarily. Fatma will absorb the initial blows, creating space to think for both of them. "We have always known that we are operating at the edges of violence. It's a matter of time before they get to us, I suppose... But let them dare... the fuckers!" "I sometimes wonder why we take this risk and if it's worth it, you know..." Fatma says.

After a short silence Alev says gently, "We take this risk because there is on one else to take it. And we feel we need to do something, we can't just sit back, condone it and so nothing. Everyone else is doing that... no one wants to touch it. It's too dangerous, too contentious. At the end of the day you are showing women that they don't have to stay and be abused sexually, physically or emotionally, that they can do something about it, but more importantly, that there are one or two women who will risk their own safety to help them. That's all we are... And in our time there was on one to help us. You know we can't just sit around philosophising or theorising about it all, like some women who call themselves feminists who can't get their fingernails dirty... you know we can't do that."

She looked at Fatma with affection and smiled. "Especially you... you are on the front-line...when you face those women, you have to help them make decisions. You can't send them back to possible death and sleep peacefully at night... can you?"

Fatma looked at her with tearful eyes — no! she signalled.

* * *

"I have nothing to give you. I am a poor woman. A peasant. I live in Turkey, in Anatolia, in a small village. I have never been out of my village, maybe down to the nearest town, rarely. And now I have travelled over seas and mountains, in a plane, to come here. To this London. I am her mother. I have come to see my daughter. I want to thank you... you, the good women who organised this meeting. Who invited me here... who invited my daughter to speak."

She touches her hair with her palms, pushes back invisible hairs out of place. She puts her broad palms on her knees. She is nervous. Her left foot does a little dance and jerks. She swallows hard, spit has dried in her mouth. She looks down to the floor for one second and then closes her eyes. Her lips move, trying to speak...

"I want to sing you this song. I've put it together myself. I have nothing else to give you. Nothing. I can't give you any money, I can't give you any presents. Nothing I can give you... please accept my humble gift..."

Alev is chairing a meeting. It is in Hackney, East London. There are around two hundred Turkish-speaking women from Cyprus and Turkey, some born in London. They have come from all over London. Machinists, shop workers, students, teachers, activists, professionals... some fluent in English, some not... young, old... refugees, immigrants, Londoners. They fill the old school room on a

145

Sunday afternoon, talking about being women, about religion, achievement, work, racism, violence... six other women are on the platform with her.

The mother opens her mouth and a strong beautiful voice fills the room. Women are silenced. She weaves her daughter's story of leaving home, coming to London with her husband, being left with no-one to help her, she curses the father and mother-in-law who torture her daughter when a mother of a ten-day-old child, she praises the strength of her daughter but praises the courage of the women who helped her even more. Wishes them life for a hundred years and more. Asks God to protect them for their goodness and generosity. Women cry as she sings.

* * *

"He beat her viciously. There isn't a single woman in this room who has not been beaten! Not one!"

Alev angrily cuts an invisible line across the air with her pointing finger. Her heavy black hair falls down to her waist as though a protective shield. Every now and again she takes the two ends on either side which have slowly fallen down over her breasts, flicks them back and secures them at the base of her neck. She is concentrating and her large black eyes are scanning the women in the room.

"We have all been beaten in life. All of us. If it's not our father, it's our grandfather or our husband or our brother. Even our younger brother has a right to beat us and if there isn't a man in the immediate family, then our uncle or brother-in-law or father-in-law or some other man obtains the privilege to beat us when necessary... and it will be necessary at some stage or another..."

People smile at her mocking tone.

"They think they have right to protect our honour and if necessary beat the shit out of us. Who are they to claim honour? Who are they to teach us morality?"

Her voice raised, challenging, women become agitated.

146

"It is not us who run after any woman they see... not us trying to seduce all women around them... not us who have affairs with English women and have children with them even when they are already married to Turkish women... the same men object to Turkish women marrying outside the community even if the young people love each other... it is them who bring diseases like AIDS into the families... it is them who do everything immoral and yet appoint themselves as the guardians of our morals! What hypocrisy! How dare they! Who gave them that right? Enough of this hypocrisy! Let them act morally before they can tell us what to do!"

The women are on their feet. They call out to her to tell the truth... to tell it as it is... to tell the truth for them, the silenced women.

"*Soyle abla! Soyloe!*" they shout at her, applauding, turning around and talking to the women around them. She waits for them to calm down.

"They try and create the illusion that we can't survive without them." Her tone is now more subdued. "Lies! All lies! We can survive without them... and they know it! We are stronger than them, always have been... and that's what they are afraid of. There is this saying where I come from, 'The mainstay of the home is the man (*Even diregi erkektir*)'. As though, if the man disappears, the home will collapse."

She smiles at them with irony.

"I don't know about you but I've seen many homes without men and they are still standing. I've seen women on their own bringing up their children, going out to work or working as home-workers, looking after their homes and surviving! They have many problems but they are surviving.

But I look and look and I can't find homes where the woman has gone. I don't see any homes where the man does the washing and cooking and looking after the children and going out to work and bringing in the money! No! I haven't seen such homes! Not one!"

147

Women are laughing and jeering.

"When the woman leaves, the home collapses! There is no home! The only time a home survives after a woman leaves, is when another woman is brought into the home to make it work! Don't tell me that the man is the mainstay of the home... he is not even the twig!"

The women are on their feet again applauding loudly and shouting their wishes of long life, and power to her mouth to tell it all. She looks at the papers in front of her and lifts her head up slowly. Her voice has become gentler. The room descends into silence.

"I want to tell you about the story of one of our women. She is an ordinary young women. She came to this country just as many of us did to find a better life. She was married off to someone who lived here. She believed she was coming to a better life from the village with its harsh life and no prospects. She was only 17. Her husband barely a year older, 18. She came trusting her husband although she didn't know him. The elders had seen it a suitable match, other villagers had recommended the family of the young man... you know the story... how many of us were given to a 'good' man? I don't have to tell you what we discovered after the wedding..."

Murmurs of agreement and shaking of heads from some of the women... "if only I knew," says a woman from the back.

"She came with lots of hopes and dreams. The dreams of a 17 year old, young, innocent, blind to the evils of life, soft, so soft... Within days she was slaving away in the restaurant and in the house. She wasn't a daughter-in-law, she was a servant. A servant to the whole family. She was the wife of the older son... they needed her to look after the younger kids as well as cook in the restaurant. She slaved day in day out... from the house to the restaurant and back again... no social life... not even a wedding once in a while.

Then she became pregnant. She wasn't well and the beatings started... she was being lazy. She wasn't working hard enough. She gave birth in the hospital and went home. Ten days later she was barely walking. The father-in-law was at home. He started shouting at her because the baby was crying. He started shouting at her bastard, at her loose morals for fucking with her husband..."

Some women are a little taken aback by the raw use of words; especially from an educated women. They are used to hearing them from others. She uses them deliberately because they were the words used. There is no place for refined words in such violence.

"...and giving birth to a bastard. Who was going to feed anther mouth? And on top of it all it was a girl, not a boy, she should take her bastard and get out if she wasn't going to work hard and earn her keep, this wasn't a place for free riders, she had to work, how long was she going to swan around pretending to be ill, how long, was she the first woman on earth to have a child, she was a lazy bitch, lazy...

He forced her to get up and cook for him. And she was trying to cook with one hand and feeding her ten-day-old child on the breast. He came in and started to hit her on the head. She pleaded for him to stop and tried to protect her baby. He carried on hitting her face and head. She knocked the pot of food on the floor trying to escape from him and protect her child. He became angrier, shouting and pulling her by the hair, calling her a whore, not a daughter, she was evil, she had brought the Devil into his house... He pulled her into the sitting room by the hair, her breast hanging out, her clothes pulled apart, the baby screaming, she was pleading for him to stop. He began to hit her with his belt." Alev takes a deep breath. She is angry, so angry, she is living through the beating herself. She tries to calm her voice and her shaking body. Some women have started to cry, silently.

"He beat the shit out of her. That's what he did this 'father' of hers. He made her black and blue. All over her body. But most of all he beat her between her thighs... yes... yes... dear women!" Alev hits the table in front of her

149

with her fist. "This man who was supposed to be her 'father', her protector, who had promised her mother to look after her when he asked for her for his son, who took her from her family, her mother, from her village and brought her to strange lands... he beat her black and blue between her thighs... Between her thighs leading to her vagina... and all over her belly... with a belt... a young mother of ten days! That's what her 'father' did to her!"

Alev stops to take a deep breath. "We found her waiting at the entrance of the hospital with her baby and one plastic bag. And the clothes she was wearing. That's all she had. She had run away. She knew no one... not a soul in this huge, big London she could go to. NO ONE! Except the women who worked in the hospital where she went to have her baby. Fatma Beyaz. My friend. She ran to her. And yes we helped her. Yes we helped her escape! If anyone wants to come and tell me we did wrong by helping her... let them... let them come!

We argued and fought with the authorities and we found her a house for battered women. With the help of my friend, Fatma Beyaz, she made it. She had a tough time but she made it. And she came here to share her story with us to make other women stronger."

Their faces covered with tears, their noses running, women stand up on their feet and applaud the young woman who is almost like a little girl in her pink top, sitting at the end of the platform wiping her eyes.

After a little while Alev continues, "She won and with her, many of us won. What she achieved was important and it is not easy. But I want you to be aware that women like me and Fatma received threatening phone calls. We were told to watch out, we were called whores. Feminist whores, because we dared to help a helpless 18-year-old escape the beatings and the torture.

We heard that religious *Hocas* talked about us in the mosque, talking of us, the sinful women, doing sinful things, against God's will, and calling God's wrath upon us.

150

Tell me, is it God's will that women should be beaten up? That we should not help them?" she demands from the women with anger. They respond with anger, "No! NO!"

"That's what they call any woman who challenges them. We are not afraid. We will not give up helping women, no matter how much they threaten us and whatever they say about us! We will not give up because they are wrong. We will continue to help women. So my beautiful women, don't shut your ears, don't pretend you haven't heard, find out, challenge what they say, educate yourselves, become strong, become determined, learn, become independent. Live your lives the way you want to live them, not how others want you to. But always be aware that if you do, you are a threat to how things are... but don't be afraid!"

She softens her voice as she looks around the room, "But you know something? They are afraid of us... those who beat us up and torture us, are afraid of us... of women! They look so strong and yet they are so afraid. You know why? Because potentially we are the ones who can change this society... because we have nothing to lose... because we have nothing to lose... because we have the worst deal possible... what else can we lose? That's why they are afraid of some of us who speak out... they want to shut us up, to marginalise us. They call us whores, call us feminists, enemies of men, marginalise us and prevent other women from hearing us. But we know, we know that women are listening... everywhere women are listening and waiting... waiting for a time which is right for them, then slowly they move... but once they move, nothing on earth can stop them.

So beautiful mothers, wives, sisters, daughters, daughters-in-law, aunts, big sisters, little sisters, all of you, but most of all beautiful women and young girls, don't be afraid. Life is out there! Go out there and take what is yours!"

When she finishes, many women come out and hug her, some are crying. She can't even get down from the platform. She is exhausted. Fatma knows she is. She comes and puts her arm around her waist, firmly holding her up. She can feel the trembling of Alev's body through the arm holding her, and she smiles at her friend. "You've done it again... you really moved those women, you made us cry... look at them, they are walking inches taller. I pity anyone who would dare stand in front of them." She turns and looks into Alev's eyes, "But you chose not to tell them the whole truth... didn't you? I wondered if you were going to..."

Alev lowers her face, "No I couldn't tell them all of it. I couldn't tell them he raped her."

---

[1] *loghusa*: a woman recovering from childbirth.

Buses

by Darija Stojnic
(Bosnia)
Translated by Jasna Levinger and E.D. Goy

London — the world metropolis, the capital, a huge city of
ten million people, full of events. Every corner marks history, has a story, is full of tradition. "The man who is tired
of London is tired of life," somebody said.

Here, to this London, the winds of war brought me and
my son. At the beginning it was only "for a couple of
months", and then a year elapsed, a second and a third,
and then more, and London ceased to be a tourist attrac-
tion. It became our city. Our home is here, my child
attends school here. We have our doctor, our dentist, our
tobacconist, neighbours, our shop and many other things
that make up our everyday life. Of course, we have our
buses too; but since we are in London they are not your
ordinary buses, they are the well-known double-decker
red buses. They are not a novelty now, we ride them
every day. We are used to it now.

Until some five years ago, I had lived all my life in
Sarajevo. We also had double-decker buses, indeed we did,
secondhand ones, from London. To tell the truth, these
buses, both theirs and ours, were not well-suited to our
narrow streets and our winter. They found our streets
somewhat confined after the boulevards of London and so
they rumbled with difficulty through the modest streets of
Sarajevo. It took a special skill to turn these monsters
round at the former Army Club, and an even more special
skill not to go nuts listening to the sound of their engines
all night in winter time. They could not switch them off
because they would have frozen.

One day they simply vanished from the streets. The story goes that the English would not give us the spare parts, but that is just one of the many Sarajevo stories.

We had survived the double deckers and became stronger, but unfortunately not strong enough to be ready for trolley buses in Sarajevo, "the ideal public transport solution"; after our town had been dug up all over, and then "decorated" with hundred of posts and miles of wire like the best protected camp, we were ready to greet our dear trolley buses. Cruelly, a minor technical detail spoiled our happiness; the fact that the pole could not grip the wire for more than ten minutes.

I can still see the driver who had to stop three or four times on the route from Ciglane to Otoka, cursing the Czech manufacturers and putting his gloves on, muttering to himself while getting out of the bus in order to replace the pole; and having done this, angrily and nervously starting again. There were murmurs, everybody was angry. The driver was sworn at for not learning to drive properly.

I had to use the Vogosca trolley bus. Every morning between 6.30 and 7.00am, I waited impatiently for it. The schedule depended on a number of factors, so you could never be sure if the bus would arrive within the hour. When it did finally arrive, overcrowded, humid, smelly, with the windows covered in condensation, the most important decision was which door to force open and how to use both elbows to push your way in. It was usually successful, although I once had four coat buttons torn off and on another occasion, my coat belt was pulled out, together with its loops, never mind the fact that my shoes were stepped on and my bottom pinched. The entire bus was united against the driver. "Slow down, you are not driving potatoes, you fool!" or "Why are you speeding, there isn't a war on", and my favourite reply: "If you don't like it, dear lady, take a taxi!"

Buses in front of my London home are more or less punctual to the minute. Everybody waiting sits quietly at

154

a polite distance from each other. When the bus arrives they board it one by one; if anybody has anything to ask the driver, they get a polite reply and the bus does not move out until all the passengers are aboard. People on the buses are usually silent. When the bus is full, the driver usually announces with a gentle hand-gesture that there is no more room. Nobody protests. Very often elegant old ladies getting off the bus say: "Thank you driver," "Thank you, ma'am," the driver replies.

I have come to like London and I have grown accustomed to living here; and it's good that nobody pulls off my coat buttons, yet my every thought, my every sense, still and for ever is of my Sarajevo. I carry my town, its atmosphere, its souls, its stories, its jokes...

I greatly miss my home town, and I even miss the Vogosca trolley bus. I miss that morning anger. I miss the loud laughter when somebody makes a passing comment. I miss my own life.

Sketching the Streets
Nafissa Boudalia
(Algeria)

I look at your face
Your hands are moving
Tracing the time
I remember
The flight of the swallow
That will never make her nest
Under the shadow
Of the juniper

I look at your face
You are passing by
The grey evening sky
Where the sun never goes
Slowly covering your trail
The time never makes sense
The women never smile
And the babes hide their faces
In the folds of the rocks

I look at your face
From the setting of the sun
And you are still hurrying by
The trees are shaking
A trail of your souvenirs
You are still in exile
And your time is near
The streets you are sketching
Are in your dreams

Earrings Old

Fahrija Hodzic
(Bosnia)

I don't look
Too much
After I've got them
My old earrings
But people do
And ask me
How old are they

In twelve twenty-three
The year of the *Hijra*[1]
They were made
In five years
They will be
Two hundred years old
When I say
I wonder
How many fingers
How many eyes
How much love
Has touched them

Did my grandad
Who I've never seen
When he gave them
To my mother as a bride
Gently handle them

Am I carrying
On my ears
All the touching
Of my family

Do my ancestors
By touch
Live with me

[1] *Hijra* — Muslim calendar for Muslim Year

There is a Fashion Show
Dursaliye Bedir
(Turkey)
Translated by Aydin Mehmet-Ali

Every Saturday in the early hours of the morning, a fashion show begins in Stamford Hill. A show of the season's clothes parades through the streets. Red brick and stone houses with high ceilings and arches, line the streets.

Although I love my early morning sleep, I would never miss these fashion shows. I can't get enough of them. The parade moves under the huge plane trees lining both sides of the main road, into the side streets. On Saturday mornings I am out on the estate before ten o'clock. At first, old men appear. Their shoulders are covered with grey, almost white, rectangular shawls. Tassles dangling at the ends look almost like the braid on an officer's uniform. Young Jewish girls follow them, slim and tall in groups of three or five, all with the same hair styles, cut at the same length; they pass in front of me, on my right or left without ever looking into my face. Isn't there ever one with curly hair? Or one who might like to have long hair? These white-skinned pretty young women have their hair cut in the style of *tessetur* wigs which they will be wearing once they get married. At times, you can't tell the difference between the wig and real hair. Who knows, maybe they are trying to get themselves accustomed to it at a very young age.

The 'young brides' are immediately obvious; most wear hats attached to their wigs, matching their dresses. They are either pregnant or next to them are pretty, small toddlers. The boys hair is already in ringlets.

Their dresses remind me of the sixties and are obviously not ready-made, as though each one has been repeatedly

159

tried on and sewn individually. What beautiful vivid colours! Who designs these patterns? Which factory weaves such fabrics? I turn the market places upside down but still can't find such beautiful material on any stall.

What designer can create such a fantastic design where beneath the navy blue coat worn in the middle of winter, a dress covered in sprouting, spring branches appears? Which model's walk can be so in tune with her dress? What other place on earth could stage such a fashion show so beautifully?

When the spring comes, the collars slip down a couple of centimetres from their present position at the top of the neck. The sleeves of the dresses stretching as far as the wrists, slip up a little towards the elbow. The dresses with pleats below the belt are generally popular with the young women and as with all their skirts, never rise above the knee, and what does the gathered material frequently used at the collars and wrists symbolise?

Even if the *tessuttur* wigs on top of their heads seem to be covering their womanhood, their clothes scream out their femininity.

And the walk of these elegant Jewish women is particular to them; it is neither too fast nor too slow. They don't look around them when they walk. If you ask them the time, many will not answer, as though they haven't heard. It is difficult for you to catch their glance. If one day, without her being aware, you come across a Jewish woman deep in thought at a bus stop, study her expression. It is as though she is listening to the sound of a flute somewhere in the distance, in silence and in thought, living outside the crowd she is part of.

I wonder if their men with ringlets who wear their black raincoats and hats, winter and summer, are aware of these beauties of theirs? I wonder what love these women live through? Do they also experience infidelity? Do they ever remove their wigs? Do they only dress up on Saturdays on their way to the synagogue? What are the designs of their night-dresses? Are the men's pyjamas also black? And their dream worlds? What are their fantasies like?

Sometimes they remind me of the Greeks who once used to live in the Balat neighbourhood, in Istanbul. Some 'patriots' persecuted them and forced them to leave.

My dear Jewish neighbours, I no longer live in Stamford Hill but I think of you every Saturday. I miss you very much. Please, don't disappear like those Greeks in Balat.

Against the Pleasure Principle
Saida Hagi Dirie Herzi
(Somalia)

Rahma was all excitement. Her husband had been awarded a scholarship to one of the Ivy-League universities in the United States and she was going with him. This meant that she was going to have her baby — the first — in America. She would have the best medical care in the world.

But there was the problem of her mother. Her mother did not want her to go to the U.S.A. Rahma was not sure just what it was that her mother objected to but partly, no doubt, she was afraid she'd lose Rahma if she let her go. She had seen it happen with other girls who went abroad; most of them did not come back at all and those who did, came only to visit, not to stay. And they let it be known that they had thrown overboard the ways of their people and adopted the ways of the outside world. They painted their lips and their faces, they wore western dress, they went about the city laughing and singing outlandish songs, they spoke in foreign languages or threw in foreign words when they spoke the local language; and they generally acted as though they were superior to all those who had stayed behind.

Her mother also seemed worried about Rahma having her baby in America. Rahma had tried and tried again to reassure her that there was nothing to worry about: she would have the best of medical attention. Problems, if any, would be more likely to arise at home than there. But it had made no difference. Her mother kept bombarding her with horror stories she had heard from Somali women coming back from America — the dreadful things that happened to them when they went to

162

American hospitals, above all when they had their babies there.

Like all women in her native setting, Rahma was circumcised, and, according to her mother, that would mean trouble for her when she was going to have a baby unless there was a midwife from her country to help her. Her mother was convinced that American doctors, who had no experience with circumcised women, would not know what to do.

Rahma had never given much thought to the fact that she had been only four years old when it happened, and 19 years had passed since then. But she did remember.

It had not been her own feast of circumcision but that of her sister, who was nine then. She remembered the feeling of excitement that enveloped the whole house that morning. Lots of women were there: relatives were bringing gifts — sweets, cakes, various kinds of delicious drinks, trinkets. And her sister was the centre of attention. Rahma remembered feeling jealous, left out. Whatever it was they were going to do to her sister, she wanted to have it done too. She cried to have it done, cried and cried till the women around her mother relented and agreed to do it to her too. There was no room for fear in her mind; all she could think of was that she wanted to have done to her what they were going to do to her sister so that she too would get gifts, she too would be fussed over.

She remembered the preliminaries, being in the midst of a cluster of women, all relative of hers. They laid her on her back on a small table. Two of the women, one to the left of her and the other to the right, gently but firmly held her down with one hand and with the other took hold of her legs and spread them wide. A third standing beside her held down her shoulders. Another washed her genitals with a mixture of *melme* and *hildred*, a traditional medicine. It felt pleasantly cool. Off to one side several women were playing tin drums. Rahma did not know that the intent of the drums was to drown screams that would be coming from her throat a moment later.

163

The next thing she remembered was one of the women, a little knife in her hand, bending over her. That instant there was an explosion of pain in her crotch, hot searing pain that made her scream like the rabbit when the steel trap snapped its legs. But the din of the drums, rising to a deafening crescendo, drowned her screams, and the women who held her expertly subdued her young strength. Then she must have passed out, for she remembered nothing further of the operation in which all the outer parts of her small genitals were cut off, lips, clitoris and all, and the mutilated opening stitched up with a thorn, leaving a passage the size of a grain of sorghum.

When she regained consciousness, she was lying on her mat in her sleeping corner, hot pain between her legs. The slightest movement so aggravated the pain that tears would well up in her eyes. She remembered trying to lie perfectly still so as not to make the pain worse.

For some time after the operation she walked like a cripple; her thighs had been tied together so that she could move her legs only from the knees down, which meant taking only the tiniest of steps. People could tell what had happened to her by the way she walked.

And she remembered how she had dreaded passing water. She had to do it sitting because she could not squat, and she had to do it with her thighs closed tightly because of the bindings. To ease the pain of urine pushing through the raw wound of the narrow opening, warm water was poured over it while she urinated. Even so, it brought tears to her eyes. In time the pain abated, but urinating had been associated with discomfort for her ever since.

She remembered being told that she had needed only three thorn stitches. Had she been older, it would have taken four, perhaps five, stitches to sew her up properly. There are accepted standards for the size of a girl's opening; an opening the size of a grain of rice is considered ideal; one as big as a grain of *sorghum* is acceptable. However, should it turn out as big as a grain of maize, the poor girl would have to go through the ordeal a second time. That's what had happened to her sister; she herself had been luckier. When the women who inspected her opening broke out into a high-pitched *mash-harad* with which women in her society signalled joy, or approval, Rahma knew that it had turned out all right the first time.

Rahma's culture justified circumcision as a measure of hygiene, but the real purpose of it, Rahma was sure, was to safeguard the woman's virginity. Why else the insistence on an opening no larger than a grain of *sorghum*, one barely big enough to permit the passing of urine and of the menstrual blood? An opening as small as that was, if anything, anti-hygienic. No, if the kind of circumcision that was practised in her area had any purpose, it was to ensure that the hymen remained intact. Her society made so much of virginity that no girl who lost it could hope to achieve a decent marriage. There was no greater blow to a man's ego than to find out that the girl he married was not a virgin.

Rahma knew that, except for the first time, it was customary for women to deliver by themselves, standing up and holding on to a hanging rope. But the first time they needed assistance; someone to cut a passage large enough for the baby's passage. That was what so worried Rahma's mother. She did not think an American. doctor could be trusted to make the right cut. Not having had any experience with circumcised women he would not know that the only way to cut was upward from the small opening left after circumcision. He might, especially if the baby's head was unusually big, cut upward and downward. How was he to know that a cut towards the rectum could, and probably would, mean trouble for all future deliveries? Nor would he know that it was best for the woman to be stitched up again, right after the baby was born. It was, Rahma's mother insisted, dangerous for a circumcision passage to be left open.

When it became obvious that her words of warning did not have the desired effect on Rahma, her mother decided to play her last trump card — the *Kur*, a ritual feast put on, usually in the ninth month of pregnancy, to ask God's blessing for the mother and the baby about to be born. Friends and relatives came to the feast to offer their good-luck wishes. It was her mother's intention to invite to the Kur two women who had had experiences with doctors in America. They would talk about their experiences in the hope that Rahma would be swayed by them and not go away.

The *Kur* feast was held at her mother's place. When the ritual part of it was over and the well-wishers had offered their congratulations, some of the older women, who had obviously been put up to it by her mother, descended on Rahma trying to accomplish what her mother had failed to do — persuade her to put off going away at least until after the baby's birth.

It did not work. From the expression on Rahma's face that was only too obvious. So her mother signalled for the two special guests to do their part. The first, whose name was Hawa, had spent two years in the U.S.A. as a student. She talked about the problems of a circumcised woman in a society that did not circumcise its women. "When people found out where I was from," she told her audience in a whisper, "they pestered me with questions about female circumcision. To avoid their questioning, I told them that I had not been circumcised myself and therefore could not tell them anything about it. But that did not stop them from bugging me with more questions." The topic of circumcision, she told them, continued to be a source of embarrassment for as long as she was there.

Hawa then talked about her experience at the gynaecologist's office. She had put off seeing a gynaecologist as long as possible, but looked for, and found, a woman doctor, thinking that she would feel more comfortable with a woman. When the doctor started to examine her, Hawa had heard a gasp. The gasp was followed by a few stammering sounds that turned into a question. The doctor wanted to know whether she had got burned or scalded. When Hawa signalled by a shake of her head that she had done neither, the doctor asked her whether she had had an operation for cancer or something in which the outer parts of her genitals had been amputated. Again, Hawa denied anything, and to avoid further questioning quickly added that the disfigurement which the doctor found so puzzling was the result of circumcision.

At that, Hawa's doctor went on with the examination without further questions. When she was finished, she turned to Hawa once more. "You had me confused there," she muttered, more to herself than to Hawa. "Don't hold my ignorance against me. I have heard and read about circumcision, but you are the first circumcised woman I have seen in my career. I didn't know it was still practised nor did I have any idea it went so far."

"You know," she continued after a moment's pause. "I cannot for the life of me understand why your people have to do this to their women. Intercourse cannot be much fun for someone mutilated like that. Perhaps that's why they do it, to make sure the women won't get any pleasure out of sex. And what misery it must be for a woman sewn up like that to have a baby."

Hawa said she went away from the doctor's office thinking how right the doctor was about sex not being fun for circumcised women. She remembered the first time her husband made love to her, how horribly painful it had been. And it had continued to be painful for her even after she got used to it. With all the sensitive parts of womanhood cut away, it was all but impossible for them to be sexually aroused and quite impossible for them to experience any of the pleasurable sensations that would redeem the act.

Hawa said she walked home feeling like a freak: what was left of her genitals must look pretty grim if the sight of it could make a doctor gasp. Why did her people do this to their women? Hundreds of millions of women the world over went through life the way God had created them, whole and unmutilated. Why could her people not leave well alone? It seemed to her, at least in this case, that man's attempts to improve on nature were a disaster.

167

The second woman, Dahabo, seemed to believe in circumcision as such. However, when a circumcised woman moved to a part of the world that did not practice circumcision, problems were bound to arise. She too had lived in America. She too had had her encounters with American doctors. She talked at length about her first such encounter. Like Hawa's doctor, hers was a woman; unlike Hawa's, hers was familiar with the idea of female circumcision. Nevertheless, Dahabo was the first circumcised woman she had seen. Dahabo told her audience about the questioning she was subjected to by her doctor after the examination:

Doctor: Did you have any sort of anaesthesia when they circumcised you?
Dahabo: No I did not, but I did not really feel any pain because I fainted and remained unconscious during the whole operation.
Doctor: Is circumcision still practised in your culture?
Dahabo: Yes, it is. I had it done to my five-year-old daughter before coming here.
Doctor: Any difference between your way and your daughter's way?
Dahabo: None whatsoever: the same women who circumcised me circumcised her.

At that point Dahabo told her listeners, something happened that puzzled her: her doctor, eyes full of tears, broke into loud sobs, and she continued to sob while she opened the door to usher her patient out into the corridor. Dahabo said she had never understood what had made her doctor cry.

Rahma had no trouble understanding what it was that had moved the doctor to tears. She was close to tears herself as she left her mother's house to walk home. How much longer, she wondered, would the women of her culture have to endure this senseless mutilation? She knew that, though her people made believe circumcision was a

168

religious obligation, it was really just an ugly custom that had been borrowed from the ancient Egyptians and had nothing to do with Islam. Islam recommends circumcision for men.

The *Kur* did not achieve what her mother had hoped. Rahma was more determined than ever to accompany her husband to the U.S.A. True, there was still the problem of her mother. No doubt her mother meant well, no doubt she wanted the best for her, but Rahma had different ideas about that. She was, for instance, convinced that having her baby in America was in her and the baby's best interest. She would like to have her mother's blessing for the move, but if that was not possible she would go without it. She had always hated circumcision. Now she hated it more than ever. No daughter of hers would ever be subjected to it.

The Traveller
Ruhangiz Sharifian
(Iran)
Translated by Niki Khoroushi

He was sitting at a table next to the window, a little way
away from me. In front of him there was a packet of cigarettes, a lighter and a cup of — I don't know — tea or coffee. He was looking out of the window and wasn't paying
any attention to anyone.

He had been alone on the coach as well. When he got on,
he glanced at all the passengers, most of whom were sitting in pairs and talking to each other or looking out of the
window. I noticed the same thing when I got on the coach.
They were sitting next to each other in such a way that
their togetherness was obvious. They were in groups of
two, three or four. I don't know what it is, but you can
always tell when people are together. A look, the way they
sit next to each other? I don't know!

He passed the empty seats next to the other passengers
and came to where I was sitting, and sat in the window-
seat on the opposite side. Everyone stole a look at him. He
had greeted the driver only. He had a clean-shaven face
and ponytail and was wearing a long floral skirt. I saw his
big, white, ugly, laced, ladies' sandals with low heels as he
sat down.

He didn't look at me when he sat down. I sighed with
relief. I didn't want him to sit next to me. I don't know
what to say to normal people, let alone him. I couldn't even
tell whether he was a man or a woman.

The first time I had seen one of these people, I was walking with my friends. He was coming towards us. As we saw
him, one of my friends said:

"Oh dear! Look at that man, dressed as a woman."

Another one said:

"No, it's not a man. He's just made himself look like that."

I said: "You can't even tell if he's a man or a woman."

Another one said: "I don't like those people."

"Why not?" I asked.

"They're not normal. They frighten you."

"Why frightened? They're not bothering you. They're harmless," I said.

He had passed by without a glance. He had vanished like a calm and silent spirit.

The coach was going to Leeds and I was getting off at Nottingham. I had been looking forward to this trip since the night before. I thought instead of staying at home, thinking about the short, dark winter days in London, I could be sitting on a bus, watching the meadows and fields laid side by side, as if they had been divided by a ruler.

He was sitting so motionless that I couldn't feel his presence. I had once seen one of them in my daughter's dancing class.

"Do you have students like him as well?" I asked.

She shrugged and said: "Yes, but no one likes him. You can't tell whether he's a man or a woman. No one bothers with him."

What a lonely person, I thought, but didn't say anything.

I didn't want to stare at him but he didn't seem to care. He took no notice of anybody. As if he knew his position, he didn't sit next to anyone, didn't talk to anyone, didn't look at anyone. He was lost in himself, calm and serene. He was leaning his head against the window and staring outside. I don't know why I felt sorry for him. It was as if he didn't exist.

The coach set off. It was a gloomy, cloudy day with not a single drop of rain. The sky was like a mouth opened up for a yawn. You felt as if you were suffocating. The coach stopped at one of the service stations on the way. The pas-

171

sengers got off, in groups of twos, threes and fours. It was warm inside the restaurant. With a cup of coffee, I went to sit at a table by the window. I noticed that he was also sitting by a window.

Sometimes I think lonely people sit next to the window to ease their loneliness. They can busy themselves looking at the outside world, pretending that the loneliness does not bother them. A packet of cigarettes, a cup of coffee and a newspaper usually complete the scene.

I looked at him, thinking, it seemed as if there were two people imprisoned inside him. I tried putting myself in his place, and wondered whether I would prefer to be a man or a woman. But it didn't work; I had no feelings. Sometimes I can't even tolerate myself, let alone trying to put up with two different people who are two halves. Two incomplete halves, who can't stand each other or make each other complete.

I looked out at the car park, where cars were arranged neatly in rows side by side. People were coming and going, some talking, some laughing and some arguing. I noticed a young couple at the pastry counter. The girl could not decide what to have. The boy pressed his face against hers and kissed her on the cheek. The girl laughed, reached out and chose a cake and put it on the tray. An elderly couple were looking for a free table. As they passed me by, I smiled, thinking they were from my coach. But they didn't respond. Maybe I only thought I smiled.

They looked at him, but his face was turned towards the window. A look came over their faces; it was neither surprise nor amusement. It was one of those ambiguous, calculated looks, which isolate people from one another. It is as if alienation and segregation have become a contagious and incurable disease of our times.

I poured milk into my coffee. It wasn't fresh and ruined its taste. I felt like taking it back, but I stayed seated, watching the people.

He had lit a cigarette and was sipping his coffee. His eyes caught mine. I became embarrassed and gave him a nod and a quick smile. He looked surprised, smiled and turned his face back to the window.

When we got back on the coach, it was raining, as if the sky was closing its open, yawning mouth. I sat in my place and stole a look at him. Although he had a bony build and a big frame, he looked thin and frail.

As the coach drove off, he pulled a packet of sweets from his bag and stretched out his hand to offer me some. I shook my head but he insisted. There was such a sincere awareness in his eyes, it moved me. I took a sweet and thanked him.

At Nottingham, a few other passengers were also getting off. I got up, looking at him. I wanted to say good-bye, but he was still looking out of the window. I said nothing. As the coach drove past, I saw he was leaning with his forehead against the window. He looked at me, smiled and waved. There was a lump in my throat. It was as if he were a kindred spirit. Who was lonelier? I don't know.

The Dog
Vida Kashizadeh
(Iran)

Tonight
I realised
dogs are not allowed
to die gradually.
My neighbour from up the stairs
asked me
if I mind him
burying his dog
in the garden
I did
but my lips were sealed
his tears
and my compassion
had decided
I heard me say
of course it was all right.
Now in the early hours of my birthday
a white dog
and the weight of his body
bearing the weight of the soil
is within me.
When my ribs move with each breath
I feel
I'm a dog's body.
Just this afternoon
I was picking another white dog's hairs
off my coat almost swearing
a dog I hadn't seen for nearly a year –
then remembering

her character
as this one has truly one
I softened
remembering Lisha now
makes it easy to accept
the still warm body of the dead dog
within the soil of the garden
within me.
A dog's life
is now
really over
for him
and for me.

Living
Memories

Scent of Saffron (extract)
Rouhi Shafii
(Iran)

My grandparents' house

My grandparents' house in Kerman was typical of desert houses. The rooms, all surrounding a desert courtyard, were spacious and bright, with high ceilings and colourful glass at the top of the door frame. The biggest room, with two doors opening on to the verandah, was kept spotlessly tidy and always looked ready for guests. Carpets covered the entire floor area of all the rooms. Mattresses were spread on the floors, on the top of the carpets from wall to wall, and handmade cushions were laid against each wall for guests to lean on. Curtains were embroidered with lace, and oil lamps, colourful crystal and glasswork, decorated the shelves. The courtyard was bordered by cypress and pine trees and all types of flower-bed. A pond stocked with goldfish was located in the middle of the courtyard and vases of geraniums were laid around it. Summer evenings began by the splashing of cool water over the hot stones of the courtyard. Water would spread on the wide verandas, in front of the rooms and over to the *pashuyeh* (borders of the pond). Moist air would fill the courtyard. The carpets were spread around and cushions laid against the wall on the verandah. Dinner was placed on a white *sofreh*, on the floor. The family shared such summer evenings, sitting around the *sofreh* cross-legged, eating and conversing. The main evening entertainment was story-telling by the elders, poetry reading or talking about ordinary events of the day.

The house had a thick wooden gate at the entrance which opened onto a long, enclosed corridor. The courtyard appeared at the end of this corridor. The gates had big metal handles, with which people had to knock hard in order to be heard. Couples had their own quarters but the kitchen and the guest-room were shared by all. Sometimes, a widowed aunt, mother-in-law or a single uncle lived in the same household. Servants had their own rooms, usually located by the gate.

Sleeping on the rooftops under the desert sky

Because of the heat, on summer nights, almost everyone slept on the rooftops. Roofs were accessible by narrow stairways. Part of the roofs were flat, apart from the ceilings of the big rooms which were dome-shaped. Most of Kerman's houses were connected through their rooftops. The houses had high walls around them which hid them from view, but only low walls separated each roof from the next. One could jump from one roof to the next and travel to another street. Rooftops were an ideal place for secret meetings and lovers' rendezvous. Young boys and girls would jump from roof to roof to meet their sweethearts. On summer evenings, women gathered on the roofs to gossip with neighbours and their giggles could be heard from all around.

At the beginning of the summer, extra rugs, mattresses and blankets were carried to the rooftops and stayed there until it was too cold to sleep under the blanket of the sky. In the morning the bedding would be rolled and wrapped in the *chadorshab* (large, square, thick woollen fabric) and covered by the rugs. Poets and writers have often mentioned the skies and the bright stars over Kerman. On cloudless nights the sky seemed so close that you could imagine stretching out a hand and touching the stars. The nights when I slept with my grandmother on the rooftop and counted the stars are unforgettable. She would hold me in her arms and talk to me in her sweet voice. I refused to sleep on a separate bed when she was around, until I was eighteen and went away to university.

180

Almost all the houses had dark, cool cellars where food was preserved. There were no refrigerators. These cellars were also used for storing bottles of distilled herbs and vegetable extracts. Rose, mint, rosemary, oregano and many other herbs were distilled each season and kept in bottles to be used either as sherbet on hot days or as medicine. For example, a mixture of mint extract in a glass of water and sugar was best for heartburn. Home-made jams, marmalades and pickles were also stored in the cellars. There were no bakeries in those days and storing home-made bread in the cellars kept it fresh for almost a month.

In each house an *abanbar* or water reservoir, kept clean water, usually taken from the household's well or purchased from the carts that toured the streets selling fresh spring water to the inhabitants. At the beginning of the spring, depending on the weather, labourers appeared on the streets, offering to clean the *abanbars*. These labourers offered other services as well; spring-cleaning and taking the rubbish out. Duvets and mattresses made of cotton became heavy and awkward after a while. They had to be undone and the cotton beaten. Cotton-beaters were on the streets from dawn to dusk singing out their services.

In the summer there was no cooling system. Instead the house had a *howzkhouneh* (a room with a huge *badgir* or wind-turret). The wind circled through the openings of the turret and travelled down into the room. In the middle of the room a round pond was filled with cool water. Rugs were laid around the pond with mattresses and cushions. Melons and watermelons floated in the pond throughout the summer. After lunch everyone had an afternoon nap around the pond, away from the heat. Some, however, took refuge in the surrounding gardens, whose tall trees kept the heat away and some went as far as the mountainous villages nearby.

Walking down to the *payabs*
A network of underground water ran for hundreds of miles from outside the city through the big houses and out

onto the streets. Sometime in the past, *payabs* or narrow stairs had been built through a tunnel which led down to these streams. Once you had climbed some hundred stairs down, it would take a few minutes just to get used to the shadowy space which was only lit by the dim light coming from the entrance high above. Although the water was warm and shallow, the darkness gave it a mysterious depth and gravity. Women often went down in groups to do their washing or to take drinking water. The houses were mostly connected through this underground water system and one could walk through them for long distances. Once in a while, when congested by mud and dirt, labourers would sweep it all away with their thick brooms.

The desert weather

Kerman has cold, dry winters that people used to endure with no central heating. They warmed their rooms by traditional means; mainly by *korsi*. A sunny room was allocated for the *korsi*. In the middle, a big, low table would be covered with a huge cotton quilt or blankets. Mattresses were laid on the floor and cushions against the walls. Under the table, a charcoal brazier would burn slowly. Families would spend the whole winter under the *korsi*. At night everyone stretched out and slept side by side. The top of the *korsi* was used to eat meals or junkets: nuts, roasted water melon and melon seeds and dried fruits. When you sat around the *korsi*, feet and arms were put under the blanket to keep warm. It was hard to come out from under the warmth of the *korsi* to go to the toilet or enter other rooms. After the introduction of oil stoves, the *korsi* was used less. Nowadays central heating is installed in almost every house.

Kerman's streets were narrow — muddy in the winter and dusty in the summer. When it rained, the mud would stick to shoes and made walking an effort. In the summer, desert dust storms and cyclones were not unusual. The only transportation available were *doroshky* (carriages) drawn by horses. The automobile did not arrive until the

182

late 1940s. People were used to walking long distances and did not expect to ride in a carriage unless there was an elderly or sick person to be transported. Women wore flat shoes which made it easy to walk. High-heeled shoes were not introduced until the 1950s. It was a custom for women to walk in pairs or in groups. This way they could chat while walking long distances. Very rarely would a lone figure be seen walking on her own. At night women were always accompanied by male relatives.

Hammam As-Souk

Haifa Zangana

(Iraq)

Translated by Judy Cumberbatch

Nabiha finally had everything ready that she and Amal would need. But she checked the bag one more time, to make absolutely sure and asked loudly, "Have we forgotten anything?"

"No, Mama."

Two bath towels and two towels for the face and hair. Pumice stone. Black mitten. *Riqui* soap.[1] Lux soap. Loofah. Her clothes and Amal's clothes... ...and two oranges.

"Hair ribbon... where's the ribbon?"

She hated going to the baths, especially since they were a long way from where they loved. Once a week, they had to trek from Haiderkhana to Aiffan in al Fadle, carrying everything in one hand, and dragging Amal behind her with the other.

Amal also loathed going to the baths. When it was time for them to leave the house, she fell prey to various illnesses. Chimerical illnesses, like stomach cramps or earache or a redness in her eyes which made it impossible for her to see where she was going. When her mother insisted there was no point in pretending to be ill, she launched her final weapon: she walked so slowly and gripped her mother's wrists so hard that she pulled her backwards every step of the way.

The journey seemed to last an eternity, from Haiderkhana to al Teppe, and from al Tippeh to Eifan through the back alleys of old Baghdad which narrowed and widened depending on how old they were. The win-

184

dows of houses opened out onto other windows of other houses, their grills covered with dampened mats made of reed and thorns, which cooled the air blowing into the interior.

Their own house was near the Haiderkhana mosque and their neighbourhood was one of the cleanest in the city, thanks to Jalil, the road sweeper. He used to say that the job of keeping the area round the mosque clean brought a reward no other job could match.

"Come on Amal, walk a bit faster."

They climbed up to al Tippeh. Up steps, so old, she was frightened they would crumble beneath her feet. She climbed carefully, cautiously, dragging Amal behind her with such force that she almost swept her into the air. On the top step, she noticed the house of Um Nidal across the alley.

"Amal, do you remember Aunt Um Nidal?"

She hadn't visited them for at least two months. Perhaps, she thought, if she finished the bath early, she could drop in on the way back.

Leila was much too preoccupied with thoughts about the Hamam to answer her mother's questions. She dragged her feet, stepping in every muddy hole she could find. When she left her sandal behind in one of them, her mother was forced to stop. She angrily cuffed her on the head and helped her to put it back on. Amal could see nothing but images of naked women. They made her think of the tale of the ghoul whose breasts were so enormous, she slung them over her shoulder to ease the weight. She could feel nothing but the soap in her eyes and the loofah scrubbing her body.

"*As-sadaqu lillah,* may God have mercy on your parents."

The man was sitting at the door of the *Hammam* reserved for men. Nabiha remembered him from the time when she was a girl of Amal's age. She had hated coming to the *Hammam* then and would trail along behind her mother. He wore a striped *dishdasha*[2], blue stripes on a light beige background. Cotton in summer and wool in winter. Over it, he wore an ancient jacket, torn but clean, which on winter days, he exchanged for a khaki army coat. He had been sitting in the same place for 20 years. There was a clean, metal dish in front of him in which there were a few coins. He sat on a low wooden stool with a knotted bundle beside him, his head shaved and his corner always spotless. Where did he sleep at night?

Amal, just as she did every week, put a *fils*[3] into the bowl and followed her mother into the *Hammam*. She lingered as long as she could in the changing room, just inside the entrance. She watched the women dress and undress. It was the midway point. A purgatory. Between the coming and the going.

The women arrive at the *Hammam* grey faced and leave sleepy and red-cheeked. They place their bundles on the benches. They take off their clothes and slip on wooden clogs, then enter the hot rooms of the *Hammam*; mothers accompanied by their children, young girls and boys under seven who have not yet transferred to the *Hammam* next door. Quickly... quickly... they hurry to reserve a good place to sit.

At the first curtain of steam, they pause and inhale deeply. The women push through them until they find what they are looking for. Somewhere clean, where they can sit down with their children and devote themselves exclusively and completely to the beautification of the body. Time passes by, unnoticed, as they sit in the gloom of the three interlocking chambers, under the arches and the domes which are like the cupolas of a mosque. One chamber leads to another.

First and nearest to the outside door and the changing room is the cool room. Here, the old congregate, and those who are short of breath, and the children. It is lighter than the other rooms and not so hot. The women here are busy and their chatter is distinctive.

Nabiha prefers the middle room. It is not as cool as the outer room, nor as fierily hot as the inner. She only ventures there to fetch water. Amal runs about and starts playing with a group of children in the outer room. The rest of the women crowd round the tap in the hot room. They remove their pails of water as quickly as possible, so as not to spend too long there.

A few women choose to remain in the hot room. They stand swaying, *Allah Hayy*, just like a circle of chanting dervishes. First to the left and then to the right. *Allah Hayy*. The masseuse kneads their flesh. Steam rises from the pails of water, from the ground and the women's bodies. Their faces glisten and glow. Their bodies ooze sweat, which trickles down drop by drop.

"Shall I wash you?"

"Please, God bless you."

First she soaps her with *riqi* soap, a light lather to remove the grease, then after a few minutes, she puts her hand into the black mitten and begins to scrub. Shoulders. Back. Upper haunches. She rinses her body and then turns to scrub the back of the woman beside her. Their bodies have an intimacy and friendship of their own. A silent language based on touch and a response of the senses. Naked bodies need no lengthy introduction. A harmony governs their nudity. A kinship unites them, the instant they are stripped of their clothes and enter the nakedness of the soul.

The young girls hate their bodies being scrubbed. They hate the mitten and loofah and soap. The *Hammam* resounds with the children's wails. The women laugh as they caress the boys' genitals, marvelling at the slight tremor which courses through their bodies, putting an end to their tears. The boys giggle, asking for more. A mother cradles her daughter and leaves the warm room for the cool to feed her near the outer door.

"Do you remember? She was a thin as a reed before she got married?"

"All the girls let themselves go once they get married."

There is a constant coming and going. The women walk deliberately, fearful of slipping. The clogs clatter loudly across the floor, the babble of noise rises like steam and the words hang from the ceiling. Stray black hairs twist and snake their way down the drain.

"Next time we ought to come at 9 o'clock."

"We would have been better off sitting next to the wall." It is cleanest close to the wall, away from where the floor slopes down toward the opening to the drains. Bodies gleam, glisten, smoothly hairless. The overpowering smell of *Dowa al Hammam*[4] mingles with the scent of henna and *riqi* soap. The rough hair from under the armpits, the pubes and the legs slides down and with every *douche* of water, forms itself into little pellets which roll over the ground to the drain. The bare feet pick their way among the strands of hair. Pails draw near, pails move away. Some women wear their underpants, others are totally naked. There are bare breasts, full breasts, pendulous breasts, firm bellies, jutting out proudly, and bellies scarred with the stretch marks of six, seven pregnancies. Here's a youthful body, and there's a women whose stomach drapes over her pubes and the upper part of her thighs like a thick sheet. She is surrounded by her five daughters.

"What a shame. Look at her, like a slave. She rushes about day and night and what's the use? She's been pregnant nine times and he's not satisfied and has gone and married someone else."

"The bastard!"

The *riqi* soap melts slowly in their hands. The warmth of the hands and the warmth of the bath transform it into a viscous jelly. Its pungent smell is familiar, a perpetual evocation of cleanliness.

In a corner, a woman hugs herself among her pails and in her stillness becomes another pail full of water. A group of women laugh. They comb their long black hair, anointing it with henna or a mix of henna and *wasma*[5] powder. A young girl shaves her legs with a razor and those nearby gape at her in surprise. The children skip about and play.

The older boys look on, fascinated at what the women are doing. Not at their mothers, for the mother's body is sacred. It is the loveliest body of all and the most beautiful. However flabby or fat or swollen, it is still their mother's body. The body of her womb, of lactating breasts and warmth. The body of solace. It is not a body to them. The boys stare elsewhere. They wink at each other. One of the women catches one. She touches his mother to alert her. The time has come for him to go to the other *Hammam*.

"The best time for a bath is Thursday morning."

She almost slips. She grabs hold of the wall to steady herself. She puts the pail down on the ground to rest and sighs loudly. Then as she bends over, her breasts sag forward. They take on a strange distended shape. The centre of gravity shifts from the centre to the outer edge. The residue hangs like a muslin bag used for straining yoghurt, the nipple at the end drawing it together like a rubber membrane. She straightens her back and her breasts return to their normal shape, dangling, pensile, as if a child's hungry mouth sucks fiercely at the nipple. She looks around. No one is watching her. Everyone is busy with their own concerns. Her drawers hang loosely. Her whole body sags. It has lost its central point of equilibrium.

Is she thinking of the past? Do bodies which belong to the past take on a different form? The women walk past her, in front of her. They don't see her.

"Look at her. She arrived first this morning and took the best spot. At least, she can lean her back against the wall."

Cries and shouts. Words. So many words. General hubbub. The whole room lies suspended between wakefulness and sleep. The pores on the skin open. The body breathes unrestrictedly and exhales through its skin.

"Shall I scrub your back?"

"No dear. No, Amina's going to scrub my back. *Amina, Amina.*"

Amina emerges from under the arch into the hot room, a bucket in each hand. She walks slowly towards them, a

189

young girl whose youth emphasises her grandmother's years. Her grandmother is relieved to see her. Childlike, she has missed her while she has been away. As she waits for the bucket of water, she sits with her back hunched, combing her hair and putting *wasma* on it, avidly, one lock at a time. Time is slowly eating away at her. She chews her *aliqat al ma*,[6] her strong gums masticating it.

A festival of the body, a celebration of the body, a purification. Water, drops, steam, liquid. They envelop the body in a fine transparent film which takes on the shape of the body in all its metamorphoses. There is a complete marriage between the metamorphosis of the body and that of the water. The body glistens after the long hours spent relaxing. There is a link between water and body, between heat of the fire and body, between body and body. The *Hammam* embraces them all in its steamy rooms, which are so suffocatingly hot: Water + Fire + Body.

The purification of the body mirrors that of the soul. Who contradicted the Day of Nudity in Babylon? The day of the sacred Priestess/Prostitute at a temple in which the scents of incense and perfumes rose, leaving the bodies shadowless.

"*Amina. Nasha allah.* How big she's grown but her mother won't let her get married. I say we're not young for ever."

"Leave her alone for God's sake. I mean, show me a happily married woman!"

Mad Hassiba, tired out, rests her head on her hands and moans softly to herself.

"And he left in the end. That whore satisfied him. After twenty years, he went after her with his tail between his legs. And what about me? After twenty years, what about me?"

She crouches in her corner as if she has come into her own room. She has locked the door, slid home the bolt and now waits. Hassiba is the first person to arrive at the *Hammam* each day and the last to leave. She always sits in the same place. The left hand corner in the middle

190

room. Once an hour, she washes her body and scrubs it with a pumice stone until it almost bleeds. From time to time, she lifts her head, and repeats her sad refrain.

"Me? What about me? After 20 years. What about me?"

A noisy quarrel breaks out. Two women against a third. The thick steam and the din mask the truth. Hands gesticulate, rising and falling, pointing at faces and hair. It starts with an exchange of insults. And ends conclusively, when one women gestures angrily and insolently at their sexual organs. Perhaps she is losing the battle and is forced to use the ultimate weapon. She bellows something incomprehensible, her voice drowning out the others. Indifferently, the two women turn away. They begin talking to each other, taking pleasure in showing their indifference, and ignore her. The tactic infuriates the other women and exposes her weakness. She slinks away from the group and sits isolated among her pails. The atmosphere of war dissipates immediately.

The body absorbs the water slowly, drop by drop, bit by bit during its passage through the three cleansing rooms. And exudes it slowly, bit by bit, when it leaves. The naked body of the women is now a part of the water. She washes, she scrubs, she primps and removes her unwanted hair. She perfumes herself, in her mind the image of a man. They are all the same, the quiet ones, the dreamers.

The fine mesh of steam, trapped in the vastness of the rooms conjures up dreams. Bodies quiver, in tune with the changes in the soul. Eyes linger on the lines of the body, on the ceiling, following the water as it trickles down, losing their way among the droplets.

Hassiba thinks about the men she hates. She dreams of a man who will protect and support her. Inside her memories die and nature rises again, searching for a secret joy, for a love which is death. She sees a wild creature take shape in the dome of the roof. It has two enormous eyes, wide open, eyelidless. Its many limbs are of different lengths, matted with short, coarse black hair. It has a narrow chest, smaller than its large belly, and vast wings. Its

191

tentacles attach themselves to anything that crosses their path. Its mouth is an extended proboscis, which exudes a white mucous, a glutinous substance like the foam on a sea wave. It coats everything it touches and draws it up. They exchange glances. A stupor invades her. Warmth courses through her. Instead of steam, droplets of the sticky mucous drop on to her arms, her breasts, her belly and her legs, thick condensed viscous drops trickle one at a time on to her exposed pubic area. Her pudenda is her core. The crystal dish forms a receptacle for the white foam. Is she about to be absorbed by this heat?

She slips quietly on to the translucent ground. While she scrubs her body, her eyes interlock with those of the strange creature. The proboscis droops gradually. Their eyes meet. The proboscis descends slowly towards her.

Her sense of excitement mounts, as she moves, the friction between her scrubbed body and the floor intensifying the reaction.

The gelatinous liquid flows out. A gauzy film of milk permeates her body. It washes it and softens the skin and makes the eyes glisten and shine. The thick heavy lips of the proboscis attach themselves to her belly, thighs and legs. They return to her core. To the crystal dish. They suck at her lazily, unhurriedly, recovering what she has given. They pull away. The woman stirs as if in sleep. She cleaves to the ground. The proboscis detaches itself. She arches her stomach, lifts her legs slightly. Warmth suffuses her. Heat penetrates her every pore. Her eyes darken. Her body shudders violently, then relaxes. She opens her eyes. She sees nothing.

Nabiha grabbed Amal by the hand.

"Come and help me. We're late."

"I want to watch."

"Come on... There's nothing to see. Someone's ill and having a fit... Come on. We're leaving in a moment."

Amal felt frightened as she looked at the shrunken body on the floor. She held on to her mother's hand but she

192

kept watching. Without understanding why, she was fascinated by the quivering body and the strange manner in which it moved. She had seen nothing like it before.

Amal walked beside her mother, but half looked back towards the twitching woman.

[1] *Riqi soap*: Traditional Iraqi soap made from olive oil
[2] *Dishdasha*: Long, striped cotton robe worn by men
[3] *Fils*: Coin worth about a cent
[4] *Dowa el Hammam*: Traditional Iraqi depilatory
[5] *Wasma*: Powder made from crushed leaves, and similar to henna, used to colour the hair black.
[6] *Aliqat al ma*: Traditional chewing gum, made from natural resin.

Yemma

Samia Dahnaan
(Algeria)

For I remember you standing
At the balcony waving
For you ask if I had a good day
For I rush revealing my love-hurts to you
For you look at me and smile
For I pinch your pleated cheeks
For I laugh and say
"Grandma, your face is a dry fig"
For I kiss you
For you scream with joy
For you exclaim,
"Girl, stop pinching my cheeks!"
For you sit quietly, listening.
For I pour you a mint tea
For I look into your eyes
I see a tear quietly drowning
Your lips touch the edges of the cup
For I join you
Between chatters and sips
Until we laugh ourselves silly.
For you Yemma I long
For the mint tea you loved
For the sea and jasmine plant I miss
For the passion you had
For the sadness you felt
For when I left you
For the day I landed,
For the grey that wrapped me all these years
For the years passing by

194

For my sight is blurred
For the tears you shed
For the youth that deserted you
For all the shattered hopes
For a country in pain,
A nation waiting in vain
For a miraculous cure.
For the enchanted years of my childhood
For the day I return
For I know you've been waiting.
For you know,
You are always here
In my thoughts.
For the pain I endure
For I know
My lips will never touch
Your pleated cheeks
For you, Yemma who saved me
and believed in me.
For you Yemma I hold a pen
For you, I revel in a language
You never spoke.

Shoulders

Fatma Durmush
(Northern Cyprus)

I was sitting down to breakfast,
when I began to be irritated.
I chased it to the muse.
Of course I went to the hills
Quietly, without wearing my coat,
Went topless in the morning dew.
No-one saw my foolishness except
For a little squirrel and it went
Climbing on and on it did not seem
To care and maybe God doesn't either.
When evening came, I said my prayers.

The Rose

Fatma Durmush
(Northern Cyprus)

I placed a red rose
on your cheek, it smothered
in your pride and self consequence.
Then went into the fields,
and placed another for dying love.

Became a woman of nothingness,
and rose to no great heights.
Doing the housework, planning nothing.

Then found a voice in things called nothings.
And called out, "Do you love me?"

There was no one and so no one answered.
It was in a particularly bad mood that surrounded
me and the housework had to be done.
I coaxed the rose and placed it upside down
and cut all the thorns but love still stung me,
despite all my precautions.

Garden Flowers

Shadab Vajdi
(Iran)
Translated by Lotfali Khonji

With your kisses, garden flowers open.
With your kisses, the nocturnal sky is filled with stars
and even day is filled with luminous atoms.

With your kisses, the spring garden comes to life
and the fiery sun of the South
in the blue sky of the shores of the Qeshm Island[1]
shines once more.

You are from the South
whose days are hot
and whose nights have skies overflowing with stars.
You are from the South
and that is why
rays of kindness shine upon our rooftop.
How kind, how warm.
For me
it's as if springtime is blossoming.
For me
the entire soil is covered with wild tulips.

[1] An island in the Straits of Hormuz

Search
Shadab Vajdi
(Iran)

Now you are here
But between us
Mistrust is entrenched like a silent wall.
Behind this wall
My hands
Burning and restless like flames
Wandering like the wind
Are searching your hands.

Thoughts and Cries of Pain

Peace to All People
Brikena Muharremi
(Kosova)

No apology
to the unjust soldiers
no apology
to the poison holders,
no apology
to the robbers of light,
no apology
to those who love to fight.
No apology
to the breakers of hearts
to those who hate the sun of life.
No apology
to the lovers of wars
no apology
to the closers of life's doors.

God, don't let people die
to the enemies of freedom
        no apology

Snowflakes

Brikena Muharremi
(Kosova)

On a train
To university
Talking to snowflakes
Old guests of my inner palace,
Ignoring a newspaper
I, the one thousandth visitor
Of the official web page
Of memories,
Constantly chatting
E-mailing my own address
Fighting the viruses
To face the millennium
And coming back
To talk to the snowflakes.
The train rushes
And rushes.

Man, the Sinful God
Nazand Begikhani
(Kurdistan)

What is my crime to be?
What was my crime to be born?

My father was waiting in the teahouse round the corner
Hearing the news of my birth, he frowned and sighed
My uncle consoled him
"Don't worry my brother, don't worry."

Whose death was my birth?
Whose death is my being?

When I was born
My mother cried
Cried and cuddled me
My father slapped her, shouted
"Throw her away and serve me."

Trickle of blood
Witness of absolute terror

Am I disappointment?
Am I agony?
Why do I bring tears to my mother?
Why do I provoke my father's anger?
Seeds of doubts:
Do I repel joy?
Me so full of tenderness
Do I plant anger?
Me so human.

My mother is justice
My father is terror

When my father died
With my watery fingers
I built the grave of terror
I painted laughter with a branch of beam
My brother threw a fistful of darkness at it
And shouted: "The realm of pleasure is male, only to him
belongs the sacredness of laughter."
I looked straight at him
My mother said a prayer

My brother is the son of my father, of force
Son of history, history of cruelty
I am the daughter of my mother, of tenderness
Daughter of history of mercy, history of justice

Woman is a sea of beauty, of mercy
Where man drinks life, drinks humanity

Oh! Dictator lover
Do you know that you are alienated?
Alienated from beauty
This is why you plant fear
Alienated from truth
This is why you are not yourself
Alienated from justice
This is why you incarnate power
Alienated from humanity
This is why you are cruel

Make yourself equal to me
In order to see beauty
Make yourself equal to me
In order to know justice
Make yourself equal to me
In order to be able to cry

My lover stripped me and said:
"I like to be equal to you."
When he did not see my virginity blood
Threw me away: "You dishonour me".

I do not know you
You do not know me
We want to be equal
Why should your greatness be embodied in my blood?
Why should the honour of the great you, emerge from the
Veil of an organ as little me?
Hey, you are not part of God, and me only your rib?
A sinful Ayet!
Sacred lie!
Sign of doubt, the terror of your fraternal Prophets

I am not you, you are not I
God you are, but not yourself
I am not you, you are not I
We are two beings
Together forming the God you created against me
Together we are humanity

Oh! Man
You are for me
Father
Brother
Lover
Son
But I am for you only shame

Oh god!
You are sinful and it is time to return to truth

The Journey
Samia Dahnaan
(Algeria)

"Let me come, let me come with you Grandma," asked Zahra.

"Okay, girl," her grandmother replied reluctantly...

Zahra's grandma was tall and slim. Her voice was raucous but soft. Her eyes were hazel-grey. A very strange colour. Sometimes they really looked grey. When she was angry, they turned from a calmer grey to a fiery one. Her pleated cheeks resembled the pleated skirt Zahra used to wear to go to school. Sometimes, Zahra used to count how many pleats she had, which annoyed her grandmother. Every Friday, Grandma prepared the *Kasdira,* a round aluminium flask which she filled with water. She packed a few dates, bread and a bottle of milk so she could give it to passing vagrants. The birds gathered, waiting for her to pour some water onto the headstones.

Zahra and her grandmother usually left before the midday prayer, then walked through a narrow street. There were many street vendors. All along, one could buy anything one wanted — sweets, clothes, perfumes, drinks, fruit, incense; all carefully laid out on large sheets. The gates were opened. Zahra and her grandmother struggled through the crowd to enter the cemetery. Zahra's grandma was relieved.

She said: "Look girl, we can see the tree from here."

Every Friday she had a date with the tree. Zahra would run down the stone path, climb the tree and sit huddled in one of its strong branches.

"Come on down, girl, you'll fall," shouted her grandmother.

The tree bore Zahra's weight, witnessed the first signs of her teens and also her grandmother's tears, weeping and wiping the immaculate cold stone.

Twenty years later, Zahra had returned and now lay on the cold white stone. She slowly opened her eyes to welcome the morning and sat up. How invigorating it felt to be breathing in the clean warm air once again. The white marble beds sought refuge in the curve of the hill, awoken by a gentle wind moving swiftly along the peaceful rows of the stone garden; hidden away from the sea and the lust of that early morning breeze. Her uncoordinated body felt heavy. Each movement she attempted to make became an effort. But she persevered and managed to get up and take a first step. It was good to feel the warmth and moistness of the earth. She could smell a heady mix of sweet jasmine, orange blossom leaves and that far-reaching ocean breeze. Zahra's face was serene and relaxed. She felt the softness of her skin and took pleasure in it. The gentle heat of the early morning sun-rays touched her face, giving it a shiny glow. The brightness of the sunlight prevented her from seeing further. In this momentary darkness, the reflections of the heaps of white stone piled high, towering into a minaret of buried and strangled voices scattered in the stone garden. She tried to hear but her ears refused to listen to the litany of those desperate voices.

The abandoned trees invited those who dared to plunge their teeth into their reddish thighs to taste their sweetened flesh. She picked a few figs, sat down and started eating. When she had finished, she felt ready to carry on. After walking for a while, she noticed a number of people coming towards her from different directions. She stopped for a moment. She was agitated but was not deterred by the bad premonition.

Zahra saw a herd of dark shadows beginning to advance towards her. As it drew closer, the shadow faded away and became an army of men dressed in long black robes floating, sweeping along its path. Zahra was anxious, but decided not to move. It seemed that the army was heading for a battlefield. All the men carried white sticks on the left flank. They also had gold belts holding polished silver knives proudly embracing their hips. Some of the men caressed the cold silver metal. They wore white turbans, which they frequently adjusted. Their footsteps followed the same pattern of repetitive, heavy, clapping sounds. What struck her was the uniformity of their beards — long, bushy beards covering their upper chests. They must be quite heavy, she thought.

She moved quickly from her position so as to have a better view of the marching army. She felt apprehensive and wanted to hide. It was too late to make up her mind. They had seen her. One of the men who appeared to be their leader, approached her and, speaking coarsely, said:

"Woman, what are you doing here alone?"

Zahra stood up and looking him straight in the eyes, said:

"Why do you ask?"

His eyes were a vivacious dark brown, under busy eyebrows, shooting beams of anger and hostility at her long auburn hair. In order to divert his persistent stare, she seized her hair and pulled it back.

"You ought to leave this place, woman. It isn't safe."

She did not like his abrupt manner and his dictatorial way of speaking to her. Where had he come from? Why wasn't it a safe place to be? There was nothing menacing here.

Zahra spoke in a soft but firm voice.

"Well, I come from around here."

He was quite tall and his costume made him look like a walking tree, in search of better soil. His hands were busy fidgeting with a green-black cloth. The two colours were striking; the green was a deep olive green and the black was a navy blue black. Both colours outlined the intensity of the dark blue sky of the hot summer evening and the green was the green of mutilated olives.

This time, he really stared at her face.

"Look woman," he shouted.

His voice made her jump. She wanted to flee from this spot. Before she could make a move, their leader said:

"Take this and cover your hair."

He gave her the cloth. Before she could say anything, he had vanished. While Zahra was staring at the cloth, she heard the heavy, orderly footsteps on the stone path.

As they moved away, the sound of their footsteps faded away. It was a rigid and repetitive drum beat which made Zahra's head spin.

She decided to carry on walking. After a while, she passed a gate which opened on to a busy street. It was comforting to see groups of women walking and chatting. To her surprise, she noticed that most women wore scarves. They were in the very same cloth the bearded men had given her earlier. The hustle and bustle of the narrow streets had a welcoming effect and she immediately felt at home. The streets looked like a rigid, patterned canvas. But an atmosphere of insecurity enveloped them. Her stomach tightened into a knot, hindering her train of thoughts. An acute shooting pain froze her limbs. For a moment, she wanted to return. It was too late.

She wanted to return to a past that was punctuated by glorious victories and eloquent speeches. A past that had given to a gullible and fervent nation a miracle recipe for economic prosperity. A past which haunted her. The sound of music made her body shake, leaving it in a state of trance.

She felt trapped. The women were looking at her, whispering: "She is not from here. She is not from here."

"Why were they saying that?" she wondered.

Was it because she was dressed differently? She understood their language very well. She had not forgotten the sensual rhythm which had been part of her all these years. The stream of words which had dried inside her, wished to flow out, healing a body which had known a long and devastating drought. She had this urge to go and look at the sea, and throw her body into the curves of the gigantic waves, feeling them on her tummy and on her breasts. She wanted to lie in the sand where her body would seek warmth and refuge in its healing power.

She longed to see her neighbourhood. She decided to take the bus instead of walking. When the bus came, she got on it and found a seat. It was quite full. The women and children were all seated. Most men were standing. Young children were sliding up and down their mothers' long dresses. The mothers were busily trying to cope with their children's bouts of energy. They were enjoying an uncontrollable game — pulling their mothers' scarves and trampling against the creased robes. She could not understand why the mothers were struggling against all the odds to keep children, robes and head scarves still. The men's arms were raised, their hands gripping the handles, while their eyes followed every movement of the women's scarves and robes.

She headed for the shopping area, expecting the market to be open. How she longed for those trivial times when she used to do her weekly shopping. The market housed one of the most popular fish markets in the country. The voices of the fishmongers and shoppers fell upon the tidy row of glossy, pink mullet exuding the last glimmers of life before being thrown into dancing flames. Outside the indoor market, small shops displayed tidy and colourful rows of fruit and vegetables. Oranges glowed like sunsets, ready to burst out their juice and to have their flesh torn. She walked past the shops and the market hallways and felt as if she was disturbing the heavy silence which had enveloped the place for many years. Isolation and a sense of loss had settled in. She felt uneasy and wary of what was to follow.

Zahra decided to move on, hoping to shake off the stubborn trails of her past. It had been a long day. She wanted to see the house, the neighbourhood close by. She wanted to be sheltered by those pillars which stood firm along the boulevard. She wanted to fill her lungs with the heady sea air.

It was a short distance to her house. She grew excited as she got nearer. Walking along the elegant boulevard, she noticed that everyone seemed to be running, rushing. Most were wearing some kind of uniform. Women wore the same robe and their heads were covered with the same green-black scarves. Bearded men wore the same outfit she had encountered when she began her journey. Were they all preparing for some kind of a national celebration parade? It seemed so.

She heard a woman's voice calling in the local accent: "Zahra, Zahra. I can't believe you are here. Is it really you?"

She was surprised to meet someone she knew. She greeted her and said: "Oh! It's you Malia, how happy I am to see you."

She stood still. She recognised her friend Malia. She was here. The present possessed her. She could not escape it. The forlorn past was behind her. They stood there in the middle of the road hugging each other.

She kept looking at Malia. Her hazel-green eyes had lost their youthful gaze, but they still had a calming effect on her. The string of words she had buried for years was about to erupt. Her face was pale, drawing out the striking lines on her forehead. Even her reddish-fair skin that had once guaranteed success and been the talk of the country, had toned down into a palish white.

She was shocked to see the green-black scarf on Malia's hair. She remembered Malia's beautiful jet black hair swaying as she walked. Why was she hiding it away?

Zahra asked: "Why are you wearing that scarf? You never used to wear one."

"You mean this," raising her hands and touching the scarf.

"Well, I'll tell you what happened to my hair. I have been wearing this scarf for two years. Well, I... Well you know... Don't you know? In fact, it's the other way round. It's wearing me. Let me explain myself. It wraps my hair, imprisons my thoughts and makes me angry. When I look

213

at my hair, it just lies flat and motionless. It needs the swoops of a Sirocco wind to feel alive again."

It was easy to pour out their lives to each other. The joy of meeting again by the tall majestic, grey pillar which bordered Kebani Street was palpable. It was a cosy corner separating them from the street.

Malia learned that Zahra had intended to come back to see her and see the neighbourhood, the town and the sea. But her writing career and her family commitments had prevented her from doing so. Malia was hungry for more information.

Malia asked: "I heard that you've become quite well known! I wish I could read some of your books. You know that they are not available here."

Zahra said: "Oh, I know that. But I am here now, I'll get you a copy."

"But tell me Zahra, why did you come back at this time?"

"Why not?" replied Zahra.

"Things are not the way they used to be. Do you remember our trip to the seaside? You wore your beautiful yellow-brown cotton print dress. My mother had prepared *Tchakchouka* (a garlic, tomato and green pepper dish topped with fried eggs) and you brought along my favourite cake. That sponge lemon cake. Oh, I can still taste it."

Zahra smiled and suddenly burst out laughing.

"I remember now, when we got to Chenoua Beach, we realised that we had forgotten our swimming costumes. For hours, we looked for an isolated spot. We found a creek. Our bodies were hot under the July sun. When I touched you, you burned with the desire to run and crash headlong into the sea, until your body had cooled down. Then, you were driven madly back to the shore. Oh! Zahra, if only those days would return."

"Those days will return," said Zahra.

"I don't think so, Zahra. Life has taken its toll on me. Every time I go on a shopping trip, I have no more energy

214

left. The shopping expedition becomes a dangerous and costly journey. It used to be my favourite pastime. It has become a nightmare trip. Some of our local shopkeepers have moved out of the area. Some of the neighbours have left town. Many have emigrated. The main market loses a stall every day.

It's a forsaken place, I tell you Zahra. You should not have come back. Even my only daughter Farida, has left and gone to Europe. I am still trying to cope with the separation. It has shattered all my hopes and dreams for her."

"Look Zahra, look around you."

"Maybe we should leave now. It's getting very late."

"We must get home before 7pm."

The streets gradually emptied. The last trail of sunrays was playing hide-and-seek with the shade. An atmosphere of uncertainty, idleness and melancholy had fallen on the place, making Malia feel estranged and displaced in her own town. Was it really her town?

As they moved from their sheltered corner, Zahra noticed men spilling onto the street. Zahra wanted to cross the road. She felt caged in. The men had sealed the street. They wore long black tunics which floated over their Turkish style trousers, making them look as if they were about to take part in some epic film.

Malia looked at Zahra and said:

"We must get out of here. Hurry, hurry. You're not wearing the scarf!" asked Malia.

"Why should I?" replied Zahra.

"You'll be in trouble. I wouldn't want anything to happen to you, Zahra."

"Don't you worry Malia. I can take care of myself".

Two men approached them and interrupted their conversation. One of them spoke in a dictatorial voice.

"Woman, where is your scarf?"

"Scarf? What scarf? I don't wear a scarf, Mister," replied Zahra.

"I've got one for you woman. Just cover your hair."

215

"I am not covering my hair."

"Ignorant, stupid, loose woman. Don't you know your customs?" he shouted.

Malia went forward to speak to the men. "Let her be. Leave her alone. She won't wear it. You need not insist."

Zahra was not intimidated. She looked at the men and said "Keep your scarf. I am not wearing it."

"You'll be punished, woman. You've asked for it."

Malia pulled Zahra's arm and said "Please Zahra, let's go. They'll get you."

Zahra's body felt light. Her hand clutched Malia's hand. "Don't worry Malia. They won't catch us."

Malia kept running, turning to see if they were behind them. Her feet did not touch the ground. She was flying too. Zahra screamed and staggered, then fell.

"Malia, Malia."

Malia stopped. She screamed too. Her scream reached far down Kebani Street.

"Zahra, Zahra."

"Ya, Yemma, Ya Yemma".

"Why, why?"

Her body was shaking. She raised her hands to her face and began wailing... Malia's tears flooded her face. She held Zahra in her arms, smelling and feeling the moistness of Zahra's hair. Her chant grew slowly into a continuous lament, sometimes interrupted by "Why, why?"

She stopped abruptly, let Zahra's head rest on the ground and launched into one of her magnificent *"yous-yous"*. She tore off her scarf and threw it at the men. "You can have it now. You cowards, murderers, butchers." She turned to Zahra and said: "Look Zahra, look at my hair, isn't it beautiful?"

Zahra smiled. In the twilight, the echoing voice of the *muezzin* calling for prayers and the haunting sound of the siren persisted.

The Barren Stick
Saida Hagi Dirie Herzi
(Somalia)

I was born in Mobileen. My childhood was weary with lack of sleep. In Mobileen one is lucky to be born male. Girls are thought of as lost labour. They are expensive to raise, and they are trouble. They are trouble because they may bring shame to the family, if God forbid they bring an illegitimate child into the house, and of course they are extra mouths to feed. And just when one could get some work out of them, in return for raising them, they go away to their husband's families, who end up getting all the benefits.

Before I left home, my family was determined to get as much as possible out of me. Long before my bones had grown strong, I was made to carry water over long distances, bring in firewood and pound grain. During the planting and the harvesting seasons, I was made to work in the fields from dawn to dusk. The routine household chores of cooking and cleaning awaited me when I got home. When there was no field work, I had to make the mats and the ropes for the family huts. I had to serve the men around the house — my father, my brothers, and any other man who happened to be there. It was my misfortune to be born the only girl in our family.

In Mobileen, the boys go to *Quoranic* schools, and when they are grown they take the cattle and sheep to the grazing lands to look after them. That is all they do, and nothing more. Herding is not tiring work. It leaves them lots of time to groom their hair and brighten their teeth with the finest brushing roots. In my village, the men are like peacocks.

217

My family could not wait to see me get married, because that would bring a dowry of cattle and perhaps sheep. In my village, a girl is given to the man who offers the biggest dowry, not to the man who would love her best. It is value for value: one side gives cattle, the other a girl. The value of a girl, like that of a cow, is based on her ability to work and to produce offspring. Preferably male offspring, of course. I often heard my family talking about what they would get as my dowry. Father would say, "If we are lucky we will get ten cows," and one of my brothers would interrupt, "No way, this can't be, we only have one and we should try to get as many as twenty."

I reached puberty at the age of thirteen and that was when I got married. My family's greed brought me a widower of my father's age. He had just lost his wife and needed someone to take care of him and his children. He gave my family twenty-five cows, more cattle than they had ever hoped to get out of my marriage. That day my mother was all excited. She came running to me in the field and said, "Sharifa, you can't believe how many cattle we are getting for your dowry! You really made your father and brothers tall among men." Those twenty-five cows made the family extremely happy. That was all they ever wanted from me.

One of the things I had to do in preparation for the wedding was to gather the sticks with which my husband would beat me. Our men believe that girls, since they all marry young, have to be beaten to become good and obedient wives. My stick-gathering took place the day before the wedding. All the girls of my age and all the newly-wed women in the village came to help me select the longest and smoothest sticks. For on that day enough sticks had to be gathered to last me all my married life. The sticks, along with a few wedding gifts, were the sum of my worldly possessions.

Nothing ever pleased my husband. He was not satisfied with anything I ever did. He made me prepare his coffee several times over. He was fond of saying, "Women were created from the crooked rib of Adam, and they should be straightened out," or he would say, "Girls were trained one way by their families, but have to be trained another way by their husbands." According to him, the only way to train a girl was with a stick. No matter what I did, I got beaten. I got beaten if I served him hot beans and I got beaten if I served him cold beans, and when I asked him to make up his mind, I got beaten. I didn't know what to do. Beating me seemed the only thing that gave him any pleasure. I wondered, "Doesn't he get enough satisfaction from the scars on my face and the limp from my hip?"

What I could not understand and what still amazes me, is that the women in the village did not mind being beaten. In fact, they believe that the more you are loved, the more you are beaten. On many occasions I have witnessed them refer to their beatings with pride. Halima, my neighbour, was always showing off her swollen face and saying, "The lover's beating is like raisin eating." I would reply, "Do you call these scars a sign of love? Any more signs like these and we will all be dead." I was in constant fear of my husband, and the only time I could relax was when he slept or was away with the cattle.

To compound my misery, I could not bear children. That made my husband hate me. He felt cheated. There were no returns for all he had invested in me. After three years had passed without me giving him a child, my husband married two other wives, who bore him children. With that I lost what little status I had in the house. I became a servant who worked for everybody and was despised by everybody. Behind my back, the new women broke eggs, to shun the evil eye from their children. The eye of a barren woman is fiercer than that of the devil.

For some time, my husband tried all the traditional cures and all the religious spells he knew on me in the hope of curing my barrenness. Nothing worked. So one morning, he called me into one of his new wives' huts. Two of his elder sons were present. He said, "I take my two

219

sons as witnesses, you are divorced." When he uttered these words three times, my marriage to him was ended.

I thought I would be glad to be free, but being back home with my family was hardly any better. There were only my brothers now. My parents had died. And my brothers did not want me. They had never liked me. Now they positively hated me. They hated me because they had to give back half the dowry when I got divorced. Moreover, they were afraid that I might claim my share of what they had inherited of livestock and land. The thought of giving something to a woman infuriated them. "The waste of it! Anything given to a woman would be wasted, just as she herself is a waste." That was how my brothers felt. And they made life as miserable as they could.

In less than two months, I was married for a second time — to the first man that passed through our village. He was an old man. As a woman who had been divorced by an old man, I could not hope for anything better, although barely twenty. My second husband was even older than the first. But being the witch-doctor of his village made him an important man. He had three wives before me and several *gheshanti*. The *gheshanti* were much like wives except that they were not married in a religious ceremony and so could be changed more easily.

I moved to my new 'home' taking with me my few possessions — some clothes, a couple of pots, and what was left of my beating sticks. I settled into the routine of work from dawn to dusk, punctuated by the occasional beating. This man was gentler. People came to him for cures and the exorcism of evil spirits. He beat me only for the sake of custom.

After two years, when it again became apparent that I could not bear children, my husband went to work on me. As the witch-doctor of the village he had to do something about my condition. If he didn't people would lose faith in his curing skills, and his credibility as well as his income would suffer. He therefore worked hard on me. He made me drink countless cups of ostrich oil. I also had to swallow vile-tasting concoctions made of herbs, roots and all sorts of other things I could not name. But in the end I did get pregnant.

The nine months of my pregnancy were the happiest days of my life. For the first time I was left alone. For the first time I had minutes, hours, days to myself. All I had to do was take care of myself and the baby growing inside me. I slept when I wanted to sleep, went to the river when I wanted to swim and ate when I felt hungry. For the first time in my life, I knew freedom.

My pregnancy also gave me status among the people of the village. Bu there was something else that made it special. My husband had prophesied that I would give birth to a boy who would inherit his profession. To be the mother of the future witch-doctor of the village was the greatest thing a woman could aspire to. I felt happy, and anxiously awaited his arrival.

Like all Mobileen women, I delivered alone. I was left by myself in a faraway hut built specifically for delivering babies. This hut was bigger than the rest. In the centre, stood a huge pillar, which branched on top into two, and on one of the branches a thick rope was tied and left hanging, almost reaching to the ground. I had a difficult delivery. My labour lasted for several days and I was screaming from severe pain. I realised then that it was because of the horror that we were left alone during our pregnancy. One of the elder women had told me previously, "Hold onto the rope which hangs from the pillar when you feel the baby is coming." The long struggle in the hut finally ended, and I gave birth to a boy.

As I held the baby in my arms, I could not believe that I had brought a life into this world. In that moment my heart was finally full of love and joy. But the baby was still. He never cried or opened his eyes. When the women came to see me and take the baby to his father for blessing, they immediately realised that the baby was dead. They took the baby for burial and returned me to my hut.

The Penelopes
of my Homeland

(For the widows of Anfal, Southern Kurdistan 1988)

Choman Hardi
(Kurdistan)

Years and years of silent labour,
the Penelopes of my home-land
wove their own and their children's shrouds
without a sign of Odysseus returning

years and years of widowhood they lived
without realizing
without ever thinking that their dream was dead the day it
    was dreamt
that what was left of life was the same as what had gone
that the colourful future had been lived in the past
that they had lived their destinies and there was nothing
    else to live through

years and years of avoiding despair
of avoiding giving up
and holding on to hopes raised by palm-readers
holding on to the wishful dreams of the nights
and to the just God who does not let such nightmares
    carry on

years and years of growing more Penelopes out of their
    daughters
and growing more Odysseuses out of their sons

the waiting women of my home-land grew old and older
without ever knowing that they were waiting
without ever knowing that they should stop waiting

years and years of youth that were there and left unnoticed
of passionate love that wasn't made
of no knocking on the door at midnight
returning from a very long journey

the Penelopes of my home-land died slowly
carrying their dreams into their graves
they died slowly leaving more Penelopes to take their place
they died slowly with no just God smiling upon them.

Recital
Ziba Karbassi
(Iran)

Translated by Stephen Watts and Ziba Karbassi

I have come   so where are your arms?
    so where is your hug for me?

A poem has come   so where is your heart?
    so where is the heart of you?

Fire   I have brought
    fire is my heat
    so open your heart

Pain I brought
    wounds I brought
    blood I brought
    traumas I brought
    snake bile
    I brought

Astonishment I brought
    heartheat I brought
    ecstasy I brought
    craziness I brought
    light I brought

These orange coloured flowers of spring
    I brought

Her hand is clenched
                she has brought all of this with
                                opened hands

Her palms are whiter than this paper
white light   white light rising off her palms
light that comes from her forehead that
                is your gift,

                        then these fingers

one is green colour of the high tree that
                        is the hanged man
                                the one dead

the second is red
                the colour of the roe deer's dream
                                when she was stoned to
                                        death

the next is yellow
                colour of the jaundiced child
                                colour of silence

the fourth is grey
                colour of tenements and tower blocks
                                in the ruined city

next is the orange one
                colour of my grandmother's calmed
                                        heart

the sixth is blue as the colour of my hair

the next is wine red like my mother's hair highlit by
                the streetlamp's light

the eighth is seven
colours of my god when I was a kid
rainbowed in the
radiant air

next to last is black
the colour of my lover and the colour
of his sleep and the colour
of night

and last is this cream
the colour of the milk between
the bodies of two close
friends

The drum heart of the world made these colours
the gong tongue of time gave these
colours their colour

these colours their colour, their tremors
their traumas

their traumas, their tremors, their
colour these colours

It is time. Sleeping is done with. It is time
to wake us
Where are you heart?
Where are you eyes?
The poem has come.
Why haven't you?

He is saying
"look how bold she is
she has come from Shams's city
she is the daughter of Tabriz
Tabriz of the Traumas."

226

She is keeping her shoulders straight
        she is keeping her head held at head height

                she is feeling good

                        she is laughing the laugh

                            of her laughter

Appendices on

Women in Conflict
and the
Literary Voice
of Women

Afghanistan

Afghan Women in War and Conflict

Afghan women have been victims of two conflicts, firstly the occupation of Afghanistan by the Soviet Union from 1979 to 1989. From 1989 to 1992 the *mujahidin* waged war against the Afghan communist regime and from 1992 to 1994 the *mujahidin* fought against each other until the Taliban came to power in 1996. A BBC World Service programme stated that there were about 50,000 widows in Kabul alone. There are about 140,000 in total.

Because of the first conflict, by the mid-eighties, over a quarter of the entire Afghan population had become refugees, while internal exile was also very high. It is estimated that five million Afghans became refugees, mainly in Iran, Pakistan, Germany and America. The political dominance of the Taliban since 1995 has been a significant factor in the acceleration in the flow of refugees. Many of the refugees are women with children but where Afghan men are present, they are no longer able to support their families by themselves. Both in Iran and in Pakistan, Afghan women are forced to work hard doing poorly paid, low-skilled work such as shelling pistachios, cleaning wool, making brooms, cleaning saffron, making chains and carpet weaving. Children usually start work at an early age.

From 1979 to 1989, a complex network of *mujahidin* movements and factions developed to oppose the Soviet military intervention with women taking an active part in the resistance. According to Doris Lessing who visited Afghanistan, it was usually women who obtained information from their connections in the administration and would pass it to urban resistance groups for their own use and for the use of commanders in the countryside. Women suffered heavy losses with hundreds of women and girls being arrested, tortured and executed. Women were also raped. There were strong female resistance movements in Herat, Kandahar and Kundiz. Young women worked with the *mujahidin* and carried arms, ammunition and information under their veils.

Following the Soviet withdrawal, there was continuing factional fighting between the various *mujahidin* groups with Afghan women being in a very insecure position and rape occurring. Rape was thought to bring shame not only on the girl's immediate family, but on the larger clan as well. 'Honour killings' of rape victims were common.

The lawlessness led to the unexpected emergence of the Taliban who promised a respite from the unruly *mujahidin* parties which had run the government since 1992. They guaranteed order based on *Sunni* Islam and vowed to restore peace to Afghanistan and transform it into an Islamic state. The Taliban is an Islamic revivalist movement which stands for radical Islam, having a strict interpretation of Islamic values, particularly in relation to gender.

The Taliban took power in 1996. In August 1998 several thousand Hazaris (Mongol *Shi'a* Muslims) were massacred by the Taliban (*Sunni* Muslims) when they captured areas of northern Afghanistan. The victims were mostly males who were killed in front of their families. Taliban militiamen in other areas of northern Afghanistan have massacred thousands of their *Shi'a* Muslim enemies, women and children as well as men. In one area, women and girls were sent to a prison camp with one report stating that Taliban men had taken young *Shi'a* women from their homes to become 'maidservants' to be married to *Sunni* militiamen. However, according to Peter Marsden, the Taliban were popular in many of the areas they have conquered.

For fifty years, women had been free and in urban areas had worked as doctors, teachers and factory workers, wearing what they wished. In Kabul the custom of veiling was not as widespread as in provincial towns such as Herat where women traditionally wore the *chowdery*.

The Taliban government interpreted *Shari'a* law in a way which placed severe restrictions on all women's lives. Hundreds of women have been beaten by Taliban guards in detention centres or in public places for defying Taliban edicts. Women were physically restricted to their homes under Taliban edicts which banned women from seeking employment, education or leaving home unaccompanied by a male relative. Other measures restricting women included the closure of women's *hammams* and girls' schools, taxi drivers refusing women passengers and shopkeepers banned from selling goods to women. The Taliban also enforced the wearing of a *burkha* in public places, with women beaten for not having the proper attire. The *burkha* covers the woman from head to foot and fits close around the head with a little grille for the eyes so that the woman inside is invisible. An Afghan refugee has likened it to a prison. The Taliban made it increasingly difficult for women to have access to health care. There are particular concerns about the increasing numbers of women dying in childbirth because of these actions. Many women and children are suffering from poverty and hunger because Afghan women were forbidden to work. Widows received food aid which had to be collected by a male relative whereas previously women, especially war widows, had taken employment outside the home to support themselves. Sima Wali states "In effect, *jihad* is being waged against women's mobility, freedom and human rights".

In July 1998, the European Union suspended all new humanitarian aid to the Taliban regime in Kabul to protest at its denial of equal treatment to women. In April 1998, the UN aid agencies gave the Taliban government an ultimatum; either it removed all edicts restricting the movement of women or it would be denied UN development assistance.

Many Afghans are refugees. Although over 2.5 million refugees returned to Afghanistan after the Soviet withdrawal in 1989, more than 1 million remain in Pakistan, with an additional 1.4 million in Iran. Some of the women and children are from villages which were bombed by the Russians, the menfolk having gone off to fight. It is mainly rural women, many of whom are widows, who live in the refugee camps of Peshawar, Pakistan. Veronica Doubleday, who stayed in Peshawar, had grave concerns about the women there. "For women in particular, it was impossible to erase memories of the harrowing experiences of bombardment, massacre or terrifying journeys into exile. Men had choices. they could take up arms and fight, they could go and find work in the city, meet new people and adapt to their new surroundings. Women had no options and nothing to distract them from the past." In the refugee camps, any infringement of *purdah*, such as not covering the face when the woman leaves the women's quarters, was reported to the Mullahs and as she is dependent on the camp authorities for food and as her children will suffer for her misdemeanours, she conformed to *purdah*. According to Sima Wali, a member of a delegation representing the Women's Commission for Refugee Women and Children, the survival rate, physical protection, nutrition, education, skills development and psychosocial well-being of female refugees and displaced women fell far below those of their male counterparts, mainly because of inequitable access to resources. According to Farah Hiwad, educated women from cities such as Kabul and Kandahar have sought refuge in cities like Islamabad and Karachi in Pakistan.

The previous and current war situation has caused upheaval to traditional lifestyles in rural areas. Although women have traditionally been excluded from public life, they were accustomed to relative freedom within their own villages and according to Veronica Doubleday who lived in Herat, the women were by no means meekly submissive or unaware of their situation. They took great delight in each other's company and were able to exert a great deal of influence on their menfolk through the management of family affairs and their socially important role of marriage-arranging. However the woman would not accompany a male family member to a place where she was likely to come into contact with alien men because if the women were molested or harassed in any way, the men would have to avenge the insult at the risk of their lives. *Purdah* is very strictly observed if the women do go out of their villages and there is segregation between men and women. According to Imran Khan, as a result of this highly-defined code of behaviour, women have immense security. They know that provided they observe *purdah*, no man will dare to harass them.

During blood feuds and tribal warfare, women are spared as it is considered cowardly for the victor to dishonour the womenfolk of the vanquished. Rape was unknown. If a woman's husband was killed, she would ensure that her sons avenged his death.

Arranged marriages are the norm with the tradition of the man paying a bride-price, a sum of money paid to the bride's father.

The attack on the USA on September 11 2001 led to the Taliban regime being attacked in Afghanistan in the search for the perpetrators, in particular Osama bin Laden and al-Qa'eda. Up to 1.5 million refugees fled the military action and within Afghanistan, women and children are considered the most vulnerable by UNICEF.

References
Mahnaz Afkhami, *Faith and Freedom*, Tauris, 1995, Chapter on Afghan Refugee Women by Sima Wali
http://www.amnesty.org
V. Doubleday, *Three Women of Herat*, Cape, 1988
Michael Griffin, Hostages, *Index on Censorship*, No.2 1998
Imran Khan, *Warrior Race*, Chatto and Windus, 1993
Doris Lessing, *The Wind Blows Away Our Words*, Picador, 1987

Peter Marsden, *The Taliban*, Zed Books, 1998

http://www.oneworld.org

C. Squire and N. Gerami, 'Afghan Refugees in Iran: the needs of women and children' *Forced Migration*, Refugee Studies Programme, Oxford, Edition 3, December 1998

W. Maley, *Fundamentalism Reborn*, Hurst 1998. Chapter 'Afghan women under the Taliban' by Nancy Hatch Dupree.

Afghan Women and Literature

Traditionally in the past, women were forced to stay at home to look after their husbands, families, relatives and the home. Attending school was forbidden to girls but some families provided private tutors at home to teach reading, writing and the verses of the *Koran*. From 1924, schooling became compulsory. The majority of women went to Koranic schools. There were no such restrictions for boys. Rural women were and continue to be, mostly illiterate.

The oral tradition is strong among Pushtus, with mothers recounting stories of valour to their children. They tell their children that a coward dies but that his screams last for ever. There is a Pushtu song in which a mother tells her son who is going to battle, that she would much rather he died a brave man than lived a coward.

At that time, women were able to introduce themselves to society as poets, writers, teachers and politicians. They disclosed the dark sides of the community and tried to eradicate them. There were two categories of writer, the first being obscure writers from amongst the ordinary people. The second group belonged to the upper class and they were well-known. One of the most famous poets was Rabia Balkhi who lived a thousand years ago and who wrote poetry in Arabic and Persian. She wrote love poems after falling in love with a slave. Consequently her brother killed her by slitting her wrists. She was then locked in the *hammam* and wrote poetry in blood on the walls. Others were Aysha Afghan, who died in 1820 and whose poems were first published in the last quarter of the nineteenth century; Mastora Ghoori, who died in 1928; Miriam Kanizak; Sanaanbar; Mahjooba Herawee; and Malehfee Badekhshi.

In the early twentieth century, opening schools for girls was a priority for King Ammanullah in order to liberate women, and in 1921, the first school for girls was inaugurated. Meanwhile, a magazine called *Ershad-Al-Nasswan* edited by two women, Asma Rasmai and Roch Afza, was published every two weeks. Through this magazine women were informed of their rights and of the menacing goals of reactionary circles towards women. During King Amanullah's reign, the Queen removed her veil (*burqa*) for the first time, so that high-ranking officials and members of the Kingdom dared to do likewise. In addition, for the first time, girls from schools were sent abroad to Turkey and other places for higher education. The obstacles and difficulties traditionally faced by women, slowly dissipated. Gradually Afghanistan acquired women professionals. Currently, there are still many educated Afghan women, large numbers of whom have migrated to the West, Pakistan and Iran, but some are still inside Afghanistan.

In recent years, there have been a large number of famous women poets and writers. The following are poets who write in a range of languages representing the ethnic groups of Afghanistan — Mastaora Shal (Pushto poet), Kubra Mazahar, Shafiqa Yaqeen (Uzbek poet), Yassamin Janah (Nooristani poet), Laila Sarahat, Khalida Feroogh, Suraya Wahidee, Pari Badakhshi, Mary Neyaz, Kamila Habib, Magga Rahmani (Dari poets). Mastoora Afghan is a major Dari poet. Writers include Roqia Aboobakr, Nafissa Abbusi, Masooma Esmali, Rahima Amini and Homaira Saljoqa. There are quite a number of well-known female poets, writers and journalists in exile. Asefa Etemadi, who was born in Kabul, is a published poet and journalist. Formerly, twenty-one journalists worked on the four newspapers published in Kabul. One poet is Safia Siddigi who lives in Peshawar, Pakistan. She is highly-educated and well-travelled, while another poet is Parvin Malal who writes in Pushtu and lives in Karachi, Pakistan. In her poems, she addresses the situation of women, Afghan refugees from the woman's perspective and the situation inside Afghanistan. Both within and outside Afghanistan, writers are compelled to use allegory and metaphor such as animal stories to mask the true meaning of their work. This applies to the work of Farah Hiwad who, although in London, continues to use this technique. Wahida Zalmai, in exile in London, addresses the concerns of women through her short stories.

The literacy rate for women is amongst the lowest in the world and even before the Taliban came to power to deprive girls and women of their education, girls' school enrolment was just 3.6% of the school age female population (*Times Educational Supplement*). This is partly because of the opposition to education for girls in highly conservative rural areas but, of course, the years of war and instability have exacerbated the situation as many schools have been destroyed and there is a chronic lack of teachers and resources owing to the poor economy. All this is having a devastating effect on the voice of women and on literature by women.

References

Farooka Gauhari, *Searching for Saleem*, University of Nebraska Press, 1996
I. Khan, *Warrior Race*, Chatto and Windus, 1993
Safia Siddiqi, *A View Through Poems*, Translated by Shah Agha Mujadedi, Peshawar, Pakistan, 1997
Times Educational Supplement
Ayesha Tarzi, *Red Death*, Islamic Texts Society, 1985
Shabibi Shah, *Where do I Belong*, Mitchells, 2000

Thanks to Wahida Zalmai for assistance with this chapter

Algeria

Algerian Women in the Civil War

Algeria was once a symbol of progressive anti-colonial struggle against the French which brought women and men together to fight for their basic human rights. Women fighters in the war of national liberation, such as Djamila Bouhired and Hassiba Ben Bouali, became the international symbols of Algeria's freedom struggle and were revered throughout the Arab world. However, in the cause of nationalism, women were expected to be bound by tradition and take responsibility for instilling Islamic culture and traditional moral standards inside the family. The slogan of nationalism was: 'Arabic is our language, Islam is our religion, Algeria is our country'. According to Marie-Aimee Helie-Lucas in her paper *Women, Nationalism and Religion in the Algerian Liberation Struggle* (1982), the projects of nationalism, socialism and religion became tools for the elaboration of an anti-women state policy. Under the post-independence Constitution, women were equal to men but this was not implemented; in fact the reverse took place — women were beaten in the streets, were forced to veil, forced marriages took place and there was a lack of jobs for women. In addition, women were angry about the 1984 law, the Family Code, based mainly on Islamic law, which reduced them to the status of minors, dependent on their husbands or fathers.

Today, Algeria is in a dire situation in a war of the secular state versus the extremists or *Islamistes* who are trying to topple the state This war has ravaged Algeria for more than six years. Several thousand civilians have disappeared without trace. *Islamistes* are defined as those

240

who are exploiting Islam for their own purposes. Algerian women are once more becoming symbols of the fight for human rights and justice in their country and using as their slogan the words of Tahar Djaout, the poet murdered in 1993 "If you don't speak out, you'll be killed, if you speak out, you'll be killed, so speak out as you'll be killed anyway." According to Aicha Lemsine, the final solution against women has become a terrorist strategy for cleansing a religion. The number of people killed since 1992 has been estimated at over 120,000. A percentage of these victims have been women who have been increasingly targeted by the extremists and are being kidnapped, raped, mutilated, tortured to death and killed by beheading. The principal armed groups are the GIA (Armed Islamic Group), the MIA (Armed Islamic Movement) and the AIS (Army of Islamic Salvation).

Women are being used for politcal purposes. In 1994, two young high school students who were unveiled, were shot by members of the GIA whilst standing at a bus station. However, two weeks later, two women wearing the veil were shot by members of a pro-government vigilante group, 'The Organisation of Young Algerians'. There is increasing pressure on women to veil. Women have also been killed because they have not conformed to the *Islamistes* view of the traditional woman's role or through their work have supported the existing system or have exposed the violation of women's human rights, e.g. school principals, writers, journalists, intellectuals or women activists. They have been targeted with threats and violence. Many women activists live in hiding, some moving every few days to avoid attack and even having to be separated from their husbands, children and families for security reasons. Many professional women have been forced into exile because of the danger to their lives. Aicha Lemsine maintains that all Algerian women have 'become a human shield, the animal brought to slaughter, marked down for the final solution by madmen'.

In the cities and towns, killers have assassinated thousands of 'liberals' who are considered supporters of the state: teachers, doctors, lawyers, journalists, academics, civil servants. Journalists are also targeted because they have sided with the intellectuals and non-religious parties who object to dialogue with the extremists. As the ultimate form of censorship, the assassination of journalists symbolises the freedom of speech lost by all Algerians because of the war. Lara Marlowe in *Index on Censorship* makes the point that for Algerian *Islamistes*, there is no freedom of expression in the established, legal media.

According to Karima Bennoune, the extremist violence against women dates from before the first round of the 1991 elections, which the FIS (Islamic Salvation Front) had won. Subsequently the elections were cancelled in 1992 with thousands of *Islamistes* being arrested and in the eyes of their supporters, becoming martyrs to the law. After the 1988 riots against the policies of the government of Chadli Benjedid, the FIS had been legalised and had addressed the problems of the poor, including women so that the Islamist parties had grown and consolidated their power and had begun to harass women. Control of women's behaviour, dress and habits, as well as its commitment to the 'policing of morality', were deeply rooted in the group's ideology and practices. In the 1990 municipal elections, the FIS had won the majority of cities and local town councils and consequently the violence against women had escalated.

In 1994, Algerian women mounted a huge demonstration against the violence in the country. Algerian women are continuing to defy the fundamentalists who are violating their human rights. An example is Saihi Horria, a leading documentary film maker who has done a great deal to heighten women's issues and explode the myths propagated by the extremists. Khalida Messaoudi, a leader of one of the biggest feminist movements for democracy, advocates resistance to the extremists. Although she had

242

been condemned to death by the FIS, she has chosen to
remain in hiding in Algeria.

References

Mahnaz Afkhami, *Faith and Freedom: Women's Human Rights
in the Muslim World,* Tauris, 1995. Chapter on Algeria by
Bennoune Karima, Margot Badran and Miriam Cooke, *Opening
the Gates: A Century of Arab Feminist Writing*, Virago, 1990
Marnia Lazreg, *Eloquence of Silence: Algerian Women in
Question,* Routledge, 1994
Aicha Lemsine, 'Death or Exile', *Index on Censorship*,
September/October 1994
Lara Marlowe, 'No End in Sight', *Index on Censorship*, 3 1995
Refugee Council, *Algerian Refugees in the UK*, Factsheet 15,
1995
Martin Stone, *The Agony of Algeria*, Hurst, 1997

Algerian Women's Writing

Algerian women writers have used literature to criticise
the patriarchal order and to champion the cause of women
in the community. Half of Algerian women cannot read or
write. Women have been marginalised, ignored and shut
away for a long time. In Algeria, traditionally women do
not speak unless men allow it.

In the twentieth century, for Algerian women writers
critical of the regimes, publication in Paris has provided a
useful escape from censorship.

There are and were a considerable number of esteemed
Algerian women writers who write mainly in French —
Djamila Debeche, Taos Amrouche, Leila Sebbar, Myriam
Ben, Hawa Djabali, Hakima Tsable, Bediya Bachir and
Yamina Mechakra. In the past, there were also Jewish
Algerian women novelists such as Elissa Rhais and
Maximillienne Heller.

There are many shared themes in the literature of
Algerian women. Taos Amrouche and Djamila Debeche
write about the problems facing the educated women,
Leila Sebbar and Assia Djebar about female bonding and

Djebar and Yamina Mechakra are among those who wrote about women active in the Algerian War of Independence. Leila Sebbar, who has lived in France for over 20 years, writes about female identity, the problems of exile and the plight of immigrants especially the way gender operates to establish and maintain social hierarchies within and between cultures. This is covered in her book *Fatima ou les Algeriennes au square*, 1981.

Assia Djebar, probably, Algeria's most famous female novelist, was born in 1936. After university studies in Paris, she returned to Algeria where she got married, and during the Revolution lived in Morocco and Tunisia, returning to Algeria after Independence. After another move to Paris, she finally returned to Algeria in 1974 to teach at the University of Algiers.

All of her novels are about women. Some of the problems dealt with by her are the relationship between spouses, infidelity, women's fear of sterility and of subsequent repudiation and the subordination of the wife to the husband. These issues are found in all of Djebar's novels as is the daring theme of women's discovery of their bodies.

Her first novel *La Soif* was published when she was only 20 and it tells the story of Nadia, a snobbish, petulant Algerian adolescent of mixed Arab-French blood, who tries to steal Ali, the husband of her childhood friend, Jedla, in order to make a former suitor, Hassein, jealous. North African critics reacted strongly to the book because although it was published in the middle of the Algerian Revolution, it did not address serious political issues nor, it was felt, did it paint a flattering or authentic picture of Algerian women. Only after the Revolution, when the anticipated liberation of women did not materialise, was the seriousness of the problems raised in the novel appreciated. Her second novel, published in 1958, was called *Les Impatients* and centred on revolt against tradition and the family, while her third novel *Les Enfants du nouveau monde*, 1962, deals with women's collective struggle.

Further novels were *Les Alouettes naives*, 1967, and *Ombre sultane*, 1987, while *Femmes d'Alger*, 1980, was a collection of six short stories. In 1977, Assia Djebar made a film for Algerian Television *Nouba des Femmes de Mont Chenona* in which old women tell of the struggle of the Algerian people to rid their land of the colonial oppressor.

Fatima Gallaire, currently in exile in France, is a leading dramatist. She won the Prix Arletty in 1990 for *Theatre Francophone* and her most well-known play: *Princesses, ou ah! Vous êtes venues... là ou il y a quelques tombes*, was written in 1988. Fatima Gallaire has talked about her motivation for writing *Princesses*. "You have to leave many times before you notice that, for those back home, you are beginning to die. Nothing will ever redeem those departures full of doubts, the interrogations, the way a country that you love can head slowly towards ruin as you watch, in despair at being helpless. The death of 'Princesse' is the expression of a wound branded in the flesh. Of an irreversible mutilation. No, I am not bitter. But I pity those who cannot express this pain by any means. I write. But I remain inconsolable." (Royal Court Theatre Programme Notes). Gallaire explores the relationship between ethnicity and gender and attempts to combine the best of the traditional culture of the Islamic community with the liberal aspirations of post-Enlightenment Europe. Her plays have been censored in Algeria and have not been performed there. She has also written two other plays — *Au loin, les Caroubiers* and *Rimm, La Gazelle*.

Aicha Bouabachi is a poet who currently lives in Germany. Her works include *l'Aube est née sur nos lèvres* 1985, *Peau d'exil*, 1990, *On assassine ma Patrie*, 1993 and works to Tahar Djaout, the Algerian poet, novelist and journalist who was murdered in 1993. Several writers are crrently in exile in London – Nafissa Boudalia, Samia Dahnaan and Chahad Fatah, who all express their concern about Algeria and about women, through their writing.

The women writers I met all talked about the alienation of women, the fact that the condition of women had not changed and about women not having a voice.

Currently, some of the writers write in French whilst others write in Arabic. This is because French was the language used in education; the French were in Algeria for 132 years. In the 1960s, education became bilingual and there was a policy of Arabisation and gradually Arabic became the sole medium for education.

Many writers denounce violence and loss of identity and deal with the writer's responsibility when faced with the loss of freedom and risk of death in a country where you die for words. One Algerian writer has assumed the pen name of Yasmina Khadra in order to hide her identity, given that her life would be in danger; even her publisher does not know who she is. Her novel *L'Automne des Chimeres*, published in 1998, uses the genre of a detective novel, to describe the Algerian crisis. Latifa Ben Mansour, born in Tlemcen and now in exile in France, in one of her three novels: *La Priere de la peur*, 1997, writes about an Algerian women intending to return home from exile in France. However, at Algiers Airport, she is seriously injured in a bomb explosion, losing both legs. The rest of her short life is spent with her cousin who relates the family history and legends. Latifa Ben Mansour is one of the activists who denounce the extremist killings in the name of Islam and in 1997 she collected hundreds of signatures for an announcement in *Le Monde*.

Hamida Ait El Hadj was forced into exile in Paris because of the play she co-wrote, entitled *El Butin* (The Booty) which is about the current tragedy of Algeria and the victimisation of women. This play was performed in London in January 2000.

References:

Algerie Litterature/Action, Marsa Editions, Paris
Irena Assiba d'Almeida, *Francophone African Women Writers*, University Press of Florida, 1994

Claire Buck, *Bloomsbury Guide to Women's Literature*, Bloomsbury Press, 1992

Jean Dejeux, *Femmes d'Algerie, La Bôite a Documents*, Paris, 1987

Jeune Afrique — magazine

Fatima Gallaire, *Princesses*, Editions des Quatre-Vents, France, 1991

Fatima Gallaire, *Au Loin, Les Caroubiers and Rimm, La Gazelle*, Editions des Quatre-Vents, France, 1993

Belinda Jack, *Francophone Literatures*, Oxford University Press, 1996

Cahiers d'Etudes maghrebines — Femmes du Maghreb, No. 8/9, 1995, Maghreb au feminin, No. 2, May 1990, University of Koln, Germany

Khalida Messaoudi, *Une Algerienne Debout*, Flammarion, France, 1995

Joan Phyllis Monego, *Maghrebian Literature in French*, Twayne Publishers, Boston, USA, 1984

Winifred Woodhull, *Transfigurations of the Maghreb*, University of Minnesota Press, 1993

Bosnia

Bosnian Women in War

Muslims were the greatest victims of the War (1992-1995) making up 66% of the dead or 'disappeared', whereas they made up only 43% of the population of Bosnia Hercegovina.

In the 1981 Yugoslav census, 83% of the urban population of Bosnia, identified themselves as 'Yugoslavs' and many people from former Yugoslavia refuse to be identified by ethnicity or 'national group'. Many people had not been believing Muslims for generations but 'Muslim' is now categorised as a nationality. Mixed marriages, of which there were many, are now considered 'impure' and nationalist propaganda calls mixed marriages 'bastard factories', polluting the biological source of family. Children of a mixed marriage suffer. The old law of patriarchy prevails in that a male child is expected to identify with his father and father's nation. In ethnic fundamentalist ideology, the procreative power of the woman is appropriated by the man and a woman's kinship with her children is overruled.

Over 80% of the refugees from Bosnia Hercegovina are women and children. During the War, males were separated from female members of the family and from their children. The husbands stayed behind and were not allowed on humanitarian transport unless they were elderly or wounded, or they stayed behind to fight. Most able-bodied men who managed to leave, paid large bribes for their escape. Men were taken away during the night while women and children had to leave their homes and were taken to another place in order to further the policy of 'ethnic cleansing'. An example is the town of Foca in the Drina Valley, which was half Serb and half Muslim in its population. The town's Muslim men were rounded up and killed or imprisoned and the women were driven out, either towards Croatia or to be jailed in Montenegro. Some women on their release, managed to escape to Sarajevo through the secret tunnel under the airport runway that kept the city's defences alive during the siege.

In the Balkans, men's and women's roles followed generally traditional patterns of responsibility. The war forced men and women into traditional roles with women providing emotional and nurturing support for their children. However, women were also forced to become independent.

As early as December, 1992, the UN Security Council condemned mass rape in Bosnia, finding that Bosnian Serb soldiers in particular, had raped Muslim and Croat women, both in detention camps and in individual towns and villages, as part of a strategy to coerce non-Serb residents to leave their homes. Serbian camps, such as Omarska, were established. There were tens of thousands of rape victims. This constituted systematic rape as part of an apparent war strategy to terrorise and eliminate a population. Many were killed after being raped. Apart from rape reinforcing the psychology of violence associated with the war, it was a humiliation within the context of a nationalist war, as the rapists intended propagating their blood line. As a result of rape, the female womb becomes occupied territory and, in addition, the female body can seem to the victim as if it has betrayed her. The child may be perceived as an enemy of the mother.

One of the most horrific events was at Srebenica in July 1995 when the Bosnian Serb army captured Srebenica, a city designed as a UN 'Safe Area' and home to 40,000 Muslim refugees. Many thousands of Muslim men and boys were separated from their wives, sisters and daughters, taken to detention camps and shot and buried in mass graves. This was Europe's worst war crime since the Holocaust. The widows were driven into exile.

The siege of Sarajevo, which lasted over 1000 days, caused unspeakable suffering for all the inhabitants. Shells were dropped by the Serbs in position in the hills above the town. Thousands of civilians were killed and wounded by shells and sniper fire while others suffered from malnutrition and hypothermia or died from untreated conditions such as diabetes and kidney disease normally treated by dialysis. People struggled to exist with spasmodic or no water, gas or electricity supplies.

Women took the responsibility for feeding their families, being dependent on UN handouts or on obtaining Deutsch Marks to buy food at vastly inflated prices. Most of the parks were transformed into vegetable patches. Women constantly risked their lives in the struggle for survival; for example, residents queueing for bread and water were killed and maimed by shells. Women had to become very resourceful to provide sustenance for family members and had to revert to primitive methods of cooking using only the very limited ingredients available. New recipes flooded Sarajevo to meet the new need.

Initially, most women were very strong and determined to resist the horrible injustice of which they were victims. However, many women gradually became depressed with the fight for physical and emotional survival and the inaction of the world community.

In Exile
Many women feel they have lost their identity and their country because they are no longer Yugoslavs but are former people from a former country. Often they take full responsibility for the children and the decision-making because they have lost their husbands. This is difficult when they may be traumatised and suffering from displacement shock.

Many women are in internal exile as well as being refugees in a range of countries worldwide. Although women may have been able to remain in their home town, they may suffer a feeling of inner exile and alienation because the character and ethnic make-up of their home town will have changed; for example, Sarajevo is now a Muslim town with many women choosing to cover themselves, lead a traditionally Muslim way of life and with loudspeakers on the minarets calling the faithful to prayer.

The women of Srebenica have still not discovered what happened to their husbands and missing male family members. The first demand of the women is that the graves of their husbands, brothers and sons should be protected and exhumed. Many of the women live in the Sarajevo area in very difficult circumstances.

The Dayton Peace Agreement, signed in 1996, is supposed to allow former residents to return to their homes. However, this will not be considered by the widows because it would mean returning to those neighbours who killed their husbands and to an area now called Republika Srpska when they are not Serbs.

According to *The Suitcase*, women find it easier to adjust to refugee life than men because they are still fulfilling their role as caretakers following the 'tradition of women's responsibility for survival, the maintenance of life and the thin thread of common sense.' A couple living in a camp in Pakistan wrote comparisons of typical days in their Bosnian home town and in the camp. Part of the wife's time as a refugee followed her familiar domestic pattern, preparing food, cleaning and taking care of the children whereas the husband's life style as a refugee was totally alien and disconnecting to him.

Many women were academics, professionals and university students, mainly from urban areas and currently their main concern is to find work or re-enter their fields. Some had successful careers in positions of responsibility with commensurate lifestyles. In exile, they are frustrated, deeply disappointed and suffering loss of self-esteem because they are unemployed, and may also be struggling to communicate successfully in English.

Rural women have had difficulty in adapting. They are very traumatised because of the war and culture shock. They are accustomed to the extended patriarchal family and often feel very alienated and isolated at home and do not have the will or desire to integrate or adapt. As many of them are older, the difficulties are compounded — day-to-day living is problematic because of financial and health problems, both mental and physical. One of the main issues for the women is their fear of going out due to lack of communication skills in English and lack of under-standing of the system in Britain. Generally, the women are often dependent on their children for accessing the system in Britain and for translating and interpreting. The children themselves may be suffering from post-trau-matic stress and may have difficult behaviour with which the mother has to cope. However, the women discuss their problems with other women whereas the men find it hard to discuss their problems and become inward looking and bitter, which can lead to violence in the home. There are a considerable number of incidents of domestic violence both in exile and in Bosnia itself, following the end of the war.

References

Issues of *Bosnia Report* published by the Bosnian Institute, London W11

Cynthia Cockburn, 'Women and Ethnic Cleansing' in *Women Against Fundamentalism*, No 5, 1994, Vol 1, London

Noel Malcolm, *Bosnia: A Short History*, Papermac, 1994

Julie Mertus, Jasmina Tesanovic, Habiba Metikos, Rada Boric, *The Suitcase: Refugee Voices from Bosnia and Croatia*, University of California Press, 1997

Zlata Filipovic, *Zlata's Diary*, Penguin, 1994

Women Writers in
Bosnia and Hercegovina

In the past women were not stimulated or encouraged to take part in the creation of a literary tradition because of the social environment and cultural heritage in Bosnia and Hercegovina over a long period of time. Aspirations to education and access to the outside world were historically intertwined with insurmountable obstacles. One of the major manuscripts of medieval Bosnia, *The Kulin Ban Charter*, does not refer to the glorification of war or celebration of a ruler's power, but to literacy, language and links with Dubrovnik and the Mediterranean. Yet, just when the effects of the Renaissance were beginning to be felt at the fringes of the Mediterranean region, Bosnia, having been conquered by the Turks, became the westernmost province of the Ottoman Empire. It was both impenetrable and conservative with oriental feudalism remaining here longer than in any other European country and even extending into the twentieth century. Another paradox has been recorded in its cultural history — the usage of as many as six different alphabets — Glagolic, Cyrillic, Latin, Bosanian, Arabic and Hebrew. However, according to the 1939 census, illiteracy in the first half of the twentieth century was as high as 88% and barely a third of children aged seven to twelve attended elementary school. It was mainly girls who were non-attenders, which in turn, led to even lower numbers at secondary level and merely symbolic representation at university.

Given these facts, it is astounding that there existed in the early eighteenth century, a poetess named Unihana Cuvidina, who was considered to belong to the so-called *Alhemijado* literature and who wrote warm, lyrical poems about a lonely woman, not in her native language but in Arabic.

Staka Skenderova was the first modern educator and feminist in Bosnia but she died in poverty, defamed and forsaken. Later, times changed, but culture and education associated with national movements was the model on which the national elites, especially those of Belgrade and Zagreb, formed their attitudes towards cultural emancipation of Bosnia and thus to women living there. The status of the Latin or Cyrillic alphabets had more importance for them than the development of literacy and women's participation in literature, because the former were the symbols of religion and nation.

During the occupation of Bosnia and Hercegovina by the Austro-Hungarian Empire, culture developed and this was a period when the modern literary tradition was established, especially in poetry and short stories. A number of papers and prominent literary magazines were published, initially in Sarajevo and then in Banja Luka and Mostar. Nevertheless, the entrenched patriarchal attitudes remained obstacles to women's access to public, cultural and literary activity. The period between the two World Wars meant another provincialisation period, both for Bosnia and Hercegovina and for Sarajevo.

Thus, the appearance of women in literature is associated with the period and the spirit which emerged after the Second World War. During the Second World War, some women had been involved in the women's anti-fascist and partisan movements and this had given them a new confidence and power. Although the proclamation of equality for women did not bring much change, the occurrence of very intensive, rapid and sometimes contradictory social, cultural and educational changes, led to opportunities for women. Not until the establishment of an urban, educated populace, however, did it become possible for women to gain entry to the field of literature and this marked the start of the proliferation of literary personalities. However, under Yugoslav communism, there were restrictions on what could be written and censorship was in place. In any case, women did not define themselves as an interest group or as feminists in the same way as western women, because sexual equality was institutionalised and the term 'women's literature' was non-existent.

Dara Sekulic is the premier poetess of the Sarajevo literary world, both in terms of her literary output and the period of time she has been productive. Her work is very personal and expressive and her preoccupation is her own world and the tragedy of existence. In contrast, Nasiha Kapidzic is more maternally enthralled by the world of children and together with a group of authors, started the tradition of literature for children. Valerija Tvrz writes for children but, in addition, writes short stories and novels. Raza Handzic and Emilija Sijacic are writers of narrative, which is the most pronounced literary tradition of Bosnia. Hanifa Kapidzic-Osmanagic writes studies on the history of literature and on contemporary literature, French literature, in particular. Antonija Bela Subic writes plays for stage, radio and television; Razija Lagumdzija wrote essays, studies and reviews on local authors. Meliha Salihbegovic wrote and published poems, after which she became more and more preoccupied by religious topics and became an enthusiastic follower of the revolution in Iran. For this reason she came increasingly into conflict with the authorities in the early eighties and was finally expelled from the association of writers. Among the published and unpublished works of Ferida Durakovic, Ljubica Ostojic, Mubera Pasic, Anita Benac, Stana Cukic, Biserka Alikadic, Milka Bozic or Marina Trumic or the works published during the lifetime of Milka Miron or Vera Obrenovic-Delibasic, can be found novels, short stories, poetry, stage and radio plays, critical essays, reviews, studies and all the productivity to be expected from a comparatively developed literary life.

In small nations, only a small number of authors can make a living from their literary work; most, including women, taking other work. Thus, Jasmina Musabegovcic, an essayist and literary critic, is a long established editor in a prominent publishing house whilst Ana Lazarevska who writes poetry, humour and literary criticism, is a journalist. Nermina Kurspahic is a television editor and Ajsa Zahirovic was a secretary whilst simultaneously writing and publishing collections of lyrical poetry. Hanifa Kapidzic is a professor at the Faculty of Philosophy, Razija Lagumdzija taught at the College for Teachers, Vojka Djikic was the editor of a prominent magazine 'The Third Programme of Radio Sarajevo' whilst publishing translations, anthologies and studies.

Literature always develops when faced with its limitations and restrictions, and this applied to literature by women authors who addressed the problems of their society. Their work was accessible to four national groups given that they lived in the linguistic centre of the language (Serbo-Croat), and this put them at an indisputable advantage over their colleagues in other centres of culture in the former Yugoslavia.

Much Bosnian literature has now been expropriated by the different nationalist groups as a result of the new structures.

The break-up of Yugoslavia and the war in Bosnia, means that many writers are now in exile, their experiences having inevitably influenced the subject matter of their literature.

References
Chris Agee, *Scar on the Stone*, *Contemporary Poetry from Bosnia*, Bloodaxe Books, 1998.

Thanks to Milan Uzelac for assistance with this chapter.

Congo

Women in the Conflict in the Democratic Republic of Congo

The government of the Democratic Republic of Congo has failed to follow through on its promises to promote democracy and human rights since it took power in May 1997, according to Human Rights Watch. More than 100,000 people were uprooted in eastern Congo prior to the civil war, due to ethnic conflicts. The number of residents who became internally displaced during the civil war remains uncertain. As many as 10,000 former Zairean soldiers and their families reportedly fled to the Central African Republic.

There is a civil war which has been raging in Eastern Congo since 1993 with full-scale civil war erupting in 1996. The violence and population displacement persisted in eastern Congo even after the civil war ended in May 1997, forcing thousands of Hutus to flee over the border into Rwanda. Women have had to flee from their villages. A 400 mile swathe of North and South Kivu region has been taken over by the Tutsi-led armed group, AFDL.

In 1998, Tutsi-led rebels opposed to President Laurent Kabila had a string of victories. A UN report has stated that the rebel forces and its allies are committing the bulk of the killings and human rights atrocities but according to Beth Verhey, major human rights abuses have been reported on both sides. Amnesty International fears for the safety of thousands of civilians persecuted on the basis of their ethnic origin and their perceived or known political affiliations.

In 1997, Zairean soldiers retreating from the country's Kivu region raped and killed with virtual impunity. Women were reported to have been victims of torture, including rape, and to have been beaten on their breasts or otherwise ill-treated, with women in many towns and villages living in constant fear of becoming the next victims. All over North and South Kivu, thousands of civilians fearing persecution and arrest are hiding in forests, trying to escape the fighting. Villages have been emptied and fields are unattended. Similar scenes have been reported in Kinshasa and Kisangani, where at different stages of the conflict, large neighbourhoods had been vacated with hundreds of thousands of displaced persons. Women dressed in mini-skirts, trousers or leggings were targeted for torture or ill-treatment by AFDL (Alliance of Democratic Forces for the Liberation of Congo-Zaire), soldiers in Kinshasa. In August 1998, at least 100 women and young girls were arrested and reportedly raped by the FAC (Congolese Armed Forces), prior to being transported to places of detention. Some of those who were raped or subjected to other forms of sexual violence, are reported to have been subsequently killed. According to Amnesty International, sexual violence appears to have been used as a weapon of war by the combatants on both sides to spread terror among the populations and to destabilise the community identity.

Ethnic Tutsi or suspected rebellion supporters have been murdered and detained in Kinshasa or Kisangani. Women with children are left to cope. On the rebel side, a particularly alarming event was the massacre of more than two hundred civilians including women, in a church in South Kivu. There have been many reports of the recruitment of child soldiers, including a special recruitment drive by the government, for youths from twelve years old. Naturally, this has a devastating effect on the mothers. In addition, there are food shortages and serious unmet health needs. Rebel forces now hold a vast swathe of Congo, including the country's third largest city, Kisangani.

Many people have fled to French-speaking countries and particularly to Belgium, the former colonial power, where there are large numbers of women amongst the 12,000 or so Zaireois.

The Democratic Republic of Congo was a strongly patriarchal society. However, in modern times, President Mobutu introduced laws to liberate women. According to Antho-Feza-Kabera, some traditions are still practised today, but generally women have gained their freedom and are free to express themselves. The first woman minister is Madame Sofie Kanza, who is symbolic of the developing emancipation of Congolese women.

In the 1970s, education was available for both girls and boys. However at secondary level, fees were charged and generally, boys were favoured. Women did nursing and secondary school studies but did not generally study to a higher level. From the 1970s onwards, women received grants and scholarships to study in Belgium. The new generation is now entering fields such as law, medicine and economics because it is felt that these lead to development and self-reliance.

The following information has been provided by two Congolese women, Lola Demoulin living in Belgium and Antho-Feza-Kabera living in the UK. It should be noted that the practices below varied according to tribe and region.

In the past, marriages were arranged and often the girl was married at or before puberty. The Bakua Lolonji who are Baluba of Kasai, stipulated that a girl had to be a virgin on marriage and in that case her mother was rewarded with a goat. There were two systems: the main one being the patriarchal custom in which the children belonged to the father. The matriarchal custom, in which they belonged to the mother, was prevalent in the West of Congo. In both cases, the woman was totally powerless. Where the children belonged to the mother, their uncle had total power over his sister's children and the uncle still plays an important role in his nieces' lives, mostly in terms of their marriages. This is beginning to disappear in the capital but is unchanged in the villages. The woman always had to sacrifice herself to the demands of her husband. In the countryside the woman was often treated like a slave and had to work ten hours a day to provide for her family. She had to sell produce to pay for her children's studies and clothes. If her children were unsuccessful, the mother would be blamed. Fidelity was non-existent with women finding out that their husband had perhaps four additional children by another woman. A man often had four or five partners in addition to his wife. Divorce was practically impossible. If life became unbearable for the woman, she left the marital home but her parents would not provide support as they were ashamed. In terms of the inheritance, males, not females, were the beneficiaries. On the death of her husband, the widow was ill-treated by her in-laws who forced her to cry continually and if she did not do so, they exposed her to the sun semi-naked. After the funeral, she was evicted and her possessions confiscated. The widow was expected to marry one of her brothers-in-law.

According to Janice Spleth in her discussion on 'Sexuality and political discourse in the Zairean novel', rape has historical importance as a normal function of conquest, characterising the relationship between victor and vanquished. Muepu Muanda in his short story *Delire*, writes about a woman whose husband has been arrested for political reasons and who is forced to turn to prostitution to support her family.

References

http://www.amnesty.org
Lola Demoulin, *International Women's News* edited by Hilary Paddon and Jan Marsh, Vol 91 No 4 1996 'La Femme en Zaire'
Jennifer Langer, *The Bend in the Road: Refugees Writing*, Five Leaves Publications, 1997 (Political/Historical background)
http://www.oneworld.org
http://www.refugees.org
B. Verhey, *Forced Migration, Refugee Studies Programme*, Oxford, Edition 3, December 1998, Democratic Republic of Congo

Women Writers in the Democratic Republic of Congo

Within the oral tradition, women played a very important part as storytellers and educators, sometimes as poets and historians and universally as participants in the significant rituals of their communities; rituals accompanying birth, initiation, marriage and death. The languages used were local languages, Lingala, Kikongo, Kiswahili and Ciluba. The literature of women was not written down however, as the act of writing went against traditional notions of what a women should be. In addition, men traditionally had the right to education while girls stayed at home and were slower to pick up literacy and a level of proficiency in French, the colonial language, which would enable them to write.

All the main writers have been male; in a collection of Zairean poetry, only four out of the 31 contributors were women. Generally, it was only during the 1970s that francophone African women writers emerged. The way was prepared by influential francophone African spokeswomen, for example Therese Kuoh, founder of the Union des Femmes Africanes et Malgaches.

An important writer and the first woman of letters is Clementine Faik-Nzuji who, between 1965 and 1970, headed a number of poetry clubs which were formed by young intellectuals. In addition, there was a new outlet for publication in *Editions Belles Lettres* and the creation of poetry competitions. Elizabeth Mweya, born in 1948, was the only female poet amongst the male competitors for the Sebastien Ngonso Poetry Prize in 1967. Her poetry collection *Remous des Feuilles*, was published in 1972. Another female poet is Ikole Bolumba who was born in 1951 and is the author of *Feuilles d'Olive* also published in 1972. Marie-Eugenie Mpongo is another poet who was born in 1948. Poetry flourished but mostly expressed the pessimism and disillusion which characterised the 1960s, post independence. Since the 1980s, poets and writers have used their voice as a means of resistance to repressive, dictatorial regimes, to express social and political realities and to call for a new just, humane system in Congo. Currently, Elisabeth Mweya (Francoise Mweya Tol Ande) is amongst poets writing about human relationships.

Clementine Faik-Nzuji who was born in 1944 and now lives in Belgium, is not only one of the first African woman poets writing in French, but also a linguist and anthropologist who produced a remarkable thesis on the Kasala chants of the Luba in addition to anthropological studies on symbolism in Africa which have extended over 25 years. Her literary works include short stories as well as poems, for example *Le Masque*, 1995, *Frisson de la Memoire*, 1993 and *Cite de l'Abondance* 1986. Her collection of poetry published in 1968 won the Senghor Literary Prize. Her poetry includes *Murmures*, 1968, Kasala, 1969, *Le Temps des Amants*, 1969 and *Lianes*, 1971. The latter is a mixture of opposing sentiments such as sadness and joy and agony and serenity. She writes about war, mourning and death.

Two further writers in exile are Amba Bongo and Lola Demoulin who both write short novels and live in exile in London and Belgium respectively. Their main characters are women battling with identity issues. Young poetesses living in France are addressing exile and false hopes in their poetry.

References
H. Gill. M. Majumdar, E. Tolansky, *Bulletin of Francophone Africa,* Francophone Africa Research Centre, University of Westminster, Autumn 1995
Pierre Halen and Janos Riesz, *Litteratures du Congo-Zaire,* Editions Rodopi, 1995
Belinda Jack, *Francophone Literatures: An Introductory Survey,* OUP, 1996
Jennifer Langer, *The Bend in the Road: Refugees Writing,* Five Leaves Publications, 1997 (Literary/Cultural Background)
M.N. Mabelemadiko, *Le Zaire Ecrit,* Horst Erdmann Verlag, Tubingen and Dombi Diffusion, Kinshasa, 1976

Cyprus

Women in Cyprus
Aydin Mehmet-Ali

Cyprus has been physically divided since 1974, by barbed wire, barricades and a guarded, mined no-man's land. As a result of forced population movements, the Cypriot Turkish communities live in the north and the Cypriot Greek communities in the south. Currently an estimated 30,000 Turkish troops are in the north following the invasion of the island by Turkey using its powers as a guarantor alongside Greece and the UK, who did not intervene.

The women of Cyprus of any age, alive today, have experienced wars. My mother at 70, has experienced six war situations. I, at the age of 50, have now gone through five. Today every Cypriot woman on the island and those of us in the Diaspora, live under the shadow of war, tanks, arms, missiles and the potential imminence of war. They wait for the slightest of signals to pack up and leave. But to go where? Only into the unknown, seeking refuge in unknown places, leaving behind homes and belongings they cherish.

Inter-communal conflicts and wars have had a devastating impact on the lives of women. As in all wars, they have suffered death, rape, separation, massacres of children and loved ones and destruction of families and all they hold dear. They have lost homes, villages, neighbourhoods, a way of life they played a part in, the right to live where and with whom they chose and the right to free movement on their island. They are the ones left behind to soak up the pain of the dead and disappeared loved ones and friends, homes and neighbourhoods. They are targeted as the mothers, wives, fiancées, sisters and daughters of the 'martyred' and used in whipping up hatred of the 'other' — the enemy. As the first teachers, they are forced to indoctrinate the young in that hatred and perpetuate it.

The division of the island and its peoples has contributed to the mythologising and demonising of the other. However, the mythology is perpetuated by the power élites and is not strong amongst ordinary people who, when given the opportunity, eagerly get together with their counterparts on the other side and search for ways of living and working together. What is encouraging and worth highlighting, is that, despite 40 years of propaganda, oppression, bans, marginalisation, intimidation and, at times, murder of those opposing nationalism and chauvinism, ordinary people, including women and children, have flocked to joint festivals and events organised in the no-man's land and sponsored by the foreign embassies and the UN. At times, meetings have to be organised in countries such as Germany, Norway, Switzerland and Britain, to avoid intervention by the power elites. Such meetings have taken place between Cypriot Turkish and Cypriot Greek women. However, even then, four women due to travel to London in March 1998 to attend the Cyprus Link conference, were prevented from doing so by an illegal decree issued by the Office of the State Prosecutor in the north.

The power élites regularly cancel planned meetings and joint projects arbitrarily without explanation. There are a number of reasons for this. Firstly, these events demonstrate to the world that the two communities are interested in peace and finding ways of living and working together, which is in conflict with the position of the power élites. Secondly, the events demonstrate that Cypriots are capable and want to take control of the processes of peace and possible solutions to the 'Cyprus Problem'. Thirdly, the plurality of views is demonstrated, rather than the monolithic positions presented in international talks which challenge the 'authority' of the power élites.

264

It is within this context of a militarised society that women and women poets, writers and intellectuals, in particular, have been involved in challenging the status quo both as citizens and as women.

Turkish Cypriot Women Writers
Aydin Mehmet Ali

there... Cyprian goddess, take and pour
gracefully like wine into golden cups,
a nectar mingled with all the joy
of our celebrations.

Sappho

Sappho, one of the earliest recorded women poets, calls on Aphrodite, the Goddess of Love, from the island of Cyprus, to bring tranquillity to her troubled heart or to bring back loved ones. Today, many women from the same Island of Love, victims of war, beg their new Gods to bring back disappeared loved ones or to rest the souls of those killed. They offer prayers for strength to live long enough to see those homes, fields, mountains, streams, trees and friends, now left on the 'other' side behind barbed wire.

The literature of Cyprus, especially poetry, is littered with the debris of war. Even if hidden, it surfaces amongst the most unexpected lines or poems of love and nature. Nese Yasin (1991), a prominent Cypriot Turkish poet, creates a striking example of prose using lines from different Cypriot Turkish poems:

Startled, the Poem woke up in a black-out night.
The stars were looking through the window and the
cicadas kept singing the same song over and over
again
Zirozi rozi
Zirozi rozi

The Poem thought about its own life and set off on a journey with sunrise. The streets were deserted and tanks had flattened the asphalt road. A young dead soldier, lying by the side of the road joined the Poem. He had written the name of his sweetheart inside his helmet and had said 'we will have children'. Unborn babies joined the Poem and young girls with tears in their eyes hung balls of jasmine on empty cradles...

Under the present military rule in northern Cyprus, opposition to a militarised society comes from the most unlikely quarter: poetry. There is a suggestion that the struggle of minorities for survival inevitably leads to the politicisation of minority literature and the creation of a poetry of common values opposed to individualism and rebellion (Deleuze and Guattari, 1986). Yet Cypriot Turkish poetry has served both the purposes of conformity and rebellion, but it is poems of rebellion which have made a more significant and lasting impact. However, some argue that such rebellion has inevitably led to the rejection of the poets by Cypriot Turkish society (Yasin, 1994).

Compared with Turkey, accepted as the centre of Turkish language and literature, there are more women poets in northern Cyprus and they occupy an important position as leading poets. In Cyprus, almost everyone reads and writes poetry. All the daily papers publish poetry as a matter of course. Poetry books outnumber any other types of books and outsell all others.

Poetry in Cyprus reflects all the political developments which have taken place on the island. In the 1940s, it was used to express a romantic longing for the far away 'motherlands', Greece and Turkey, in the wake of new discovered nationalisms. In the 1950s and 1960s, it dripped with blood, hatred and revenge as it served nationalism to accentuate the irreconcilable difference of the two communities, their mutual hatred throughout history and in the creation of the demonised 'other', the enemy. The denial of separate

Cypriot identities and Cyprus as the motherland, was central to the creation of those myths. Any attempt to challenge these nationalist, official definitions was considered a treasonable offence. The war in 1974, the occupation of the island by the Turkish army and the Turkification process which followed, provoked the assertion of a separate Cypriot identity amongst Cypriot Turkish intellectuals, as distinct from the hitherto accepted Turkish identity. However, as late as the 1980s, because of humanist poems written in the 1970s referring to the Cypriot Greek people and their suffering in the wars, the poets were accused of being traitors and enemies of the people. The vilification and pressure led to enforced exile for some poets.

Nese Yasin, one of the leading poets, is well-known in both the south and north, as well as outside Cyprus. She regularly recites at international poetry festivals and her work has been translated into a number of languages. She is probably one of the most courageous poets, continuing to break the arbitrary rules, bans and human rights violations imposed on Cypriots. In one of her earliest poems in the 1970s, she challenges the ruling elite by asking:

> People should love their country
> So my father always says
> mine has been divided
> through the middle in two
> which half must I love?
> *(Translated by Aydin Mehmet Ali)*

With this poem, she voiced the feelings of many who loved the whole of Cyprus and regarded all of it and not just the part they were imprisoned in, as their motherland. This poem was composed by a Cypriot Greek and became the unofficial anthem of Cyprus, symbolising the desire for the unification of Cyprus. In contrast, her father had been the poet laureate of extreme Turkish nationalism in the 1950s and 1960s, barking rivers of blood, hatred and war from the rostrums of the ruling élite.

267

Nese Yasin has been witch-hunted in the north where she lived until recently. She was sacked from all her posts under pressure from the authorities; has been harassed, followed and her house broken into. After a number of years, unable to find a job and refusing to be driven out of Cyprus, she went to the south and now works as a lecturer at the University of Cyprus. This has earned her the title of enemy of the Cypriot Turkish people. In her poems, she challenges the nationalism and chauvinism of society and the state, both on individual and political levels. She writes about all aspects of women's lives; their aspirations, dreams, fears, hopes, struggles and passions. She challenges the taboos and stereotypes, be they political, social, sexual or erotic. Her books have been published by well-known publishing houses in Turkey, but not in Cyprus. She is involved in many peace activities amongst women as well as men, trying to bring the two communities together on joint projects.

Filiz Naldoven is another leading poet who has a fine command of the subtleties of the Turkish language. She uses unique Cypriot sensibilities and sensitivities in her poetry full of island imagery, smells and sounds. Her poetry is unique amongst all Cypriot Turkish poets, and is enriched by her sensitivity to the use of language as a woman. She is barely tolerated by the power élites. The performance of her award-winning play in the mid-1980s was banned and prevented from being performed in any of the state theatres. She had to find a private sponsor to publish her first poetry book as the Ministry of Education and Culture refused to publish her work. She is a refugee from the south who feels imprisoned in 'half-an-island' and her poetry reflects that sense of dislocation and alienation very eloquently.

Both of these poets have suffered displacement because of the conflicts and wars in Cyprus. They have been subjected to oppression, including the banning of their work, isolation and marginalisation as independent women and poets living in a militarist society. At times, they have been branded as immoral women because they have dared to challenge the official morality.

All women writing now, share a common identity and consider Cyprus as their motherland as distinct from the generation writing in the 1940s. While women comprise half of all the famous poets writing during the syllabic-romantic period in the 1940s, they do not seem to be represented in the nationalistic, abstract and communal periods of Cypriot poetry which lasted until the mid-1970s. Amongst those identified as the 1974 Generation or its followers, and other independent, leading poets writing now, more than half are women.

Other women poets and writers such as Feriha Altiok, Neriman Cahit, Ozden Selenge and Ilkay Adali have focused on the special position of women in society, dealing with many issues. The theme of war and conflict is ever present. Faize Demirciler is one of the new generation and probably the most promising, with her powerful use of the Turkish language and the imagery and melodies of Cyprus. She has published two collections of poetry and numerous articles.

Women poets and writers in the diaspora are not well-known and very little has been published. The annual poetry and short story competition organised by FATAL (For the Advancement of Turkish-speakers' Art and Literature) in London, is encouraging some women to emerge, by organising readings and publicising their work through radio and newspapers. Some of these women are: Alev Adil, Fatma Durmush, Ergul Nur and Aydin Mehmet Ali. FATAL is in the process of preparing an anthology of writing by Turkish-speaking women in London who have had their work published.

These words of Nese Yasin (1991) sum up the role of poets in situations of sharp conflict, such as in Cyprus:

"Yes, but is a poet not a genius who with her intuition and perception would walk ahead of her people, society and time? Undoubtedly that is true but poets are also created by their society and history."

269

Inevitably poets in our societies and communities take on a social role. I would only add that in societies such as ours, against all odds, poets also create their societies and histories. That is certainly the case for Cypriot Turkish women poets. They are certainly heroines of resistance!

References

J. Balmer, *Sappho, Poems and Fragments*. Brilliance, London, 1984

G. Deleuze, and F. Guattari, (1986), *Kafka: Towards a Minor Literature*, London

M. Yasin, (1994), *Kibrisliturk Siiri Antholojisi* (Anthology of Cypriot Turkish Poetry), Yapi Kredi, Istanbul.

N. Yasin, (1991), The Cypriot Peace Operation by the Young Cypriot Poem in Mehmet Ali, A. (ed. and trans.), Turkish Cypriot Identity in Literature, FATAL, London.

Iran

Women in the Conflict in Iran

According to Mahnaz Afkhami, the history of Iranian women is bound inextricably to the history of Shi'a Islam which defines women as being procreators and guardians of the family. Islam prescribes the position of women relative to men in the household and society with the woman being defined primarily as a mother and also as a wife, sister and daughter. Shi'ism is defined by the Shi'a cleric who have the political and moral power.

During the nineteenth century, western ideas entered Iran as a feature of the colonial process but there was, inevitably, a tension between religion and modernism. The right to vote was achieved in 1963 and suffrage was a prologue to the acquisition of other rights, as women began to exercise political power in the major patriarchal institutions: the family, society and state. It was the beginning of a serious struggle for women to become involved in higher liberal and technical education, the production and managerial job market, and law, and also in defining the ethics of family relations and in the struggle to raise women's consciousness. During the 1960 and 70s, women organised themselves in earnest. Through the provision of the Family Protection Law, Iranian women finally achieved the right to participate significantly in decisions about their own marriage, and divorce and decisions about their children. It took almost a century for women to move from total public invisibility to a visible, political, social and economic presence.

This process was reversed in the Islamic Republic, created after the revolution of 1979; a strictly traditional,

271

patriarchal society with Iran's clerical order as the sole interpreters of the values, norms and aesthetic standards of Shi'a Islam. Gender philosophies and gender policies which suppressed women were instigated and women lost significant ground in the struggle for gender equality. The regime deprived women of almost all their civil rights and turned them into second-class citizens required by law to be at the disposal of their husbands at all times. The legal age for marriage was reduced to 14, polygamy was re-legalised and in cases of adultery it was mainly women who were punished by being executed by stoning. Separation of men and women was carried out in all walks of life. The regime tried to force women out of the job market including segregating women and enforcing full Islamic cover in offices and public places and closing nearly 140 university fields of study to women. Women fought seriously for their rights but the regime succeeded in putting women back in the veil in public places but not in resocialising them into fundamentalist norms. However, there were women's groups who supported the Islamic Republic's policies and who felt that poorer women were empowered and that Muslim women needed to be united, for example in liberating Palestinians. These women felt that the *chador* was liberating, as women were no longer viewed as sex objects.

Iranian women have been the primary target for Islamic fundamentalists. They have been the victims of the male-defined revolution that betrayed them; many supported the end of the Shah's regime, hoping for a socialist, fairer society as described by Rouhi Shafii in *Scent of Saffron* and Manny Shirazi in *Azadi Square*. The left-wing movements had implied that their revolution included women. Women have to contend with a modern theocratic regime which claims absolute authority for defining correct behaviour in all aspects of life. Ruhangiz Sharifian has described the difficulty of living democratically inside the home in Iran but having to adopt different, covert behaviour outside the home because of the secret security police.

Women also had concerns about their children being brainwashed at school. It has been suggested in *In the Eye of the Storm* that gender roles are embedded deep in Persian history and culture and do not just originate from the Islamic Republic's creed.

Under President Khatami the practice of execution by stoning has fallen into disrepute. However, according to the 1998 Amnesty International Report, at least five women were sentenced to death by stoning and three women were reportedly stoned to death. Zoleykhah Kadkhoda was reportedly arrested and charged with having sexual relations outside marriage and was sentenced to death by stoning.

Although the laws still enforce the wearing of the *chador* and *hijab*, there is a weakening of restrictions on the dress and decorum of women, with female modesty becoming a matter of individual choice. Increasing numbers of women are found in all fields of employment with women lawyers seen increasingly in court. Literacy is more than 80 percent among Iranian women, which is one of the highest rates in the Muslim world. Iranian men are no longer allowed to divorce in the traditional Islamic manner simply by saying 'I divorce you' three times and divorce cases must now go through Islamic courts. Farideh Farhi, a political commentator, feels that although there is a fundamental grassroots change in people's behaviour, nevertheless, nothing has been resolved. A Teheran housewife recently commented "It would be odd indeed if we were to campaign for the right to wear a mini-skirt before we can get a decent job or have custody of our children."

The reformist, President Khatami, owed his election landslide in May 1997, to women, the vast majority of whom voted for him. Through women's organisations, protest marches and the media, women exert pressure on the government. According to Martin Woollacott, 'The most important single political force is undoubtedly that represented by its thirty million women, who have in all kinds of ways resisted the regime's efforts to isolate and subordinate them'. Maryam Poya points out that secular feminists have now joined forces with Muslim feminists. Shared experience 'closed the gap between religious women who supported the Islamic system and the secular women who opposed it'.

In the Iran-Iraq War (1980-1988), women suffered from stress, anger and worry and believed that the war was foolish. Thousands of boys and men were killed and were then glorified as martyrs. The suffering of a mother is well described in the short story *The Hejleh* by Esmail Fassih.

Overall, since the Iranian Revolution, the number of Iranian exiles has been estimated at two million. According to Gohar Kordi, the novelist in exile, loneliness is a problem for women who often feel depressed. Their families have disintegrated and are scattered and there is a feeling of rootlessness and of being forced to spend old-age in an alien land. Many women are caught in a poverty trap and in addition, there is often cultural conflict between the parents and children.

References
Mahnaz Afkhami and Erika Friedl, *In the Eye of the Storm*: Women in Post-Revolutionary Iran, Tauris, 1994
http://www.amnesty.org
http://www.iranian.com/LalehKhalili/March99/Women 'To live or to be alive? That is the question for Iranian women'.
http://www.oneworld.org/
Maryam Poya, *Women, Work and Islamism*, Zed Books, 1999
Refugee Women's Voices, Refugee Council
Rouhi Shafii, *Scent of Saffron*, Scarlet Press, 1997
M. Shirazi, *Siege of Azadi Square*, Women's Press, 1991
M. Woollacott, 'The old men of Iran can no longer skirt women's issues', *The Guardian*, January 2000

Iranian Women Writers

For centuries, the written literary potential of Iranian women had been repressed. Women had no voice, and occupied the private space of female seclusion, whereas men controlled the public domain. For centuries, veiling inhibited women's verbal self-expression. Women were coerced into silence and adopted *Sharm,* meaning shyness and shame. The price pioneering literary women paid for not remaining silent was high. Tahereh, the pioneer of Iranian women's literary tradition, was charged with heresy and executed at the height of her creativity, aged 36. Parvin E'tessami, the first woman who published a poetry collection, died at the age of 34 and several other writers attempted suicide. Suicide for these women was an expression of public defiance as well as of individual despair.

Towards the middle of the twentieth century, a new tradition of women's poetry came into being in Iran, a tradition of women intensely involved in self-reflection and self-revelation, not sheltered or restrained by the anonymity or opacity of the veil. These poets include Jaleh Esfahani, Lobat Vala Sheybani and Tahereh Saffarzadeh amongst others. This poetry has been considered offensive to Muslim 'fundamentalists' because to them it deviates from traditional male-female relations and destroys cultural authenticity. However, according to Farzaneh Milani, even the modernised, educated elite could not reconcile themselves to the changes affecting women's status.

One of the major contemporary Iranian women poets was Forough Farrokhzad who was born in 1933 and died in a car accident in 1967. Five collections of her poetry were published: *The Captive (Asir), The Wall (Divar), The Rebellion (Esian), Another Birth (Tavallodi Digar) and Let us Believe in the Dawning of a Cold Season (Aghaz Fasl-e Sard).* She rebelled against traditional values, old social norms and hypocritical religious restrictions. In subject matter, she was daring and brave enough to express the hidden feelings and emotions of the Iranian woman who had been suffering a double repression, deprived of many civil and fundamental human rights in a patriarchal, Muslim society. She bitterly criticised her society, especially its injustice against women. She understood that

275

young women wished to free themselves from the prison of veiled chastity and enforced modesty, to express their natural desires. She was also rebellious in freeing herself from the influence of the neo-classical poets. After this phase, she established her own style and her poetry and became deep and philosophical. She wrote about life; death; happiness; sorrow; the beauty of nature; the ugliness of social injustice; hope in love's triumph; despair and other notions and emotions, but especially about the sacredness of women and the mystical beauty of sex.

Farrokhzad influenced many women poets such as Shadab Vajdi, Maimanat Mir-Sadeghi, Zhila Mosa'ed and Mina Asadi.

Until 1947, women had no written or published fiction. This was a male domain. Oral storytelling, traditionally the province of women in Iran, was not only an outlet for women's creativity, but also an artistic arena in which they found expression for their life stories. These unwritten tales were handed down orally from generation to generation. Whereas unveiled women had produced significant short stories and novels during the last few decades before compulsory veiling implemented by the Islamic Republic, women had not published works of fiction.

It was only in 1947 that the first collection of short stories by a woman was published. This was *Atash-e hamush' (Fire Quenched)* by Simin Daneshvar. The first novel by an Iranian women was Simin Daneshvar's *Suvashun*, published in 1969, in which the author tries to explore the sensibilities of a happily married woman, who suffers because of the uncompromising and heroic stance her husband takes against the corrupt Iranian regime and its foreign masters. At the end, when her husband is killed, the wife takes up his political cause loyally and with conviction. Daneshvar makes social statements through her characters.

Shahrnush Parsipur is considered to be one of the foremost Iranian novelists. Her first long novel *The Dog and the Long Winter*, 1976, is a first person narration about the trials and tribulations of a young middle-class Iranian girl. In the first part, she creates the illusory relationship the girl is caught in but in the second part, the narrative suddenly breaks down and switches from realistic presentation and description to a stream of association and consciousness involving the girl's dead brother, his imprisonment and sufferings. Her second novel, *Tuba and the Meaning of the Night*, 1989, opens at the end of the Qajar dynasty, when western thought and new ways of living directly began to influence and change the traditional, closed society of Iran. A humiliating incident with a foreigner causes the heroine's father to contemplate the connections between the roundness of the earth, the foreigner's presence and the changes and upheavals to come. His conclusions are "Yes, the earth is round; women will start to think and as soon as they begin to think, they will become shameless."

Farzaneh Milani states: "Fiction writing is now a historical imperative for Iranian women. It not only pulls the women storytellers out of anonymity, it also proclaims voice, visibility, the mobility afforded by and through writing, and the right of access to writing."

Despite compulsory veiling and changes affecting women's personal freedom, women's literature both inside and outside Iran is flourishing and in the last decade or so women's writing has become very politicised with a resistance against repression of any sort. Despite various forms of censorship, the number of books published and sold in the last decade far exceeds pre-revolutionary levels. Simin Behbahani, the poet, has become a major literary figure. There are a large number of writers in the UK such as the poets Shadab Vajdi, Ziba Karbassi, Jaleh Esfahani, Lobat Valah, Nazanin Rakhshandeh, Vida Kashizadeh and the writers Pari Mansouri, Rouhi Shafii, Rouhangiz Sharifian and Gohar Kordi. Gohar Kordi's autobiographical novel *An Iranian Odyssey* was published in 1991 and *Mahi's Story,* about her mother, in 1995. A second generation

Iranian writer is Dorit Rabinyan, who lives in Israel and is author of *Persian Brides*. The story is steeped in the passion, emotion and superstition of the Persian culture which came to dominate the lives of the Jewish women characters. Nahid Husseini, an exiled journalist, believes that it is difficult for Iranian writers to write openly and directly, given the censorship and the fact that this style is not customary in the Iranian culture. Instead, metaphor and allegory are used.

It was believed by many that there would be more freedom of speech under Khatami, but this has not proved to be the case because of stiff opposition to reform from the conservative clerics in his government. There is still rigorous censorship and in the winter of 1998, several writers disappeared or were killed. An attempt to resuscitate the Iranian Writers' organisation was suppressed. However, the situation may be changing, instanced by President Khatami criticising agents who had murdered and terrorised dissident intellectuals since November 1998.

References

Mahnaz Afkhami and Erika Friedl, *In the Eye of the Storm: Women in Post-Revolutionary Iran,* Tauris, 1994

Mahmud Kianush, *Modern Persian Poetry*, Rockingham, 1996

Kordi Gohar, *Mahi's Story*, Women's Press, 1995

Farzaneh Milani, *Veils and Words: The Emerging Voices of Iranian Women Writers,* Tauris, 1992

Soraya Sullivan and Farzaneh Milani, *Stories by Iranian Women Since the Revolution,* Center for Middle Eastern Studies, University of Texas, 1991

Martin Tucker, *Literary Exile in the Twentieth Century*, Greenwood Press, 1991

Shadab Vajdi, *Closed Circuit*, Forest Books, 1989

Shadab Vajdi, *To the Memory of the Thirst of the Southern Mountain Slopes*, self-publication

Dorit Rabinyan, *Persian Brides*, Canongate, 2000

Zohreh Sullivan, *Exiled Memories = Stories of the Iranian Diaspora,* Amazon, 2001

Iraq

Women in the Conflict in Iraq

There were women's active public organised movements in Iraq from the 1920s to the end of the 1960s; for example, in 1951 the Iraqi Women's Union presented a petition to the government demanding changes in the constitution to guarantee women their rights. In theory, Iraqi women enjoy equal political rights with men but both Iraqi women and men live under one of the most repressive regimes in the world.

Suha Omer states that women appointed to high political positions are tools of the Ba'ath Party regime and adopt male ways of thinking. The General Federation of Iraqi Women is effectively part of the state security system, which is headed by Saddam Hussein and his male relatives. Nevertheless, Haifa Zangana is of the opinion that large numbers of women have developed a mistrust of men in power because of the turmoil and chaos caused by the Ba'ath regime. However, patriotic women are deployed to spy on men who are suspected of being against the regime and these women are then rewarded by the state. In these conditions, women's equality before the law and their right to vote and hold office are sources of pain and oppression rather than pleasure and liberation.

Women who are political activists face imprisonment, torture and ill-treatment, which continue to be widespread. The fate of thousands of people who 'disappeared' in previous years remains unknown. They include hundreds of suspected members of opposition groups and their relatives, who were arrested when Iraqi government and

279

KDP forces took control of Arbil in August 1996; thousands of Shi'ite Muslims arrested in the aftermath of the March 1991 uprising and an estimated 100,000 Kurdish civilians who 'disappeared' in 1988 in 'Operation Anfal' (see 'Iraqi Kurdistan').

The regime has a planned, systematic policy of demolishing family life by using fear through divisive measures such as rewarding, threatening and spying. This includes dishonouring women which is one of the powerful means of attacking social cohesion in order to secure political control. The ideology of shame and honour is thus exploited by the regime for their own purposes because if a woman is thought to have behaved sexually dishonourably it brings shame on the whole extended family and clan as honour has a high moral value to be preserved at all costs. According to Sana Al-Khayyat in *Honour and Shame*, oppression by the patriarchal system is practised upon women by women as well as by men. 'Women probably feel a greater direct oppression by members of their own sex, than by men, as women practise social control by adopting male ways of thinking and male roles in policing each other'.

Throughout the 1950s, 60s and 70s, an increasing number of women entered the public sphere engaged in office and professional jobs. By 1980, women accounted for 46% of all teachers, 29% of physicians, 46% of dentists, 70% of pharmacists, 15% of accountants, 14% of factory workers and 16% of civil servants. The Iran-Iraq War (1980-1988) caused labour shortages and therefore forced women to take on economic and administrative functions on an unprecedented scale and to do 'men's work' such as driving lorries and directing traffic but the overriding pressure was both to work and to have large familiesy. The latter was encouraged with financial rewards from the state and with the banning of contraception. The war lasted eight years with a huge loss of male life, estimated at 500,000 to one million. Women were expected to celebrate having given a 'martyr' to the war and the regime

280

rewarded anyone marrying a widow. The years of war have left women having to cope with damaged husbands, sons and fathers or surviving without male relatives. There has been a significant increase in the number of widows.

The Gulf War (1990-1991) also had a catastrophic effect on women. A day-to-day description of living in Baghdad during the bombing raids is described in *Baghdad Diaries* by Nuha al-Radi. In addition, the effect of the international sanctions has been crippling A study has revealed that there had been a four-fold increase in child mortality and a high incidence of health problems among women, resulting from shortages of food and medicines. The UN-imposed international sanctions of the past seven years continue to cause immense hardship and to make survival very difficult. There is now evidence that the uranium coated ammunition used in the Gulf War is causing babies to be born with serious congenital defects and there is an increased incidence of leukemia and other cancers and deformities in children. In December 1998, the British and Americans bombed Iraq for 70 hours (Operation Desert Fox), ostensibly because of its arsenal of biological and chemical weapons of mass destruction, following Baghdad's barring of American weapons inspectors.

Suha Omar feels that the most distressing effect for women of the dictatorship has been the damage to family life resulting from repression, fear, forced deportation, war and economic impoverishment. There have been many reports of increased domestic violence and an intensification of patriarchal attitudes and practices.

References
S. Al-Khalil, *Republic of Fear*, Hutchinson Radius, 1991
Sana Al-Khayyat, *Honour and Shame: Women in Modern Iraq*, Saqi Books, 1992
http://www.amnesty.org
Fran Hazelton, *Iraq since the Gulf War*, Zed Books, 1994. Chapter on Women by Omar Suha
http://www.oneworld.org

Iraqi Women Writers

Samira Al Mana in her paper 'Witness of her time' presented at the SOAS conference 'Mapping Arab Womanhood', describes how Arab women gradually became more emancipated after the collapse of the Ottoman Empire during the First World War, as girls attended the new schools opened for them. In the thirties, women began to think of casting aside their black cloaks called *aba'a* and the word *sufoor* began to be heard — 'taking off the veil'. This took place peacefully, and generally with the support of men. However, in the last few years, new decrees have restricted young women's rights to travel alone and allowed men to kill any female relative who is considered to be tainting the family's reputation. Muslim girls are now prevented from attending school after the age of eight. Samira Al Mana expresses the hope that Iraqi women will not have to wait for another five centuries to make their voices heard and pleads for learning from the lessons of the past.

In *Arab Women Novelists*, Joseph Zeidan states that Arab women writers were scarce until fairly recently and what writings they did produce, usually imitated the norms established by the existing male-dominated literary tradition. These however provided the foundations for the modern literary accomplishments of Arab women.

According to Fatima Mohsen in her article 'Cultural Totalitarianism', the link between culture and politics was firmly established in the 1940s and 1950s with most Iraqi literature in the twentieth century, and especially poetry, being influenced by politics. Women have mainly written short stories and poems that question the social norms that systematically oppress women. There have been very few Iraqi women dramatists.

Much of the best poetry by women as well as men, has been accused of being 'modernist', and has never been accepted in Iraq and has been opposed by conservative critics and by state publishing houses. In Iraq, the pioneering women writers were exclusively poets. Umm Nizar (1908-1953) was pre-occupied with two main topics in her poetry: patriotism and the cause of Arab women. She glorified the role of Arab women throughout history and emphasised the predicament of women of modern Iraq — victims of ignorance, stagnation, and narrowmindedness and urged them to try to overcome these difficulties. In the sphere of patriotism, Umm Nazir wrote about Iraq's struggle for independence, the Palestinian issue and other liberation movements in the Arab world. In the 1960s, work by Nazik al-Malaika, a highly gifted poet and the daughter of Umm Nizar, was published.

The short story is now women writers' favoured medium and it is only in the second half of the twentieth century that there has been significant fiction writing. However, women have few opportunities to be published with publishers interested only in those with established reputations. Many Arab readers and critics dismiss fiction by women as simply autobiographical and focused on the relationship between the sexes. The first novel by a woman, Maliha Isaac, was published in 1948. Daisy al-Amir, who was born in Iraq in 1935 but lived in the Lebanon for some time, wrote of a society reconstructed with a feminist consciousness after the Lebanese War (1975-82). Her first collection of short stories *The Distant Country that You Love* appeared in 1964. In 1969, she published *Then the Wave Returns*, a collection of short stories dedicated to the Palestinian woman writer, Samira Azzam. She has published two collections of short stories about the Lebanese Civil War. May Muzaffar was born in Baghdad in 1948. She is the author of two volumes of short stories, a novel and a collection of poetry. She describes physical violence towards women in her collection of short stories entitled: *The Swan*, published in 1973. These writers usually described women's lives as a constant struggle to find a space of their own. Safira Jamil Hafiz, a writer now in her seventies and living in Iraq, was a prominent political activist who was imprisoned and tortured in 1973. Her first collection of short stories was entitled *Dolls and Children* and was published in Baghdad in 1956.

Fatma Moussa-Mahmoud in the *Bloomsbury Guide to Women's Literature* feels that the new feminist discourse works mainly by writing about the female body. Aliya Mamduh has written the novel *Mothballs*, 1986, which is set in Baghdad and has its central figure, Huda, the inquisitve, tomboyish girl of nine who is confronted with the truth of female flesh. The subject is the women's world in the crowded city of Baghdad and the characters in the book are mainly women. This novel is considered to be a remarkable contribution to the genre of the feminist novel in Arabic.

Hoda Al-Sadar whose pen-name was Bint Al-Huda, was a novelist who had several novels published including *The Lost Aunt*, 1978 and *Meeting in a Hospital*, 1980, both published in Beirut. She was executed in April 1980, having been persecuted by the regime because she belonged to a Shi'ite group.

Throughout all the tragic events Iraq has experienced since 1979, Iraqi writers inside and outside the country have been unable to express themselves freely; individual creative activity and intellectual dialogue having been crushed. It has been estimated that there are only about 20 Iraqi women writers inside and outside Iraq, in spite of women's involvement in society since the 1920s.

Haifa Zangana in her lecture entitled *Writing in Exile: The Dilemma of an Iraqi Fiction Writer* at SOAS, 1998, stated that Iraqi writers inside Iraq have three choices — to follow government ideology; to choose silence; or to continue writing through the use of allegory and mystification. Writers have been imprisoned, tortured or executed or forced into exile. Instead, a 'mass culture' has been created which serves purely as a means of Ba'ath Party control over the hearts and minds of the Iraqi people. The Ba'athist regime has a cultural code of its own with Ba'athist literature centred on the role of the absolute leader as a savoiur with whom the destiny of the nation is identified. Since 1980, when the Iraqi Writers' Union was abolished by a decree, writers have been organised in an association controlled by the Ministry of Culture. In literature, only one theme was sanctioned: the actual victory (Iran-Iraq War). The function of literature was to romanticise war and glorify martyrdom, making life inferior to death. The realistic school in literature was attacked as being critical of society.

The most important writers are now part of the Iraqi Diaspora and amongst the new generation of writers, the novel has flourished, with new writers able to express themselves freely and enjoy the freedom of publishing. According to Fatma Mohsen in *Banipal*, the novel became the pre-eminent tool for exiled writers with which to break the silence over the political tyranny in their country, and to communicate with their national community and with their own memory so that the novel became an instrument of resistance against political oppression. Some of the Iraqi women writers in exile in the UK include Haifa Zangana, Samira al-Mana and Salam Khayyat. The latter has had four or five novels published, one of them focusing on the life of an Iraqi soldier who refuses to fight in the Iran-Iraq War. Salima Salih, who lives in Germany, is considered as one of the most prominent writers. In her short stories she focuses on memory and interaction with the new society. Recently, in 1998/9, she had a novel published on the theme of memories of life in her city, Mosul.

Haifa Zangana has talked about some important issues affecting the Iraqi writer in exile. Language is a key issue, the exile being cut off from the new society because of it and having to rely on translators. However, translation is a problematic area with huge cultural differences to bridge, as well as the difficulty in translating phraseology for which there seems to be no equivalent. Secondly, memory is used as a substitute for the past and present and is preserved intact so that it often becomes life itself. However, memory is not always reliable and a sifting and purifying process takes place. Thirdly, there is limited active exchange with the new society and an initial adjustment to personal trauma is necessary before any interaction with British society can take place. Fourthly, writers are struggling with political independence, given that many were allied to the Communist Party and suffered a sense of loss after the collapse of the Soviet Union. Fifthly, there is the lack of an immediate presence of readers, given that publication and distribution in Arabic is very limited in Europe and that in the Arabic world there are controls and strict censorship. Finally, it is difficult for writers to liberate themselves from ideological slavery and style is often sacrificed for ideology.

References
Samira Al Man'a, *Witness of Her Time*, 1999

Margot Badran and Miriam Cooke, *Opening the Gates: A Century of Arab Feminist Writing*, Virago, 1990

Claire Buck, *Bloomsbury Guide to Women's Literature*, Bloomsbury, 1992

Fran Hazelton, *Iraq since the Gulf War*, Chapter on 'Cultural Totalitarianism' by Fatma Mohsen, Zed Books, 1994

Margaret Obank, *Banipal No. 2,* Article by Fatma Mohsen 'The Iraqi migrant novel'

Haifa Zangana, *Through the Vast Halls of Memory*, Hourglass, 1991

Joseph Zeidan, *Arab Women Novelists*, State University of New York Press, 1995

Kosova

Women in the Kosova Conflict

For centuries, the Serbs had oppressed the ethnic Albanians in Kosova where 90% of the population was Albanian and 10% Serb, with the control being in Serb hands. Tito had tried to defuse Albanian national aspirations and had granted Albanians special status, a process which culminated in the constitution of 1974 making Kosova an autonomous province. Nonetheless, nationalist unrest persisted and combined with dissatisfaction at the province's dire economic backwardness. In 1989, the Belgrade government abolished Kosova's status as an autonomous province within the Republic of Serbia. The Albanians of Kosova then set up the institutions of a separate republic, such as education and healthcare systems. Since 1989 Kosova has been ruled by Serbia with brutal policies which amount to apartheid against the Kosovan majority.

Tensions escalated from 1997 onwards, when the Serb government enforced a clampdown. The situation deteriorated drastically and levels of violence steadily increased throughout 1998. In January 1998, Serb helicopter gunships targeted and destroyed villages in central Kosova with the dead including women and children.

The Serbs had a policy of bombing whole villages and regions and 40% of villages were destroyed. Villages were shelled and burnt by the Serbs with civilians, including women and children, being driven from their homes. It was estimated that as many as 400,000 people had been forced to flee their homes and UNHCR estimated that about 200,000 people had been displaced internally. In September 1998 the horrific killing of women and children who had been displaced, was reported. The Serbs committed appalling atrocities, murdering women and children and civilian men. Huge numbers of women had been left alone when the Serbs arrested men as 'suspects' and widowed when their husbands were killed in cold blood. Mothers and daughters were themselves victims. In one testimony, Nushe Hadrijonaj, tells how she and her five children fled their village but met the Serb police on the road. Their 18-year-old daughter was questioned and the family was forced to return to their village without her. The mother never saw her daughter again.

Up to December 1998, about 1700 people had been killed and about 450-500 had disappeared. There was unconfirmed evidence of mass graves. In January 1999, the Serbs bombarded central Kosova for five days, forcing Kosovans out of their villages into the freezing hills. In Racak, 45 male civilians were slaughtered, causing the women and children to flee.

The Kosova Liberation Army which was formed to launch a separatist uprising and to fight Serb oppression, recruited women, mostly the under thirties, who bore arms alongside the men. It was a way of reviving history because in the past, some women, whose memories remain cherished, had fought. Some were imprisoned in Serbia while those who were killed fighting with the KLA were considered martyrs for freedom. Clearly those women who were unable to join the KLA because of family responsibilities, were separated from their menfolk and many women had been widowed because their husbands had been killed fighting. The KLA suffered a string of defeats in summer 1998 and Western diplomats had argued that it was a spent force and refused to involve it in talks on Kosova's future. A cease-fire was agreed in October 1998 but, having used the peace to re-arm and to introduce better training methods, the guerrillas emerged stronger than ever.

In March 1999, the indiscriminate use of armed force, violence and widespread killing of Kosovar civilians escalated into genocide, 'ethnic cleansing' and brutal expulsion, with the Serbs intent on driving out all the Albanian population. Refugees numbed by fatigue and fear, fled the Serb death squads. The overwhelming majority of refugees were women, children and the old with few men aged between 16 and 60. Thousands of men went missing, young Albanian men having been rounded up and shot by Serb forces intent on reducing the swelling ranks of the KLA. There was evidence of mass graves. The people remaining inside Kosova were desperate for food and medical supplies.

Systematic rape, as part of Serb policy, took place. Women were separated from refugee columns, taken away to be raped in a Yugoslav army camp and then were possibly killed. Women and girls fleeing in family groups were publicly stripped by the roadside and then raped by the Serb militia. The victims have even tried to conceal the raping as it would bring too much shame on them in Kosovar society. One Kosovan woman was quoted as saying "Where we come from, it is better to die than to be raped."

The crisis was the largest refugee crisis in Europe since the Second World War.

It was estimated that over 600,000 refugees had fled Kosova and that in total, 1.4 million Kosovan Albanians had been displaced. Refugees escaped to Albania, Macedonia, Montenegro and Bosnia. About 16,000 refugees were evacuated to countries around Europe, with many coming to Britain on the Humanitarian Evacuation Programme. Large numbers of women who arrived without the male members of their family were extremely traumatised and struggled to cope alone in London and provincial towns. By May 2000, 49% of the evacuees had returned on a permanent basis, with Kosovans continuing to return.

References
www.ipr.net/balkans/news
Wendy Bracewell, '*Rape in Kosovo: Masculinity and Serbian Nationalism*', 'Nations and Nationalism' (Gender and Nationalism issue), London, 2000
Alush A. Gashi, *The Denial of Human and National Rights of Albanians in Kosova*, Illyria Publishing Co. New York, 1992
Noel Malcolm, *Kosova*, Papermac, 1998
Kosova: *Oppression of Ethnic Albanians*, Minority Rights Group International
Briefing on Kosova, pub. Refugee Council, 1998
http://www.refugees.org
Save the Children Emergency Bulletin Three, August 1998
My Name Came Up, Refugee Council, 2000

Kosovar Women and Literature

The situation has been particularly dire for both female and male Albanian writers in Kosova. Generally, the development of literature has been restricted because of suppression by the Serbs, contact with writers in Albania being forbidden. The public use of Albanian was also forbidden under the Serbs when Kosova was incorporated into the Kingdom of Yugoslavia in 1918. This ban precluded the development of any Albanian theatre.

After the Second World War, for more than half a century, Albanian writers creating in conditions of socio-political and cultural repression were forced to be influenced by non-literary factors, producing work based on socialism, social revolution and on the working class and the peasants. The writer had to beware of decadence, formalism, bourgeois-revisionism and modern influences. In addition, the writer had to be a party member while the books had to be permeated with party inspiration and the proletarian-communist class. The writer had to rely on the experiences of social realism authors, especially those from Russia. Literary work had to be a means of propaganda and the writer had to be an 'educator of the masses'.

In his paper, Xhevat Ademi argues that de-cultural-isation leading to marginalism, occurred through the policies inflicted by the Serbs and that the sub-culture atrophied, accelerating the assimilation of the group which the Serb ideology could not tolerate. Albanians expressing discontent were labelled as nationalists, chauvinists, reactionaries and separatists. All the literature which was considered contrary to the Serb programmed project, was blocked and stopped.

Yugoslav drama dominated the professional theatre in Kosova with the presence of just a small number of international writers, while space for national Albanian drama was absurdly small. A large number of staged dramas were removed from the theatre repertoire after just a few performances for political reasons. However, in the late forties, a new type of theatre, the Professional Theatre of Kosova, was founded. In Pristina, where the national culture was strictly dictated, theatrical life developed very slowly with many obstructions and limitations imposed. Until the end of the seventies, the presence of national drama in the repertoire of the Albanian ensemble at the Professional Theatre of Kosova, barely reached ten per cent.

After the onset of relative liberalisation and expanded rights which followed Brioni Plenum and especially during 1971 when the Yugoslav centralist regime broke down, theatre life developed. The repertoire was partly set free from ideological censorship and Albanian and contemporary drama were included in its programmes. During this time, a new professional theatre was formed in Gjakova while in Pristina, the youth theatre 'Dodona' began. At that time, contacts with Tirana, Albania improved, with the mutual exchange of professional cadres such as professors, directors, actors and stage designers.

Unfortunately, after the protests in Kosova for more independence in 1981, this activity was crushed and the destruction of institutions of political, economic and cultural life continued. The violation reached its summit in

1989 with the closing down of Albanian cultural, scientific and educational institutions and with the dismissal of all their Albanian employees. All the professional cadre and workers were replaced by Serbs and Montenegrins. The professional Theatre of Kosova and the youth theatre 'Dodona' were under a Serbian-controlled, coercive administration. The Albanian ensemble was evicted, together with their works and repertoire. The Academy of Sciences and Arts was abolished, the financing of other cultural institutions was cut and the financing of the Writers' Association of Kosova and various magazines was halted.

In 1991 laws about the official language were passed by the Serbs. The Albanian language was forbidden for official purposes with the official language deemed to be Serbo-Croat, using the Cyrillic alphabet rather than the Latin one used by Albanians. The closure of Albanian schools started in 1990/91 and, as a result, the Albanians organised their own parallel system of education. However, the teachers and organisers were frequently subjected to arrest, intimidation and beatings by the Serb police.

More recently, university lecturers who clandestinely taught Albanian literature and history as part of their courses could be imprisoned for 20 years, if caught. Writers were forced to use allegory and Valbona Luta commented that she still finds it difficult to write openly, even though she is outside Kosova.

The number of women writers and poets whose work has been recognised and published is very limited. In an anthology of modern Albanian poetry which included eight Kosovan poets, there were no women poets represented at all. Women used to write quite a lot but did not have the means to have their work published. Nevertheless, literature is published in the women's journal *Teuta*.

Poetry has always been the main form of literature in Kosova and has always been more popular than prose. The poetic imagination has solid roots in the soil and land and in its people; their aspirations, sufferings and dreams. Up to the early eighties, about 300 volumes of poetry had been published compared to only 70 novels and 50 plays. The transition from an oral tradition to written poetry, with the essentially oral appeal of its rhythms and rich sonority, is made more readily than the one to longer works of prose.

The lack of a strong prose tradition in Albanian literature can also be attributed to the recent development of mass literacy in Kosova. It was the founding of the literary periodical *Jeta e re* (*New Life*) in 1949 which gave a voice to the younger generation of Albanian writers in Yugoslavia and served as an initial forum for literary publications. It was not until the mid-sixties that Kosovan Albanian literature began to appear in print in Yugoslavia on a significant scale. However, the Serbian authorities fiercely opposed all progress in education and culture for the Albanians and the intellectuals constituted the greatest threat to those in power. The first generation of writers was annihilated politically, with many leaving to live in exile and some being imprisoned.

The initial work in the eighties of the poets of the present generation is reflected in the variety and dynamism of contemporary Kosovan verse. Edi Shukriu, born in 1951, is probably the most esteemed woman writer. She is both a poet and a playwright and finds her inspiration in the Illyrian past about which she has special knowledge given that she is an archaeologist. Her first drama *Kthimi i Euridikes (The Return of Eurydice)* was published in 1987. Lindita Aliu, born in 1963, is another poet who is a former English lecturer at the University of Pristine. Other female poets are Lindina Ahmeti and Flora Brovina. The latter, who is also a doctor and women's activist, was jailed by the Serbs, having been arrested in 1999 in Pristina.

One diaspora author is Nexhmie Zaimi of New York, who wrote *Daughter of the Eagle: The Autobiography of an Albanian Girl,* published in 1937.

References

Xhevat Ademi, *Learning through Drama*, 1995

R. Elsie, *History of Albanian Literature*, Columbia University Press, New York, 1995

R. Elsie, *An Elusive Eagle Soars: Anthology of Modern Albanian Poetry*, Forest Books, 1993

Kurdistan

Kurdistan is the homeland of about 25 million Kurdish people and was shared between Turkey, Iraq, Iran and Syria during the 1920s. The Kurds have been battling for their own homeland ever since.

Women in the Conflict in Kurdistan/Iraq

One of Saddam Hussein's policies is to destroy the social fabric of the Kurds in order to exert control over them, with women and girls being victims of this policy.

In Iraqi Kurdistan, the 'widows' towns of Gushtapa demonstrate the outcome of this policy. In 1983, Iraqi soldiers removed all the Barzani tribe men and boys over ten from their detention camps, having destroyed the Barzani villages. Eight thousand Barzani Kurd males disappeared. The women and children were left vulnerable, far away from their homeland. Without male protection, girls lost any hope of a decent marriage and wives were left in limbo as their husbands had disappeared but were not definitely dead. Left without an income traditionally provided by the males, the widows' economic circumstances are dire. Some women have been forced into prostitution. Women are murdered by their families if they have relationships outside marriage or outside the tribe as it is considered that they have brought shame and dishonour to the extended family.

In 1998, a wave of forcible expulsions of 1,468 Kurdish families from Kirkuk to the Kurdish provinces in the north, took place. In addition, the food rationing tickets as well as the properties of the targeted families were confiscated by the Iraqi authorities.

During the Iran-Iraq war (1980-1988), the Kurds were perceived by the Iraqi government as supporting Iran, a charge that incurred brutal reprisals by the army and security forces. *The Anfal* was a special operation of genocide bureaucratically engineered from 1987 to 1989 by the Ba'ath Party against the Kurds of northern Iraq. This included the razing of thousands of frontier villages and the internal deportation and disappearance of 182,000 Kurdish men, women and children. Inhabitants were also imprisoned and executed. In 1988 came clear confirmation that Iraqi government troops had unleashed chemical weapons on the town of Halabja in Iraqi Kurdistan. There is a widespread legacy, from the Iran-Iraq war, of landmines and unexploded ordinance throughout the Kurdish region. 'Safe havens' were established in some of the Kurdish areas of northern Iraq in 1991. Kurdistan was a safe haven until Saddam Hussein took its capital, Arbil, with his tanks in 1996.

In Iraqi Kurdish society, the younger urban generation has access to education and to traditionally female dominated careers such as teaching, nursing and clerical work. Raising children and caring for the home are among other roles which have to be performed alongside their outside careers. However, the role of rural women is primarily to raise children and care for the home. Kurdish women have a difficult struggle for greater independence and equality within a traditionally patriarchal society and according to Sheri Laizer in *Kurdish Women: Identity and Purpose*, the ruling male elite restricts the development of female identity. In *Frontiers under Fire*, Sheri Laizer states "It was the lives of Kurdish women that were most in need of urgent reform. Their situation was little changed from that of their great-grandmothers and the lives of village women were still virtually pre-historic, so basic were their labours and daily concerns. Many of the young Kurdish women I met wished for more freedom and appealed to intransigent fathers or husbands, but the majority felt that they had to resign themselves to their fate and remain in the shadows." As in other societies covered in this book, the honour ethic is paramount. This is based on the belief that women cannot be trusted to protect their chastity in the best interests of the patriarchal society. A woman may be killed for exerting her will, for choosing a man to marry that the family has not selected — or of whom they disapprove — for having a love affair or sexual relationship, for eloping or being discovered in a compromising situation or for joining a political party. Punitive killings are carried out by a woman's father, husband, brother or other male relatives.

Kurdish women MPs and others worked on a women's agenda for the fragile parliamentary system established by the elections of May 1992. This was to draft proposals for the reform of family law which had been developed by the Ba'thist regime from Islamic law. The proposed reforms were in three main areas — marriage, divorce and inheritance. The marriage law around polygamy would reduce the number of wives a man could have from four to two. The proposed divorce law reform would abolish the *talaq* method by which a man could divorce his wife by saying three times 'I divorce you'. Other proposals are the outlawing of forced prostitution and domestic violence with the same penalties for an adulterous husband as for an adulterous wife. Thirty-five Patriotic Union of Kurdistan MPs signed but the Kurdish Democratic Party MPs refused to sign as they were traditionalists.

However, equality is to an extent being won by some Kurdish women fighting as *peshmergas* for a free Kurdistan alongside their men; the poet, Berivan Dorsky, who writes in Badinani, was a guerrilla for two years. In an *Anthology of Contemporary Kurdish Poetry*, an unknown, nameless woman guerrilla, dedicates a poem 'Karnveli Hill (How I Love These Mountains)' to a male fighter who was killed. The last verse is:

Life is one, the struggle is one
the path is one, the comrades are one
and as I vow to follow in your path
to death, I shout your name

Martyr Beritan!

References

Fran Hazelton, *Iraq since the Gulf War*, Zed Books, 1994. Chapter on women by Suha Omar.
Resistance: Women in Kurdistan, KIC/KSC Publications, Kurdistan Solidarity Committee and Kurdistan Information Centre, 1995
Kurdistan Solidarity Committee and Yashar Ismail, *Anthology of Contemporary Kurdish Poetry,* 1994
Sheri Laizer, *Into Kurdistan: Frontiers under Fire*, Zed Books, 1991
Sheri Laizer, *Martyrs, Traitors and Patriots: Kurdistan after the Gulf War*, Zed Books, 1996
P-J. Luizard, *Monde arabe Maghreb-Machrek*, pub *La Documentation Française,* 1999 (Article — *etre femme Kurde et Irakienne en Europe* by Nazand Begikhani)

Kurdish Women Writers in Iraq

Singing and story telling are an important part of village life, with women performing for each other and their children. Laments for the dead are performed by women. One lament sung by Barzani women (*shin*) mourns the loss and disappearance of their males and also expresses hope they are still alive (see 'Conflict in Iraqi Kurdistan'). However, the world of literature is dominated by men. Although Kurdish poetry is five hundred years old, until recently all the writers were male. Women have only been able to read of the male experience, which did not reflect their experience and struggles.

However, younger Kurdish women from Iraq, are now starting to write short stories and poems in Sorani which are published in newspapers. There are some women writers and poets such as Kajal Ahmed, Ahlam Mansur, Kharshida Baban, Daiky Solaf, Muhabatt Karadakhi and others whose work has, unfortunately, either not been published or only in a limited way. The centre for cultural and artistic activity is Suleimanya.

The subject of their writing covers gender, Kurdish identity and more recently, exile. Most of the younger generation of writers are influenced by western feminism. They began writing as a result of reflecting on the effect of feminism on women world-wide, as well as on their personal experiences of women's oppression on a daily basis. The French philosopher and novelist Simone de Beauvoir has had a great influence on new modern women writers in Kurdistan. In addition, they have been very much affected by the Egyptian woman writer, Nawal El Saadawi, whose writing has had a great influence on the development of feminism in the Middle East.

Successive regimes have always sought to contain Kurdish aspirations and limit Kurdish autonomy, language and culture. The campaign of genocide against the Kurds and the collapse of the Kurdish movement in 1975, had the effect of forcing writers to flee to safety abroad, the main centres being Germany and Sweden. A number of Kurdish Iraqi women are writing in exile in the UK, such as Choman Hardi, Sozan Mohamed, Nazand Begikhani and Berivan Dorsky.

References:
P. Kreyenbroek & C. Allison, *Kurdish Culture and Identity*, Zed Books, 1996

Women in the Conflict
in Kurdistan/Turkey

Women are very much a part of the liberation struggle in
Turkish Kurdistan and are represented at every level of
this struggle. They are considered to be equal contributors
to the struggle and their representation has increased as
they have become more visible so that they have gained
status and power. Many have given their lives in the struggle against Turkish colonialism and racism. They are
fighting everywhere, in the cities, towns, villages and in
the mountains where they fight as *peshmergas* on the
front line alongside men. Kurdish women struggle on two
fronts — for the liberation of Kurdistan and for women's
rights and most rural women have become politicised. It
should be noted that different Kurdish political groups
have different attitudes to women, some being traditionalists and some modernists.

Leyla Zana was the first Kurdish woman to be elected to
the Turkish Parliament in 1991. She added a reference to
the 'Turkish-Kurdish brotherhood' in her inaugural oath
and spoke in Kurdish in Parliament. As a result, she has
been in prison for many years and has become a symbol of
Kurdish resistance.

The situation of Kurdish women who fall into the
clutches of the Turkish security forces is indescribable.
Women in Turkish prisons are subjected to humiliation,
torture and rape, women being sexually assaulted when
they are tortured. The imprisonment of women in Turkey
represents a gender-specific form of human rights violations (Amnesty International).

The families of women who are persecuted because of
their political activities are harassed by state security
operations in Kurdish neighbourhoods in the towns as
well as in rural Kurdish areas. Some women whose husbands have fled to seek political asylum had to undergo
gynaecological examinations to ascertain whether or not

the husband went to the mountains and occasionally visited the wife.

Kurdistan is still a male-dominated, patriarchal society with men being the head of the family and having the final say over issues ranging from how to spend the family money to whom their children should marry. Women in rural areas have little control over their own lives. Poor self-confidence and lack of education have allowed women to be oppressed for centuries. When they marry, often at an early age, they are merely transferred from the all-powerful authority of a father to that of a husband. If the marriage runs into trouble, the young woman will get very little support from her own relatives. Legally, parents cannot force a girl to accept a husband but psychological pressure is often applied. Such a marriage would be legally invalidated, but the girl would have to pay a heavy social price for such an action. Such situations, often leading to family tragedies — murders and suicides, are not the result of an unjust legal system, but tradition.

Large numbers of Kurds, perhaps two million, including women, have been forced to migrate, because of crimes committed by the state against its Kurdish population, such as the scorched earth policy by the Turkish army. They arrive in Anatolia jobless and homeless. The majority live in poverty in large cities such as Istanbul. The political movements are very active in exile with women being highly involved and often forming their own women's groups. In February 1999, Kurdish communities in exile demonstrated vociferously against the abduction and imprisonment of their leader, Abdullah Ocalan, by the Turkish Government. Women were equally involved in the protests, with one Kurdish girl setting fire to herself in London to demonstrate the strength of her feelings.

References
Newspaper articles including 'Turkish Delight' by Julie Flint, *The Guardian*, December 1, 1998

Internet — www.one world.org
Index on Censorship, 1, 1995
'An Impassioned plea for free speech in Turkey' published by
Friends of Ozgur Gundem and Action for Kurdish Women, 1994

Kurdish Women Writers in Turkey

For seventy years Kurdish language, identity and culture have been banned. Kurdish cannot be taught in schools and Kurds have been killed merely for speaking Kurdish on the streets. There is a policy of cultural genocide by the Turkish government. Whilst writing in Turkish Kurdistan, writers may be known as Turkish with those using Kurmanji (Kurdish language) being imprisoned or worse. Their true identity may only be revealed when in exile. The main centres for Kurdish Turkish culture and literature in Kurmanji are Sweden, Germany and France. Because of the Turkish government's policy of neglect and the lack of resources, facilities and opportunities in Turkish Kurdistan, it has been difficult to develop culture, especially given that the language is forbidden. Literature has not been a priority for women, as fighting and politics have long dominated Kurdish life.

The Kurdish community generally lives in villages and women have the role of transmitting traditional stories which are spoken and not written. However, Bejan Matur is a young poet who has recently travelled widely to read her work. She uses the imagery of the south east and imagery common to women.

Some Kurdish women express themselves by writing as journalists, which is an extremely dangerous occupation. Gurbetelli Erzos, the female editor of *Ozgur Gundem,* the radical pro-Kurdish daily newspaper, is in prison along with nineteen members of her staff. In December 1993, the entire staff of 150 was arrested and tortured. The newspaper lost nine of its correspondents, killed by unknown assailants, and was officially closed down in 1994.

References
Estella Schmid, Sheri Laizer, Kamal Mirawdeli, *Anthology of Contemporary Kurdish Poetry*, Kurdistan Solidarity Committee and Ismail Yashar, 1994

Somalia

Women in the Somali Conflict

The ousting of Siad Barre in 1991 did not ease the Somali crisis and the war in Somalia between the clans and the war-lords continues unabated. Human rights abuses against unarmed civilians, including women and children, are still being carried out by militias of clan-based factions. Abuses include scores of deliberate and arbitrary killings, as well as rape. In March 1997, for example, members of the Bantu minority, including four women and eight children, were killed and seven women were raped.

The Amnesty International report for Somalia, 1988, states that women prisoners were raped, sexually assaulted or sexually humiliated, for example by being paraded naked in front of security officers. Many of these women were members of Islamic organisations and were treated in degrading ways because of their religious beliefs, for example being forced to bare their heads, arms and legs in front of men or being forbidden to pray at the set times. Women were also arrested at that time for being alleged members or sympathisers of the SNM which consisted mainly of Isaaqs from the north. Sufia Hashi Madar is serving a life sentence for this reason and there are also other women political prisoners.

Fatima Giama, a London women's group organiser, has said "The world only hears the man's voice, not the woman's voice but the war affects women in economic terms and as refugees." The civil war has had drastic consequences on living standards and the general health of the community and has resulted in increased maternal mortality and morbidity. Disease and famine are wreaking havoc in parts of Somalia, prompting clan leaders and relief agencies to appeal for emergency assistance. A Somali male refugee has reported the current Somali situation: women do not have rights and are raped and sexually abused, the fighting men taking their possessions.

Nuruddin Farah, the eminent novelist, in his article in *International Pen* maintains that women have a radical role in Somali politics. He describes how a few dozen women in Kismayo bared their breasts in public in front of a crowd of men. Fists raised, voices harsh, they shouted 'Rise, Rise!' challenging the men to action, reproaching them for their failure to confront the excesses of dictatorship. By challenging the men in this manner, the women implied that they would no longer defer to them as husbands, fathers or figures of authority.

Somali clans are based on male bonding, reaffirming the power of men over women. Where men mystify politics, glorifying their role in it, women are distrustful of the warring and peacemaking processes. Women are aware of the importance of the multiplicity of connections the warring communities have, seeing themselves as mothers to children of one family, now as daughters of another, and on remarriage, as mothers to offspring from yet another lineage. The men remain true to their father's ancestral identity; the women do not. Women are turned into spoils of war or into gifts of peace given away in marriage to settle a dispute between men.

Somali men think that a woman's identity is incomplete without reference to a male relation or husband. Women and men have very clear, different roles. Many women are now single-parent families bringing up children on their own. Their husbands may have disappeared, been killed or be languishing in refugee camps in Ethiopia or Kenya. The Somali Diaspora is now very large, with women having settled in the UK, USA, Canada, Australia and mainland Europe. In Canada, women comprise about 60% of the total adult Somali population. The traditional extended family usually ceases to exist in this situation and women are left very isolated and vulnerable and may suffer from mental health problems. In exile, they have to function as individuals whereas they are accustomed to being part of a group — the tribe being the passport to identity. Women who were raped or assaulted in the war situation in Somalia, may choose to remain silent for fear of being ostracised or blamed for the abuse within their community. They may also be victims of racism. Women may be working in unskilled jobs as well as looking after their children on their own, thereby challenging men and the traditional male role. An area of concern amongst the women is the identity of their children. They feel that they are being exposed to bad influences, both at school and in society at large. In addition, there is also conflict between the generations; families being disfunctional and girls leaving home.

References
Mohamed Dahir Afrax, *Hal Abuur* Vol 1 No 4, Article 'The Single Mother Phenomenon' by Ladan Caafi
http://www.amnesty.org
Nurrudin Farah, *PEN International*, Volume 48, No. 1, 1998, 'The Women of Kismayo'
www.oneworld.org

The Somali Woman's Voice in Literature

Somalia's poetic tradition is closely associated with its history and national identity, and the tradition of oral poetry is held in the highest esteem. Poetry has a specific function in Somali society — both to educate and to reinforce the sense of community.

Jeanne D'Haem in her book *The Last Camel*, states that although Somali women no longer wear *purdah* 'they will always see the world through the veil of their experiences'. She maintains that people describe themselves by the stories they tell about their lives and are defined by their experiences.

Margarent Laurence, writing in 1952, stated that there was a good deal of women's poetry in Somali literature, i.e. poetry written by women for women. Generally, performing poetry is the function of the man, as women are not officially recognised as full clan members. The classical genres, i.e. those poems traditional Somalis consider highest in the rank of serious poetry, and noble enough with which to discuss politics and important social issues, are performed by and for men only. The public forums where men perform are male oriented and are places where they sip tea and chew *quat*. However, women have on occasion taken part in poetry reciting competitions and won respect for their words. Women also traditionally pass on a huge store of folktales, sayings and chants as well as the songs associated with everyday tasks. Women's poetry is becoming known through cassettes. There are five structures in Somali poetry. Four of these are considered to be male and one is considered to be female. This is called *buraanbur*. Somali poetry is sung or chanted. However, dance songs are performed for the benefit of both sexes. Standing in a circle, the crowd takes the line of the chorus, while one person chants in the role of the cantor. Two or three dancers, possibly including a woman, perform in the centre.

Work poetry is chanted or sung whilst weaving, loading camels, fetching water etc. There are differences in work poetry depending on whether the workspace is male or female. Work songs are segregated and women's work poetry is composed for women and covers personal issues such as family, home and husband, or gender issues such as the sex of a baby — a male being more valued. It is passed down through the generations and has no authorship. Women sing these songs while they are working in small groups. However, they are not usually seen and this work poetry is not taken seriously.

Another type of poetry is ritual and religious poetry where again there is segregation between men and women. Women have their own brand of religious poetry which is for a different audience. The women will pray to Allah to come to their side. The older women may chant or sing the poetry to younger women in late pregnancy or where the family, children and child-bearing are concerned. Sometimes they pray to Fatima, the daughter of the Prophet. In pre-Islamic times, prayers were made to female gods. The women use Somali while the men tend to use Arabic because they usually have more education.

A third type of poetry is classical poetry by women. Classical poetry is the most respected form of poetry, which men see as their own. However, women's classical poetry was not presented in a public forum because of the constraints and barriers in society for women. It has now become better known because of radio broadcasting.

Nowadays, because of the experience of exile in urban centres, as opposed to the traditional pastoral society, different versions are being performed, depending on the environment. Young girls are now composing in English. There are concerns that young people are not interested in traditional Somali poetry. Nevertheless, poetry and song performed at events such as weddings are crucial in unifying clans and are a symbol of memories of being one people.

Some women writers in exile in the UK are Anab Sheikh Abdi who writes poetry in *beramble* form, Qali Khalif who writes both in *beramble* and *gabay* form, and Zenab Jama.

References
B.W. Andrzejewski with S. Andrzejewski, *An Anthology of Somali Poetry*, Indiana University Press, 1993
Aman, as told to Virginia Lee Barnes and Janice Boddy, *Aman*, Bloomsbury, 1994
A Song for Carrying Water and other stories from Somalia, Gatehouse Books
J.W. Johnson, Heelloy: *Modern Poetry and Songs of the Somali*

pub. Haan, 1996
Margaret Laurence, *A Tree for Poverty*, McMaster University Library Press & ECW Press, 1993
Mama East Africa Women's Group, *Shells on a Woven Cord*, Yorkshire Arts Circus, 1995

Turkey

Women in Turkey

According to Amnesty International, the 1990s have seen a steady erosion of human rights in the name of national security, both women and men being victims. The authorities attempt to excuse, ignore or cover up abuses such as torture, political killings and 'disappearances'. Hundreds of people, including women, were detained because of their non-violent activities. Trade unionists, students and demonstrators were frequently taken into custody, most released after a short period of police detention but others being sentenced to terms of imprisonment. Torture continued to be widespread and female detainees were frequently sexually assaulted. A woman lawyer, Sevil Delkiliç, has been sentenced to thirty years' imprisonment after legal proceedings which were marked by the serious abuse of investigative and detention procedures, including the use of torture.

The 'Saturday Mothers' are the female relatives of those who have 'disappeared' in police custody. Every Saturday they hold a vigil in Istanbul demanding that the authorities account for the fate of their relatives. They are frequently harassed and. throughout the years of their vigil, they have suffered ill-treatment, detentions and prosecution.

Leyla Zana, a former parliamentary deputy, is continuing to serve her 15 sentence, imposed in 1994 for alleged membership of the PKK (Kurdish political organisation) and her criticism of state policy in the predominantly Kurdish south-eastern provinces.

310

Thousands of women students wear the Islamic head-scarf but Turkey's strictly secular society forbids the wearing of religious dress in state-owned buildings. The laws are now being enforced at all universities and in June 1998, thousands of students protested and there were injuries and numerous arrests by the police. In 1997, Turkey's army had forced the country's first Islamist government out of power.

Turkish women enjoy nearly all the rights accorded women in Western democracies. Yet under Turkish law, men are the head of the family and have the final say over issues ranging from how to spend the family money to whom their children should marry. Until recently, Turkey was also one of the few Muslim countries where arbitrary virginity tests were legal. In addition, until recently, although women found guilty of committing adultery faced a prison sentence of up to three years, adultery was legal for men.

Women in rural areas, however, have little control over their own lives. Poor self-confidence and lack of education have allowed women to be oppressed for centuries. When they marry, often at an early age, they are merely transferred from the all-powerful authority of a father to that of a husband. If the marriage runs into trouble, the young woman will get very little support from her own relatives. Legally, parents cannot force a girl to accept a husband of their choice, but psychological pressure is often applied. Such a marriage could be legally invalidated, but the girl would have to pay a heavy social price for such an action. These situations, often leading to family tragedies such as murders and suicides, are not the result of an unjust legal system, but of tradition and taboos. The family's honour is all-important.

References

www.amnesty.org
Index on Censorship, 1, 1995
www.oneworld.org

Women Writers in Turkey

The *Penguin Book of Modern Turkish Verse* includes only one woman poet: Gülten Akin. She was born in 1933 and is one of Turkey's most distinguished poets for whom 'poetry is synonymous with social responsibility'. She is the author of many collections and recipient of many awards. Her first book, *Hour of the Winds*, 1956, won the Turkish Linguistic Society's award for poetry in 1961 and again in 1971 with the *Epic of Marasli Okkes*. She currently lives in Ankara, Turkey.

Melisa Gürpínar, born in 1941, is a poet and playwright living in Istanbul. She studied drama in London and prepared programmes for the BBC. She has published many books of poems.

In the past, after the creation of the Turkish Republic in 1923, several major writers were forced into exile. These included Halide Edib, the leading woman novelist who published many books in England and the US while in exile, including a critically acclaimed novel entitled *The Clown and his Daughter*, 1935. Her literary output was enormous. She wrote many novels of modern Turkish life, covering the whole range of Turkish women's problems in a time of fundamental change.

The modernisation of Turkey with the establishment of the Turkish Republic, officially revolutionised the position of Turkish women. Women writers had to cope with problems caused by the new ethic, by the new social forces and with problems of the new language, Modern Turkish. Sukufa Nihal Basar was a writer who was active in women's rights movements in Turkey. Seven volumes of her poetry were published between 1919 and 1960 and six novels between 1928 and 1951. Halide Nusret Zorlutuna was affected all her life by the political upheavals and was a poet and novelist who wrote in the new style. Other writers are Suat Dervis, who studied literature in Berlin and was a novelist, and Güner Ener who wrote short stories.

Many women writers continued to write traditionally, for example Damiha Ayverdi, who wrote of Turkish life as being dominated by the ideals of Islamic Jihad, and Nezihe Araz, who composed Sufi poetry.

Other modern writers are Sevgi Soysal, Adalet Agoglu, Furuzan, Leyla Erbil and Sevim Burak. The difficult positon of women in Turkey and the conflict between old and traditional ideas are described in Aysel Özakins's novel *The Prizegiving*, 1980. Erendiz Atasu is considered a feminist writer — she is author of *The Other Side of the Mountain*. Latife Tekin, author of *Tales from the Garbage Hill* and *Dear Shameless Death*, is one of the most original of all Turkish writers, using magical realism in her writing, which is set in villages and about those who migrated from the *gece kondu* shanty towns. Buket Uzumer is a very popular writer and author of *Mediterranean Waltz*.

There is considerable concern about the lack of freedom of expression in Turkey. The Penal Code is used against writers and journalists who criticise the Turkish state and any advocacy of separatism is punishable. In 1988, 184 members of the literary and cultural elite were brought to trial for publishing a book entitled *Freedom of Thought*. Journalists, for example, are imprisoned for interviews with Kurdish leaders. There were at least 29 Turkish journalists in prison at the end of 1997 and close to 20 journalists were tortured in Turkey. Women journalists are frequently sexually assaulted.

'Exile Literature', particularly as a result of the psychological problems of the large numbers of Turkish workers in Western Europe, has become a branch of modern Turkish literature. There are at least a million and a half Turks in Germany where a new generation of German writers of Turkish origin is growing up. Aysel Ozakin is a path-breaking feminist-marxist novelist with a considerable range of work. Emine Seugi Ozdamar writes auto-fiction about her life in and between Turkey and Germany. Other writers are Dilek Zaptcioglu, Zehra Cirak (poet),

Alev Tekinay, Saliha Scheinhardt, Renan Demirkan and Fatima B. Güueli Gün, in exile in New York, who wrote the novel *On the Road to Baghdad*. The reasons for the paucity of known Turkish-speaking women writers in exile in Britain have been considered by Aydin Mehmet Ali in *'Breaking the Silence of the Soul'*. FATAL gives Turkish-speaking women a voice.

References

Nermin Menemencioglu, *Penguin Book of Turkish Verse*, 1978
Claire Buck, *Bloomsbury Guide to Women's Literature*, Bloomsbury, 1992
Martin Tucker, *Literary Exile in the Twentieth Century*, Greenwoood Press, 1991
Mehmet Ali Aydin, Breaking the Silence of the Soul from *Mother Tongues*, edited by Stephen Watts, (MPT, 2001).

The
Contributors

The Writers

Samira Al-Mana was born in 1935 in Basra, Iraq and studied Arabic Language at Baghdad University. She now lives in London where she completed her studies as a librarian and worked for the Iraqi Cultural Centre. She has published four novels, a volume of short stories and one play. Her first novel, *The Forerunners and the Newcomers*, was published in Beirut and a collection entitled *The Song* was published in Baghdad in 1975. *Another London* was published in 1979 in London. Since then, she has written several short stories and a novel *Look at me, Look at me* which was published in Cairo in 1998. With her husband, she edits and produces a journal called *Al-Ightirab al-Adabi*, which publishes the work of Arab writers in exile.

Nuha al-Radi was born in Baghdad, Iraq in 1941, trained at art school in London in the early 60s and later taught at the American University of Beirut. A painter, ceramist and sculptor, her works have been shown throughout the Arab world and in Berlin, London and Washington. She sees herself as a citizen of the world, 'a nomad'. *Baghdad Diaries* is her first book.

Dursaliye Bedir was born in Turkey in 1958 and has lived in London for about ten years. She has written since childhood. She won second prize in Turkey in 1988 for her book *Londrada bir kadin Dondu* and first prize in Northern Cyprus for her short stories. She currently writes for a Turkish feminist magazine *Pazartesi*.

Nazand Begikhani is a poet from Iraqi Kurdistan. She started writing when she was still at school and her themes are exile, gender and Kurdish identity. After

317

studying English Literature in Iraq, she completed a Doctorate in Comparative Literature. She lectures part-time at the Sorbonne Institute of Oriental Languages and Civilisation and worked at the Kurdish Cultural Centre, London, focusing on gender issues. She is currently researching media representation of refugees.

Amba Bongo is from the Democratic Republic of Congo (formerly Zaire) and now lives in London. She was brought up in a literary atmosphere, her father being a publisher. She studied English and English Literature at Brussels University. She has completed one novel in French about her own experience as a refugee, *Une Femme en Exil*, l'Harmattan, Paris, 2000. She is currently working on a second novel about a woman with AIDS.

Nafissa Boudalia is from Algeria and now lives in London. She is both a poet and painter and occasionally returns to her country to paint at great risk to herself. She has worked as a journalist since 1969, originally working for Algerian newspapers *El Moudjahid* and *Algerie Actualites*. In 1967, she won the Prix St Germain des Pres in Paris for her poetry. Her collection of poems *Reflexions sur l'Algerie* (1989) focused on the political situation in Algeria, especially the position of women.

Samia Dahnaan who was born in Algeria, studied languages and now works in the care industry. She feels very strongly about Arab women, and Algerian women's issues, in particular. She is co-founder of the Algerian Women's Association. Much of her writing is about 'home' from 'home'.

Aida Derguti was born in 1972. She is an historian on Albanian issues. Her work has been published in Kosova with her mentor being the departed, well-known poet and intellectual, Latif Berisha, who was killed by the Serbs. She was in exile in Switzerland but left to join the KLA.

Amna Dumpor was born in 1968 in Mostar, Bosnia and Hercegovina, where she was involved in the media and theatre. This included appearances on the local radio station, television and theatre. In October 1998, she published her first book of poetry *Tears in the Heart* in her home town of Mostar. She has been living in London since 1992.

Fatma Durmush is a member of a Turkish Cypriot family and came to Britain when she was one month old. She sees her identity as being British-Turkish as she speaks Turkish and is steeped in Turkish culture. She worked in her father's café in south London, simultaneously writing and studying for the Open University. After a violent attack, she gave up working in the café to write full-time and paint. She has been a feminist since the age of twenty-one. She writes both poetry and prose and has completed a novel entitled *Dual Self*. She writes mainly in English but also in Turkish. Her work has been published in *The Big Issue, Daily Express* and read on a radio magazine programme. She has won seven literary awards, including first prize in the London Turkish Literature Festival (1998). She edits the *Morley College Literary Magazine*.

Farooka Gauhari, formerly an associate professor at Kabul University in Afghanistan, currently works in the Department of Biology at the University of Nebraska, USA.

Choman Hardi comes from Iraqi Kurdistan and is the daughter of a well-known Kurdish poet. Her mother tongue is Sorani. She came to Britain in 1993 when she was 17, attending school in London. She read Philosophy and Psychology at Oxford University and is a Master in Philosophy of University College, London. She has published two collections of poetry in Kurdish: *Return with No Memory* (Denmark, 1996) and *Light of the Shadows* (Sweden, 1998). During the summer of 1998 she travelled around European cities with a Kurdish cultural group comprising poets, artists, musicians and dancers. She is Chair of 'Exiled Writers Ink!'

Saida Hagi Dirie Herzi was born in Mogadishu, Somalia. She has a BA in English Literature from Jeddah, Saudi Arabia and a Master's degree in Teaching English from the American University, Cairo, Egypt. Until recently, she was teaching at the King Abdul Aziz University, Jeddah. She specialises in writing short stories. She now lives in the United States.

Fahrija Hodzic is from Sarajevo, Bosnia. She originally studied Economics and then edited an Economics and Politics magazine. During the war in Bosnia, she lost members of her family, including her brother. She came to England as a refugee in 1993, first settling in Leigh-on-Sea. She now lives in London. Unusally, she writes in English. Her poetry has been published in a number of anthologies and also in *Muslim News*. She visited Ghana to read her poetry.

Ziba Karbassi was born in Tabriz, Iran in the 70s and came to England in the late 80s. She has had four books published, the first three in Farsi and the fourth in Farsi and English: *A Scorpion Under the Pillow, With a Broken Star in my Heart, The Sea will Drown* and *Water or the Blue.* She has participated in many international poetry festivals.

Vida Kashizadeh was born in Abadan, Iran and is a singer, poet and songwriter. She started writing poetry as a teenager and developed her songwriting at a later stage. She has been in the UK since the late 70s.

Valbona Ismaili Luta is an Albanian from Kosova who was born in 1966 in Pristina. She started writing at an early age and her first poems were published when she was a teenager. She used to write for a student newspaper, *Bota e re*, published in Pristina. She came to London in 1993 and is a correspondent for a Kosova Albanian women's monthly magazine, *Teuta*. She is currently a freelance reporter for *RFI* and is also teaching Albanian.

Dieudonnee-Marcelle Makenga was born in Lubumbashi, Democratic Republic of Congo, in 1978 but originates from the Kasai region. She followed her family into exile in Algeria where she lived from 1982 to 1990. She is currently a student at l'Ecole des Infirmieres de la Croix-Rouge Francaise. She has written several poems about the state of being exiled and she also works with a group of African dancers and musicians in Limoges, France.

Pari Mansouri is an Iranian, writer and translator who was born in Tehran. She studied at Tehran University and has a BA in English and Literature and an MA in Social Sciences. She was a teacher of English Language for 20 years until 1975 when she came to Britain with her family. She has translated and published ten books by foreign authors and her own novel *Above and Beyond Love* and a selection of short stories for young adults *The Winged White Horse* were published in 1990 and 1995 respectively. Her latest work, published in 1997, is a book of short stories entitled *Entertainment in Exile*. She writes in Farsi.

Aydin Mehmet-Ali is from the Turkish part of Cyprus and lives in London. She writes short stories and, in addition, runs a Turkish-speaking women's writing group to give women a voice and in connection with this, has initiated an annual writing competition. She has completed a Master's in Adult Education. She is chair of Hackney Action for Racial Equality.

Brikena Muharremi was born in Kosova in 1978 and came to England in 1995 when she was 16. She has a degree in Law from the University of Westminster. She is a poet who started writing when she was nine. She has had 30 poems published in Albanian and in 1994, won first prize in Literature for the Young Poetesses of Kosova. Her first poetry book was published in Albanian in Kosova in 1996 *Pallati Zemres*. Brikena also writes stories, one of which was published in *Teuta* in February 1998. She writes mainly about the reality of life in Kosova and about life in general, using both Albanian and English.

Shahrnush Parsipur is an Iranian who is considered by some to be the most famous contemporary Iranian novelist. She now lives in exile in America. Her first book, for children, was published in 1969 (*The Little Red Ball*) and her first novel, entitled *The Dog and the Long Winter* in 1976. Her collection of short stories, is called *Crystal Pendant Earrings*. Subsequently, she was imprisoned for four years and then wrote her novel, entitled *Toba and the Meaning of Night*. *Women without Men*, was a short, surrealistic novel which was banned by the Iranian Government in the mid-1990s which put pressure on her to stop such writing. *Blue Logos* is another surrealistic novel, written in the USA and published in 1989.

Rouhi Shafii is a social scientist and author. She has a BA in English Literature and an MA in Social Sciences from Tehran University and an MA in Women's Studies and Education from the University of London. For 17 years, Rouhi worked at management level in the Iranian private and public sectors. The revolution of 1979 brought an enforced end to her career. Since 1985, she has made London her home.

As a social scientist, Rouhi has focused on social problems, particularly those of women. She writes articles and lectures on women's issues and she has translated and published two books in Iran: *Women of Vietnam*, 1982 and

Argentina, National Resistance and Peron's Dictatorship, 1981. She has edited a book on the history of women's movements throughout the world. Her latest book, published in Britain, is entitled *Scent of Saffron*, Scarlet Press, 1997. She is currently completing a historical novel.

Ruhangiz Sharifian was born in Iran and now lives in the UK. She studied Child Psychology in Vienna and has written essays about children's education. She started writing short stories twelve years ago. In 1989, she had a book of short stories published and her novel *Silk Skein* about a wealthy Iranian family, was published in 1995. Her story *My Sons* was shortlisted in the London Short Story Competition in 1995. She writes in Farsi and her daughters translate her work into English.

Shehrazad was born and raised in Iraqi Kurdistan until the completion of her degree in Oil Engineering, and has since lived in exile. She has an MA in Screen Writing and Research for Film and Television and now works as a freelance writer, researcher and translator.

Darija Stojnic was born in Sarajevo, Bosnia, and now lives in London where she is a counsellor. Whilst studying Law, she worked as a journalist on a local paper and after gaining her degree, worked in the District Attorney's Office. She subsequently worked as a manager in the radio and TV stations of Sarajevo. Her stories were published in the bulletin produced by Sarajevo Radio/TV and in local papers and were stored in drawers but when the UN burnt furniture in Sarajevo for fuel, her stories were also burnt, "for a good cause" she says with characteristic humour. She says that writing stories keeps her alive. In the UK, they have appeared in the Sarajevo/London bulletin (*SALON*). She is currently writing *Stories of London*.

Ayesha Tarzi was born in England of Afghan parentage. She went to live in Afghanistan at the age of ten. Her collection of short stories *Red Death* was published in 1985 and she has completed a first novel entitled *Night Letters*. She has degrees in Science and Russian literature and since 1963 she has worked with several international organisations. In 1980 she took refuge in England from the turmoil and terror caused by the Soviet invasion of Afghanistan. She has worked for the Inner London Probation Service for 15 years.

Gjeraqina Tuhina is a young journalist from Kosova who studied Law at the University of Pristina. She reported for Radio Free Europe. At great risk to herself, she continued to send reports to Britain until she was forced to flee Pristina. She is currently working in Prague as a reporter.

Shadab Vajdi was born in Iran and is a poet and a linguist, who writes in Farsi. She studied Persian Literature and Social Sciences in Iran and has a doctorate in Linguistics. Three collections of poetry have been published in *Farsi: A Bend in the Alley, A Song for Little Hands* and *To the Memory of the Thirst of Southern Mountain Slopes*. Her collection translated into English is entitled *Closed Circuit*, published in 1989. Her poems reflect the cultural influences of East and West. She now lives in London and lectures at the School of Oriental and African Studies.

Haifa Zangana was born in Baghdad in 1950. She graduated from the University of Baghdad School of Pharmacy in 1974. A year later she left Iraq to work with the Palestinian Red Crescent in Damascus, Syria. As a painter she participated in various European and American surrealist publications and group exhibitions, with one-woman shows in London and Iceland.

She edited and published *Halabja* in 1989. *Through the Vast Halls of Memory,* her first novel, was published in English in 1990 and in Arabic in 1995. Three collections of short stories followed: *The Ant's Nest* (1996), *Beyond What the Eye Sees* (1997) and *The Presence of Others* (1999). Her other publications are the novels *Keys to a City* (2000) and *Women on a Journey,* (2001).

Lily Al-Tai was born in Baghdad, Iraq and came to England for her studies in 1974. She studied Fine Art at the Bayam Shaw School of Art, London. She has participated in various group exhibitions in London and Europe.

Jennifer Langer works in the field of further education and has co-ordinated various refugee education projects. She is director of "Exiled Writers Ink!" and edited *The Bend in the Road: Refugees Writing,* published by Five Leaves in 1998.

Further Reading

Al-Mana Samira,

The Forerunners and the Newcomers, Beirut, 1972

London Sequel, London, 1979

The Umbilical Cord, London, 1979

The Oppressors, Damascus, 1997

Look At Me...Look At Me, Cairo, 1999

Only A Half, London 1985 (English and Arabic)

The Song, Baghdad, 1976

The Soul And Others, Beirut, 1999

Al-Radi Nuha,

Baghdad Diaries, Saqi Books, 1998

Begikhani Nazand,

Yesterday's Tomorrow: A Collection of Poetry, pub. Association des Artistes Kurdes, Paris, 1995 (Kurdish)

Bongo Amba

Une Femme en Exil, L'Harmattan, 2000

Dumpor Amna,

Tales from the Heart, published in Mostar, Bosnia, . 1998 (Bosnian)

Gauhari Farooka,

Searching for Saleem: An Afghan Woman's Odyssey, University of Nebraska Press, 1996

Mansouri Pari,

Entertainment in Exile (Farsi)

Muharremi Brikena,

Pallati I Zemres, published by Forumi I Krijuesve te Artit, Pristina, 1996 (Albanian)

Shafii Rouhi,

Scent of Saffron, Scarlet Press, 1997

Tarzi Ayesha,

Red Death, Islamic Texts Society, 1985

Vajdi Shadab,

To The Memory of the Thirst of the Southern Mountain Slopes (Farsi and English)

Closed Circuit, Translated from the Persian by Lotfali

Khonji, Forest
Zangana Haifa,
Through the Vast Halls of Memory, Hourglass, 1991
The Ant's Nest, 1996 (Arabic)
Beyond What the Eye Sees, 1997 (Arabic)
The Presence of Others, 1999 (Arabic)
Keys to a City, 2000 (Arabic)
Women on a Journey, 2001 (Arabic)